DYKE LIFE

ing out and life beyond the closet

Beyond the Closet

FROM GROWING UP TO GROWING OLD

Dyke Life

A CELEBRATION
OF THE LESBIAN EXPERIENCE

EDITED BY

Karla Jay

BASIC
BOOKS

A Member of the Perseus Books Group

Designed by Jessica Shatan

Library of Congress Cataloging-in-Publication Data

Dyke life : from growing up to growing old, a celebration of the lesbian experience / edited by Karla Jay.
    p. cm.
Includes bibliographical references.
ISBN 0–465–03907–3 (cloth)
ISBN 0–465–03908–1 (paper)
1. Lesbianism. 2. Lesbians—Identity. 3. Lesbian couples. I. Jay, Karla.
HQ75.7D95 1995
305.48'9664—dc20   95–18423
                                                                          CIP

98 99 ❖/HC 9 8 7 6 5

℮ONTENTS

PART II: RELATING TO EACH OTHER

PART III: SEX AND GENDER IDENTITY

PART IV: THE PUBLIC WORLD

PART V: THE LESBIAN BODY

$\mathcal{A}$CKNOWLEDGMENTS

Many people contribute to the successful completion of a book. For this particular anthology, credit first and foremost goes to Marny Hall, a loyal friend as well as a tireless, generous, and good-humored mentor. I'd also like to thank Sydelle Kramer, Elizabeth Meese, and Karen Kerner for providing feedback on various stages of this project and Jo Ann Miller, Linda Carbone, and Juliana Nocker of Basic Books for their editorial advice.

Grateful acknowledgment is made to the following sources for allowing me to reprint material:

Parts of Joyce Hunter's "At the Crossroads: Lesbian Youth" have appeared in *National NOW Times,* Nov.–Dec. 1990, reprinted by permission of the National Organization for Women; and *Crossroads,* American Friends Service Committee's Bridges Project Newsletter, Fall 1993, reprinted by permission of the publisher.

"Procrasti-dating" is reprinted courtesy of Jacqueline Lapidus. © 1993 Jacqueline Lapidus.

Kath Weston's "Guessing Games" is an abridged version of a chapter from her forthcoming book, *Render Me, Gender Me* (New York: Columbia University Press). Research was supported by the National Science Foundation, the Rockefeller Foundation, the

Center for Advanced Feminist Studies at the University of Minnesota, and the Center for Advanced Studies at the University of Iowa.

"Double Trouble" originally appeared in the July 14, 1994, issue of *Metroline* and is reprinted by permission of the author. © 1994 Lesléa Newman.

"After the First Visit," by Margaret Robison, is reprinted from *The Disability Rag & ReSource*, January/February 1994.

WELCOME TO DYKE LIFE:
AN INTRODUCTION

According to the media, lesbians have arrived. Lesbian-spotting stories are everywhere. In 1994 alone, lesbians graced the covers of magazines ranging from *Newsweek* to *The National Enquirer,* and television covered everything from life in "Lesbianville, USA" (still labeled Northampton, Mass., for postal purposes), to Melissa Etheridge's coming out and Martina Navratilova's retirement. We have certainly come a long way, sister queers, from sinister images like the one of Sister George forcing her lover to eat her cigar butt.

Most of the public, including many lesbians, seems to assume we are finally getting the true picture of lesbian nation in all its quirky and queer diversity. After all, don't we see those dykes on bikes at the pride parades? Didn't a *20/20* segment feature a lesbian splashing on aftershave before an evening on the town (although we might have wished she hadn't used a fragrance, or at least used a more politically inspired product than Obsession for Men)? But despite this welcome new visibility, many of us feel that the vast majority of lesbians we know have been totally ignored.

Lipstick lesbians, business executives, and movie stars may be all the rage, but where are the granola dykes, lesbian separatists, waitresses and construction workers, fat dykes, old lesbians, lesbian adolescents, butches, disabled lesbians? Where are the lesbians who look like your grandmother, who may in fact be your grandmother? Where are the women of color? Northampton may be fairly white, but the real Lesbianville is not. Perhaps it's too complicated for the media to introduce (or comprehend) more than one concept at once. If they focus on one or two Generation X dykes, they must feel they can discount the rest of us. Next, they can discount our numbers, which range in recent surveys from 1 percent to just under 10 percent of the entire female population. Just counting all the lesbians who are married to men would make the numbers skyrocket, but that would mean male pollsters would have to acknowledge that some of these lesbians are their wives.

Gay and lesbian political organizations counter media homophobia by emphasizing success and affluence. Of course, there are rich, famous, and prosperous lesbians other than k. d. lang and Martina Navratilova. Such organizations feel that making us seem just like successful heterosexuals will help influential nongays empathize with us. And in truth, most of us want the same things as heterosexuals: marriage (with all its entitlements: health insurance, survivorship benefits, and so on), children, job security. Lesbians and gay men run the same gamut of political and religious beliefs as heterosexuals, from ultraliberal to archconservative. Spurred on by Bruce Bawer's *A Place at the Table,* conservative homosexuals are beginning to emerge from their teak-lined closets.

The assimilationist, homogenized images favored by the media are endorsed by most gay and lesbian rights organizations and media groups. Such groups as GLAAD (Gay and Lesbian Alliance Against Defamation) praise any positive portrayal or image of a gay man or lesbian, while calling on us to write letters denouncing negative stereotypes. There is nothing wrong with positive press or attractive representatives, but why are white, straight-looking, ultrafeminine clones chosen to represent us? Sometimes the only lesbian on television seems to be Camille Paglia busily attacking other lesbians and managing to offend as many lesbian as straight women. And some-times the only TV images of a pride march are of leather dykes and festively gaudy transvestite men. We know conservatives use this kind of footage to scare their audiences into thinking that we all look like that—and would like their children to look like that, too. The fact that most of us look no different from heterosexuals fright-ens the media. But would the picture of lesbian nation be any truer if we eliminated leather dykes and obvious butches from the family portrait? In truth, the portrait of Lesbianville won't be realistic until many, many more of us are included in it.

The contributors to *Dyke Life* intend to help define—and cele-brate—who we are in all our wonderful diversity. The chapters in this collection attempt to demarcate the borders of lesbianism with-out collapsing differences in race, ethnicity, class, age, or other fac-tors. Although no book can ever be completely representative, I attempted to paint a broad canvas to counteract the trend of books by and about lesbians that address only fragments of our communi-ties—books on butches, softball, separatist philosophy, coming out, or S/M, for instance. Books on lesbian parenting often speak exclu-sively to those who want or already have children, instead of appeal-ing as well to the larger childless community in which these families will live. We seem to have stopped listening to those outside our cir-cle; we no longer share our inner lives even with other lesbians. If we believe that our sexual orientation is the most defining part of our lives, we have to understand and celebrate our own lives and those of other lesbians, while drawing sympathetic nonlesbians into our space as well. Many of the chapters of this book investigate in new ways what it means to be a lesbian and how we live our lives. Our unique lifestyles and experiences give us the capacity to enrich the world around us, provide new visions, and generate new solutions and alternatives.

Creative alternatives emerge from the very real differences between lesbians and nonlesbians. Two lesbians in a relationship are not an imitation of a husband and wife. Since fewer lesbians have children than our heterosexual peers do, we tend to have more time and energy for work. At home, lesbian partners tend to split the chores and the cooking fifty-fifty and to take turns helping each other out, rather than emulating the traditional and still common pattern of a heterosexual woman putting her husband's career first.

For those women with children, as Sondra Segal-Sklar points out in "Lesbian Parenting: Radical or Retrograde?" the very existence of two-mommy lesbian families (which the *New York Times* estimates at over 30,000) questions gender roles, division of labor, and the definition of motherhood. I don't think lesbians would be willing to give up these differences to be accepted.

Our greatest strengths lie in the very diversity of the lesbian community and in the ways we differ from both gay men and straight women, not in how closely we imitate them. Monique Wittig has written that "lesbians are not women." Harry Hay, one of the founders of the Mattachine Society (a homophile rights organization founded in 1950), liked to say that homosexuals are different from heterosexuals in every way, except in bed. If Wittig's stance seems too radical, perhaps Hay's is a tad timid. I'd like to take their thinking a step further and proclaim that lesbians are not (like) either gay men or straight women either in or out of bed.

In the early 1970s, lesbian feminists were vocal about the need to include a distinct lesbian perspective/agenda in the women's and gay liberation movements. But since then we have been consumed with the battle for the Equal Rights Amendment and with maintaining reproductive choices for women—although equal access for lesbians to reproductive technology apparently has not been part of the publicly articulated goal. In pursuing the "right to choose," did we inadvertently abandon the right to choose our lifestyle? It seems clear that if anyone lost the struggle for equal rights, lesbians did.

Although large numbers of lesbians joined the feminist movement, we saw our perspectives and goals subsumed into the larger categories of "woman" and "gay." Many feminist authors simply presume that lesbians are exactly like other women. Susan Faludi's *Backlash* mentions us only once or twice in its 460 pages; the word *lesbian* is not even listed in the index. Other books, like Gail Sheehy's *The Silent Passage,* implausibly align the lesbian experience with that of straight women, as if we, too, experienced "perimenopausal panic," as if a lesbian reacted to her lover's menopause the same way a husband does to his wife's.

At the same time, the public continues to conflate our identities with those of gay men. Both gay men and the media have coopted the word *homosexual* and use it to describe situations, conditions, and events that apply only to gay men. In other situations, the media completely overlook lesbians' presence; for example, on the cover of the June 20, 1994, issue of *New York* magazine, celebrating the twenty-fifth anniversary of Stonewall, is a male "Doonesbury" character completely surrounded by white gay males. Inside the magazine only two of the many photos documenting the history of gay and lesbian liberation include women (and all are of whites). In this volume, Shelley Anderson's "Something About Pride" reminds us, for example, that lesbians are also members of the armed forces; in fact, they are discharged for homosexuality about three times as often as gay men. Until the appearance of Colonel Margarethe Cammemeyer's book and the subsequent television film, the gays-in-the military debate seemed to focus almost exclusively on straight men's fears about having to share the showers with openly gay men.

Like the struggle for choice, AIDS has pulled us into another arena that does not focus primarily on lesbians. E. J. Graff has pointed out some of the more blatant errors in the AIDS debate, like a *New York Times* op-ed piece warning that "'gay men and lesbians' must be careful not to fall back into pre-AIDS sexual practices like anal sex . . . as if the writer really believes lesbians have the same anatomies as gay men, or comparable AIDS risk." Most of us are deeply affected by the AIDS crisis. More than half of the gay men I knew have died of AIDS. Yet many of the women I knew have also died—from breast cancer, brain cancer, or male violence. Others have been totally disabled by crippling arthritis or CFIDS (chronic fatigue immune dysfunction syndrome). In this volume, several chapters and sidebars attempt to deal with illness and loss as they affect lesbians. In "Health Care Issues," Karen F. Kerner outlines illnesses that seem to affect lesbians disproportionately, such as breast cancer and CFIDS. She points out that almost no mainstream medical studies focus on lesbians, so it's impossible to know whether our lifestyles are healthier or not. At the same time, the smug assumption that we have one of the lowest rates of AIDS obliterates the reality that lesbian adolescents, who tend to have sex with their gay male friends, have an alarmingly high rate of AIDS, as Joyce Hunter points out in "At the Crossroads: Lesbian Youth." Jane Futcher ("Outlaws and Addicts: Lesbians and the Recovery Movement") reminds us that alcoholism in the lesbian community is found at a much higher rate than among nonlesbians. In "We Never Promised You Role Models," Jeanne Adleman notes that while some old lesbians may have health problems, none of us has a guarantee of good health at any period in life. Jeannine DeLombard explores the difficult problem lesbians face as primary caretakers of elderly parents, children, friends with AIDS, and ailing lovers ("Who Cares? Lesbians As Caregivers"). And in "A Letter from Anita," Kitty Tsui poignantly reminds us how much the loss of friends hurts everyone, whether gay or straight.

If we agree that lesbian lives diverge from those of straight women and gay men, then it's not difficult to agree that the rhythms and times of lesbian life also differ. Childhood and adolescence can be much lonelier for lesbians, who often lack the words to name our feelings of being different. Though lesbian adolescents as a group are much more open and self-aware than those of a generation or two ago, they are still much more likely than nonlesbians to run away from home, to commit suicide, and to be attacked by peers in school. Few cities offer groups for young lesbians, probably because of a fear that heterosexuals will think lesbians are "recruiting" the young. Even fewer cities have gay high schools (the Harvey Milk School in New York City is one exception). As a result, lesbian adolescents live with both isolation and misinformation.

Despite such hardship, several studies indicate that lesbians obtain a higher level of education than our straight peers, in part because a woman who defines herself as lesbian early in life knows that she will not be able to depend on a man to earn more than she will. Lesbians, Maria De La O notes ("Lesbians in Corporate America"), are apt to enter high-paying professions that have a reputation for tolerance; for example, they become professors in universities where the First Amendment is sacred, or computer programmers in companies that provide domestic partnership benefits. But, as Donna Allegra points out in her chapter ("She Tickles with a Hammer"), a high number of lesbians can also be found in the blue-collar trades, such as construction work. They are attracted by the high pay, the good benefits, and the possibility of working with other lesbians (though they're more likely to find sexist men). Ironically, in spite of this work ethic, lesbians earn less than our heterosexual sisters.

Lesbians generally have a much more positive attitude than straight women toward aging. Most of us don't share the culture's phobia about becoming senior citizens. We don't have to please gay or straight men, who tend to enshrine youth and slim waistlines. We don't see midlife as a time when our partner might desert us for a younger woman, though, of course, this scenario does happen occasionally. We see ourselves becoming more attractive, maturing into those older lesbians we always admired! (See "Lesbian Baby Boomers at Midlife," by Esther D. Rothblum, Beth Mintz, D. Brookes Cowan, and Cheryl Haller.)

Some old lesbians are organized, active, and energetic. In "RV Life Begins at Seventy," Shevy Healey points out that retirement can be a time to visit new locales, make new friends, or embrace a new lifestyle. Old lesbians are more likely to find partners than are heterosexual women, who face a quickly dwindling coterie of men (see Mary Meigs's "About Being an Old Lesbian in Love"). Many old lesbians have already overcome self-consciousness about doing things alone or only with other women.

The one rite of passage all lesbians go through, which may occur at any point in our lives, is coming out. Surveys have found that the process of discovering that one is sexually different may happen to children as young as four as well as to seniors. Coming out to ourselves and to others is a cornerstone of gay and lesbian existence and is the topic of several popular anthologies and memoirs. It liberates us and changes the way people perceive us forever. Because telling others that we are lesbians is never a completed act—we are always meeting new people who assume we're heterosexual—it is a central rite of passage to which the contributors to this collection repeatedly return. Just as coming out is a necessary rite of passage, recounting how, where, and when we did it is a common topic of conversation and a good way to get to know other lesbians. Whether or not a lesbian is open with her family of origin is often the acid test for learning how she feels about her own lesbianism or what her politics are. All of us weigh the pain of possible rejection against the destruction to our psyches caused by having to pretend to be someone else or having our families of origin simply assume we are someone else.

In "Are We Family?" Laura S. Brown points out that the benefits of coming out to families of origin may be both more illusive and more elusive than they seem. In most cultures, for instance, lesbian commitment ceremonies are not accorded the same level of celebration as heterosexual marriages, nor do our families of origin help set up lesbian couples financially, as they often do for their heterosexual children. There are exceptions, of course, as Kitty Tsui notes in her chapter, "Lesbian Marriage Ceremonies: I Do."

In addition to dealing with our relatives, we must constantly decide whether to be open with our friends, at school, on the job, and with friends or parents of our children or grandchildren. Professional women often choose work environments that make it less difficult to come out, but in construction work, if you are working on high scaffolding, it might prove dangerous to your health to announce your lesbianism to a sexist male colleague. Every new person brings another moment of decision. Even I, who am totally open about my lesbianism, have found myself the startled object of heterosexual pursuit at work. For some, public self-identification may become an act of courage: Antigay initiatives like those in Colorado and Oregon spurred many to become involved in lesbian politics (see Lee Lynch's "Something Snapped"). A person's poor reaction to a coming-out announcement, not to mention antilesbian laws and initiatives, constantly reminds us that others have made an issue of our sexual orientation. We can also see how complex the issue of coming out is, as Jessica Morris and her co-authors discovered when they tried to map coming-out narratives in "Finding a 'Word for Myself.'"

No matter what family of origin we grow up in, the vast majority of lesbians were not born and raised in a milieu composed of other homosexuals, and so most of us migrate to congenial environments like Northampton, Massachusetts, or San Francisco (see Anna Livia's "San Francisco Spice Rack"). In an unpublished paper, Lee Lucas Berman and Jeffrey Jones of the University of Kentucky refer to "push-pull factors." What pushes us out of the towns and cities of our birth is hate, bigotry, intolerance, physical or verbal abuse. In "Our Relationships and Their Laws" and "Our Children and Their Laws," Ruthann Robson points out that since laws were not fashioned for the benefit of lesbians, we may find that we lack legal protection regardless of where we live. Indeed, some studies suggest that as many as 80 percent of homosexuals have been victims of verbal abuse, and more than 15 percent have suffered physical assault as well. Other studies report that assault against lesbians is rising rapidly, perhaps a sadly inevitable by-product of our increased visibility. Positive factors, in contrast, pull lesbians to various locales. According to the 1988 National Lesbian Health Care Survey, over two-thirds of us live in communities that offer such amenities as a lesbian bar, all-lesbian sports teams, and gay/feminist coffeehouses or bookstores. Of the 18 percent of lesbians who live in communities without any of these activities or cultural institutions, about half are within fifty miles of them.

It might be argued that bars are still the central cultural institution for the majority of lesbians in North America. It is difficult to find a lesbian who has never been in a women's bar. And despite the popularity of twelve-step and other recovery programs, alcoholism, as mentioned earlier, remains higher among lesbians than non-lesbians, in part because of the important role that bars play in our social lives (see Jane Futcher's "Outlaws and Addicts"). Fortunately, today we have music festivals, women's centers, coffeehouses, dyke pot-luck parties, and softball teams, to name but a few alternatives to bar life.

Though the early efforts of post-Stonewall lesbian feminism favored setting up rural separatist communes or communal urban households, the majority of lesbians live in large metropolitan areas, though less so than gay men do. Even in the twelve largest cities that are perceived to be gay-oriented, lesbians tend to live in neighborhoods other than the "gay ghettos": Manhattan's Greenwich Village and Chelsea, San Francisco's Castro, Houston's Montrose, South Florida's Coconut Grove, New Orleans's French Quarter, and Southern California's West Hollywood, to name a few. Although the media refer to these places as centers of gay life, in truth most lesbians cannot afford to live in them. Instead, we frequently reside in tangential areas such as the Mission District in San Francisco or even much farther away from the gay center—for instance, Park Slope in Brooklyn, or Jamaica Plain, near Boston. In male homosexual resort areas, such as Cherry Grove, until recently gay men often resented lesbian presence: They didn't want us intruding in their private paradise. Esther Newton reports in *Cherry Grove, Fire Island* that "during the 1960s at least one of the Grove hotels and many landlords wouldn't rent to women." Lesbians venturing into resort areas such as the Grove or Provincetown or Key West were often treated as though they had wandered into a private, all-male reserve.

I suspect that the advent of the AIDS epidemic in the early 1980s shifted the dynamic of habitat for both lesbians and gay men. Resort areas such as Cherry Grove were among the hardest hit by the early wave of AIDS-related deaths. The men who survived started to vacation elsewhere, in part to avoid the painful memories of their friends who were deceased and in part to avoid the many temptations that might lure them to the same fate. Lesbians, in contrast, had no such negative associations. Furthermore, after a decade of visibility in the gay and feminist movements, lesbians were more likely to want to associate together in both urban and resort areas. Unfortunately, those who choose to remain in lesbian towns like Provincetown or Northampton often have to give up something for the privilege of being able to hold hands on the streets (in a feature in the *Boston Phoenix,* Liz Galst noted that this was a big attraction). Unless they are enterprising enough to establish their own small businesses, they often find themselves earning much less money than they had in their hometowns. In Provincetown, for example, a computer technician might wind up waiting tables or cleaning rooms.

The lure of major metropolitan areas and cultural centers, aside from better job opportunities, is the larger pool of lesbians to socialize with, whether or not we are seeking a relationship. The very concept of "dating" is problematic for lesbians: Since we have been socialized as women, many middle-aged and older lesbians in particular find it difficult to "make the first move" and call up another woman (see Jacqueline Lapidus's "Procrasti-dating"). Being a small minority group, lesbians sometimes have problems finding potential partners in their city or town who share their professional or leisure interests. Even in large cities, lesbians of color, a minority within a minority, find that they face special challenges in forming relationships with other lesbians, as Beverly A. Greene points out in "Lesbian Couples."

Another attraction of major metropolitan areas, or Lesbianvilles, is that the many lesbians who choose to have children find it easier to adopt, to be awarded foster children, or to locate suitable sperm donors there than in a small town in a conservative state. But, as

"Creating Lesbian Families" (Heather Conrad and Kate Colwell), "Lesbian Parenting: Radical or Retrograde?" (Sondra Segal-Sklar), and "Our Children and Their Laws" (Ruthann Robson) point out, a home of dykes with tykes is legally, medically, and socially complicated. Support groups for mothers as well as appropriate schools and a social network for children are important considerations in creating and maintaining a lesbian family.

Probably more lesbians are in committed relationships than any other group. A common joke in our communities is that on the second date, a lesbian brings her U-Haul and moves in! (A gay man, the joke continues, brings his lover on the second date!) Although monogamy and commitment ceremonies would have been anathema in the politically correct 1970s, today they are a popular rite of passage, as Kitty Tsui points out. They might range from a private ceremony for two on a moonlit lake to a large party (see E. J. Graff's "June Brides"). We should not forget, however, that single, celibate, and bisexual lesbians also have valid and potentially pleasurable lifestyles (see Greta Gaard's "Black Lace Hairbow").

Lesbian couples, families, and rituals are not simply duplicates of heterosexual lives. As several of the contributors to this volume make clear, lesbian commitment ceremonies, relationships, families, communities, and culture all call patriarchy into question. When a lesbian couple shows up at the company picnic or a family wedding, or when we ask for a king-size bed in a motel or hold hands in a restaurant, we are questioning patriarchal institutions and heterosexual privileges. We are also destroying assumptions that two women of the same race together must be sisters or cousins or "just good friends"—categories nonlesbians tend to read into us when they detect a relationship, but can't conveniently label it. We challenge the limits of vision: Things are not always as they seem.

Many of the chapters and sidebars in *Dyke Life* challenge readers to consider the ways in which we are unique. Our differences both make us outcasts and offer us new perspectives on institutions, rituals, and privilege. Nevertheless, it is our sexuality that makes us stand out most conspicuously in a heterosexually dominated world. For most of history, lesbian sexuality has been erased. Many scholars, including Lillian Faderman, Caroll Smith-Rosenberg, and Martha Vicinus, have posited that relationships between women prior to 1900 were affectional rather than sexual. While most of us would agree that relationships between women were not the same for Sappho and her circle of poets as they are for contemporary lesbians, we still are not certain about the origins of passionate, genital sexuality between women.

Today, lesbians are on the cutting edge of sexual radicalism, as Marny Hall reveals in "Clit Notes." She uncovers an enormous capacity in many lesbians for fantasy, fun, and a variety of relationships. Some lesbians now claim the right to an erotic freedom that was once associated with gay men. A few large cities have sex clubs and S/M bars for lesbians, while pornographic magazines and videos produced by lesbians for other women have proliferated across the United States. Our sexuality has become as public as our tattoos and our pierced bodies (see Judith P. Stelboum's "Psychic Armor" and Yemaya KauriAlecto's "Body Piercing"). Many forms of current lesbian sexuality are daring and transgressive. Where we once were careful to pretend that we didn't convert nongays, the motto of Lesbian Avengers is "We Recruit," and lesbian "vampires" actively seek to seduce straight women (see Amanda Kovattana's "Confessions of a Lesbian Vampire"). Dildos, once derided by many lesbians as "imitation penises," now make penises seems like imitation dildos (see Slick Harris's "My First Dildo"). In this volume, sidebars and a short chapter on "Safer Sex" explore a few, but by no means all, facets of lesbian sexual experience, as well as the need to have safe fun in the age of AIDS and herpes.

Our sexuality and our sexual identities set us far apart from heterosexuality. Though most of us have all too little time to spend making love, it is what we do in bed that defines lesbians in the minds of most people, including other lesbians. And, however we may feel about butch and femme identities, they are a core part of a significant number of lesbians. In the years after Stonewall, activists denounced butch/femme, S/M, and transgender identities as role playing, but many of us have since learned to appreciate our diverse sexual communities. Unlike either heterosexual men or butch gay men, butch lesbians strive almost solely for the pleasure of the femme. In "Guessing Games," Kath Weston demonstrates that lesbian sexual identification is not as simple as either heterosexuals or many homosexuals would like to believe; for example, even women who label themselves butch find they have characteristics they would consider femme. In "Butch Mothers, Femme Bull Dykes," JoAnn Loulan concurs that butches may be mother figures and femmes may be tough ladies, indeed.

The joyous look at lesbian life and sexuality in this collection follows a loosely chronological order, starting with coming out, which, of course, may occur at almost any age, and then following our lives from adolescence to old age. The book also tries to follow our lives from the private sphere of relationships, sexuality, and families into the public arenas of work and political activism, including outing other lesbians (see Victoria Brownworth's "Outing and the Politics of the Closet"). The last section, "The Lesbian Body," encompasses issues of health, life, and death that we must all face regardless of our age, race, or social status.

Because no one speaks for all lesbians, each piece in this volume has its own voice or distinct perspective. Most are accompanied by sidebars that act as counterpoints or dissenting voices to the material in the longer piece, offer ideas that aren't covered in the chapters, and give added dimension. Many of the chapters end with suggestions for further reading and additional resources to remind us that other voices have spoken on these issues.

The felicitous tone of most of this volume is not intended to make the pernicious suggestion that lesbians are "better" than non-lesbians. We certainly have problems in our communities, as discussed in Paula Ross's "What's Race Got to Do with It?" We don't often deal with our own racism or anti-Semitism, and we can also be callous to the voices of the young, old, disabled, and different among us. Many lesbians would like to deny that problems such as battering exist in our relationships. Lesbians in general tend to be knowledgeable about racism, ecofeminism, and other issues, but reading books or magazines is not the same as taking positive action to bring about social change. But we are proud of active, lesbian-oriented organizations such as Old Lesbians Organizing for Change, the Lesbian Mothers National Defense Fund, and the National Center for Lesbian Rights. A handful of foundations, like the Astraea Foundation, have shown a true commitment to funding projects by lesbians of color.

This anthology, I hope, represents a commitment to lesbian diversity. We can be proud of our heroes, but women as diverse as brick-layers and physicians have lesbianism as a common denominator. The spirit of "we are everywhere" is reflected throughout this book.

—Karla Jay
October 1995

PART ONE

RELATING TO
OTHERS

ONE

ARE WE FAMILY? LESBIANS AND FAMILIES OF ORIGIN

Laura S. Brown

Every year at Seattle's Lesbian and Gay Pride Parade, I observe a familiar scene. Among the floats of men in leather and the cowboy-booted women doing the two-step and all the other representations of our communities, there is one group whose appearance always calls forth the loudest cheers, and not a few tears. These are the marchers from the Parents and Friends of Lesbians and Gays (PFLAG), usually graying heterosexual women and men carrying signs that state "I love my lesbian daughter" or "Proud parent of a gay son." How all of us watching wish our mothers and fathers were among them. The lesbian and gay onlookers are profoundly moved and grateful that parents would publicly proclaim their love for their lesbian and gay children.

But why should such an outpouring of excitement and longing be inspired simply by parents saying they love and accept their children without condition—especially without the condition that they be, or pretend to be, heterosexual? Even suggesting that something might be wrong with this picture seems at odds with a sentiment so many lesbians share: how wonderful that So-and-so's parents have "accepted her"; how nice that her relatives treat her partner just like a member of the family. Is acceptance so rare and important that it should be sought at any cost and should be cause for celebration? What's wrong with this picture is the implicit message that lesbians can expect little from our families of origin.

We hear a great many stories about the trepidation and hard work that lesbians bring to the process of coming out to our families of origin. In our writing and in our music, we tell of our struggle to have civil or, if possible, close and loving relationships with parents, siblings, aunts, uncles, cousins. Most of the time, it is the lesbian family member who takes the risks, does the emotional work, makes the concessions, takes responsibility for staying connected. Rarely do we hear of families reaching out, initiating the arduous task of reconciliation and reintegration.

The relationship of lesbians to the families in which we were raised reflects heterosexism and patriarchal models of family relationships. If we make *acceptance* the gold standard for these relationships, we set the stage for being invaded by heterosexist and sexist norms—a sure sign that our efforts have been derailed by sentimentality and assimilationism. Instead of praising our gains in acceptance by our families, I would like to examine the effects that such norms have on our well-being. I want to suggest a radical shift in our vision of family connection, to explode the notion that acceptance is the sine qua non of good relationships between adult lesbians and our families of origin, and to ask, "Who's accepting whom?"

THE PATRIARCHAL FAMILY

Let's look first at the patriarchal underpinnings of the concept of family. In *The Family Interpreted,* the feminist family therapist Deborah Luepnitz cogently shows how the roots of the patriarchal family of white Western cultures can be found in the Roman family, in which the father, the "paterfamilias," was the owner and sole source of power and life. He literally declared whether a child would live (and become his possession) or be left on the hillside to die of starvation and cold. Girl children were of value primarily for exchange with other families to build or cement alliances.

Adult women were similarly disenfranchised in this historical backdrop to the Western family of today. Traded from one man (father) to another (husband), they were slightly elevated slaves of the household who could be divorced at will, ordered to commit suicide or killed outright, disposed of like any other household possession. Women had no legal right to custody of (or even access to) children after divorce, since any offspring in the marriage were the sole possession of the husband. Since his wife was also his possession, he was within his rights to beat and rape her, and her assets were his.

Most contemporary Americans were raised in families that, if not blatant in their expression of heteropatriarchy, contained persistent elements of that Roman family model. Until the 1970s, a married woman did not have the right to retain her own name or to have credit separate from her husband's; she was not legally defined as a person. There were other, more painful expressions of men's rule over women. The term "battered woman" may not have been coined until the late 1970s (lesbian Del Martin's much-forgotten book *Battered Wives* was published in 1976, two years before the now better-known work of heterosexual feminist Lenore Walker), but battering has always been common in family life. And even in so-called liberated heterosexual families of the 1970s and 1980s, as the sociologist Arlie Hochschild has documented in *The Second Shift*, women continued to carry most of the burden of child care, homemaking, and emotional development of the marital relationship, even when employed full-time outside the home.

In the recovery movement craze of the 1980s, it became fashionable to decry the American family as "dysfunctional" because of alcoholism, denial, and harmful parenting styles. But lesbian commentator Elana Dykewomon has asked whether it is ever possible for a family to be functional within the context of patriarchy. This is not to say that some individual families can't transcend these dynamics, but lesbians must cast a critical eye on nostalgic mythologies of the family so that we can begin to reexamine our relationships there.

SO WHY DO I LOVE MY FAMILY?

This brief analysis of the dangers of the patriarchal family may not seem to match the emotional experiences and recollections of many lesbians. How can their positive emotional experience co-exist with a structure that is inherently harmful to women and makes lesbians invisible because they are the property of no man? First, as I just mentioned, there have always been exemplary families in which the individual members have struggled to ameliorate or even transcend the messages of heteropatriarchy. Other families, even those with some evidence of patriarchal values, have been powerful sources of warmth and affection from which the lesbian daughter benefited. This love is especially valuable in counteracting the societal bias and oppression against American lesbians of color, Jewish lesbians, and others whose culture of origin is devalued. When family is a refuge, it can be hard to notice its flaws. Then, too, memories are not always accurate. Most of us want to have had happy childhoods. So we tend to reconstruct our memories of events to create such thoughts, even if this means rationalizing or minimizing our knowledge of violence and violation.

Thus, for a variety of reasons, lesbians may come to idealize the families in which they were raised. Their desire to fit into their families can become the driving force behind a number of scenarios in lesbians' lives that do not empower them. Only by looking realistically at the problematic aspects of the traditional family, by questioning the value of those scenarios of attachment, can we begin to see how these patterns can damage the well-being of lesbians. Only

Judy MacLean

I'm watching a grown man guide tiny airplanes around the sky by remote control. Mark is my lover's brother—my brother-if-there-were-a-law. I'm glad, I really am, that Jenny's family accepts our relationship, and me, enough to include us in this outing.

It's just that it's hot out here. And boring.

When you fall in love, everything about your lover is bathed in enchantment, from her recovery history to her root canals. Yet when you meet her family, you have about as much in common with them as k. d. lang has with Rush Limbaugh. And while *not* being accepted by your lover's family can hurt like hell, being accepted can pull you into activities that are only slightly more enjoyable than an afternoon at the Motor Vehicle Department.

As a lesbian, I've been so busy trying to get *into* the family circle that I forgot to ask whether I would be interested in what goes on inside it.

I've had genuine in-laws. During the 1960s, I was heterosexually married. My mother-in-law wanted me to join her in the Junior League. I preferred dropping acid, protesting the Vietnam War, and studying existentialism. And I had a stockpile of nightclub comedians'

jokes about mothers-in-law to keep me from feeling guilty about turning down her offers.

Not so today. There's only one excuse for less than absolutely harmonious relations with my if-there-were-a-laws, and that's if they show homophobia. If not, I have a duty to go along with the family program, whatever it may be.

Let's face it: Your lover's family being hostile to your existence has advantages. My previous lover's father was a card-carrying member of the National Rifle Association. He had a whole basement full of guns. I remember my ex in tears because her father wouldn't let me into his life. It was a problem for her. For me, it was a way to avoid our differences. He hated lesbians. I hated guns. If he'd been willing to bend, I would have had to bend, too. At least when he refused to meet me, it kept me from having to stand around at a target range while he explained the difference between his AK-47 and his Uzi.

But today, I am holding a black box that will make an itty-bitty green jet do a loop-the-loop. Still, I'll get revenge. Next time Mark comes to visit us, I'll broaden *his* horizons by taking him to a poetry reading. Or maybe campaigning for a lesbian candidate.

then can we begin to lay a foundation for new forms of relationship between lesbians and the families from which we come.

PATTERNS OF RELATING

Through my experience as a psychotherapist, my readings of auto-biographical lesbian literature, and examinations of my own life and those of my lesbian friends, I have observed and analyzed some common patterns and styles of relationships between lesbians and their families of origin. I have concluded that the primary function of that relationship is to uphold the heteropatriarchal family by means of marginalizing lesbian existence in the family context. These relationships can be unhealthy and denigrating for lesbians. They are disrespectful of our lives and our intimate relationships, making us invisible at worst and diminishing the value of our life choices at best. Here I would like to describe briefly several of these patterns and analyze the problems they present. The examples offered here are composites of different women, with details changed to protect anonymity.

In the Closet

When the relationship between a lesbian and her family is characterized by denial of her identity, she becomes defined as a sexual neuter, a "spinster" sister or aunt, an unmarried daughter. Such a lesbian is invisible as an adult who may have a rich sexual and intimate life. She is thus construed as still belonging to the family—not being "owned," so to speak, by a man and not defined to the family as being in intimate connection with women.

For the many lesbians whose family of origin is blatantly anti-lesbian, hiding the self is seen as the only way to maintain a relationship with parents, siblings, and other loved family members. When these lesbians fear that their families' acceptance is conditional, or have seen other relatives cut off for different "sins," they take it to be too risky to let the truth be known.

The price for this choice can be high. If she is thought of as the single daughter, the lesbian may find herself at the beck and call of the family, since any commitments to a relationship with a partner are invisible. She is likely to be expected to put in appearances at family holidays and celebrations on her own, since the presence of the "roommate" may raise suspicions. She may be the target of misguided matchmaking attempts and have to tolerate invasions of her privacy for the sake of maintaining the fiction that she is heterosexual. This mask can at times be destructive to any lesbian relationship in which this woman finds herself, as her partner will be caught in the bind of being important to the closeted lesbian, yet having to pretend not to be to her family.

Andrea, a lesbian in her mid-thirties from a middle-class, white, Catholic family, knew her parents disapproved of homosexuality because they actively participated in a religious group that advocated the conversion of homosexuals. She needed their financial help to complete her advanced degree program and did not want to be cut out of what she believed would be a considerable inheritance from her parents, which she felt entitled to after years of dealing with their difficult relationship.

Though she lived with a series of female lovers, Andrea had an ongoing dating relationship with an unsuspecting man whom her parents could see as a possible husband. She pressured her lovers to date men as well, to help her cover. In this manner, she was able to invite some of her longer-term lovers to various family gatherings as the "roommate" (with heterosexual credentials). She freely admitted to her lesbian friends that she had never been attracted to men; nonetheless, she would occasionally force herself to have intercourse with the man she dated.

The stress on Andrea as an individual and on her relationships with women was profound. In order to continue in the relationship with the man, she began drinking more and more before, during, and sometimes after her dates in order to tolerate his increasingly intimate behavior, as well as her own shame at deceiving and exploiting him. Over time, she began to depend on alcohol as a coping strategy for other facets of her life, especially her relationship with her parents.

Not surprisingly, the women lovers who had initially been willing to go along with the cover-up found themselves frustrated and often enraged, particularly on the nights when Andrea went out with her "boyfriend." One female partner threatened to leave unless they went to couples therapy. Andrea, fearful that she would never be able to make a lesbian relationship work, reluctantly came to my office but insisted that she would never come out to her parents because she felt it was unreasonable to ask them to accept her as she was. She did not see how she could maintain her cover as a heterosexual woman without continuing to fake relationships with men, even though she loved her current partner. She could see no way out of her terrible dilemma short of her parents' deaths. She commented with irony on how she, in the name of family closeness, had almost come to hate her parents at times and to feel increasingly estranged from them because of her deception. She dropped out of therapy after a few months, and her lover left her soon afterward.

While not all lesbians who are closeted to their families engage in as extreme a deception as Andrea did, many suffer similar losses of self-worth in the process of stripping away their identity each time they interact with their families. Is it worth it? The bargain struck by such women often reflects their own strong sense of unworthiness and a tacit admission that, as lesbians, they dare not seek acceptance and tolerance by their families because they have so profoundly transgressed.

One Foot Out of the Closet

Some lesbians manage to be open with one or two members of the family, often a mother or sibling, with whom they conspire to keep the secret from the other family members. Commonly, this configuration repeats earlier alliances in the family that were forged to keep secrets in the name of preserving family unity or to protect a

Terri de la Peña

I was thirty-one, the shy middle daughter, when I came out in a whisper to my younger sister. Blanca (not her real name) kept my secret from our Chicano Catholic family for five years. When the others began to suspect, I gradually edged out of the closet.

Mom offered novenas to save my soul; Dad seemed unsurprised. I gave everyone coming-out books. One Sunday Mom invited my lover to play Scrabble. I began to relax. With time and the realization that I was the same person they had always known, calm returned to the family.

Three years later, Blanca began dating Oscar (not his real name). Instinctively, I distrusted him and told her so. Nobody in the family liked him. He made inappropriate comments—racist, sexist, homophobic. I confronted Blanca to no avail.

Though she had been my first ally, Blanca outed my lover and me to Oscar. He then committed acts of vandalism against family members, putting sand in our gas tanks, flattening tires, breaking windows. My otherwise closeted lover left me.

I felt despondent and betrayed, but eventually began to date again. A year after Blanca married Oscar, I met a new lover.

One night Oscar pounded on my door, claiming he wanted me to sign a neighborhood petition; I refused to let him in and insisted that he go away. He stomped off, but waited the next afternoon at my mailbox. He called me "cunt, pussylicker, pervert." I grabbed my mail and hurried upstairs. When he repeated the scenario the next day, I phoned the police; they never came.

That weekend, Oscar continued his verbal harassment as my lover and I arrived home. Furious, yet afraid he might harm her, I persuaded her to leave. Blanca watched as Oscar began to follow me; I slammed my apartment door and called the police again. The dispatcher asked whether Oscar were a former boyfriend. "No," I said. "He's my sister's husband. I'm a lesbian."

When the cops arrived, I came down to meet them. They informed Oscar that his aggressive behavior constituted a violation of my civil rights; I could sue him on that basis. The cops agreed he was a "powder keg." One gave me his business card, warning me to be careful.

Since I could no longer believe or trust her, I cut all ties to Blanca. Now I can never think of her without being reminded that homophobia begins at home.

weak or ill family member. Subtle attempts at subverting the authority of the paterfamilias are played out in the manner of slave laborers attempting to sabotage factory work. In such families, the power of the father and the hegemony of patriarchy are explicit, creating a false closeness among the oppressed members that is intensified when the lesbian daughter shares her secret under a pledge of strict confidentiality.

In this strategy, the price paid by the lesbian is usually less than when the secrecy remains total. The family member(s) in the know usually include the partner in family events, inquire into the well-being of the relationship, and in general behave supportively as long as the lesbian relative does not violate the secrecy compact. But this special, secret relationship reinforces the notion that being lesbian is dangerous ("If your father finds out, it will kill him"). Accidental "slips" by the lesbian may make her the target of anger from the knowing family member, who fears the possible unraveling of the conspiracy.

This strategy is illustrated in the poignant lyrics to Meg Christian's song "Momma," in which a lesbian daughter sings of her love for her mother, who knows of the daughter's sexual orientation but will not admit to it, thus creating silences between them. The lesbian daughter is distanced from family members when the price of playing hide-and-seek becomes too high. The familiar lesbian cartoon in which a couple frantically "de-dykes" the house before the arrival of visiting parents demonstrates in a small way how energy that could be turned to productive ends is channeled into keeping the secret.

Ginger, an African-American lesbian in her late twenties from a working-class family, utilizes this strategy. She is out to her two sisters, who insist that she not tell their parents, who would be very "disappointed." Ginger describes encounters with her family as a frantic juggling act, as she talks openly with her sisters, all the while making sure that Mom or Dad doesn't accidentally overhear. When Ginger is dating African-American women, she has been able to integrate her lovers into family events as "friends." One time she trembled with anxiety when her mother got close to one of these women, then became confused when she completely disappeared from their life after Ginger broke up with her. She and her sisters agree that her parents probably sense something about Ginger's sexual orientation, but are happy to stay ignorant of it. And Ginger has the illusion of including her lovers in her family life.

But Ginger's most recent relationship, with Becky, has badly strained this system of coping, since it is much harder to explain a white Jewish friend to her parents. While she continues to be open with her sisters, she finds herself the target of questions and criticism, particularly from her father, with whom she has had a close and important relationship. His profound and painful experiences with racism have left him suspicious of whites; his daughter's seemingly inexplicable alliance with Becky angers and upsets him, and he and Ginger have argued over it. She finds herself caught between wanting to respect her sisters' pleas for continued silence about her lesbianism and her desire to clear the air and tell her parents who Becky really is in her life. Ginger has also become acutely aware that she is not accepted by either her parents or her siblings, the latter seeing her lesbianism as something too terrible for the parents to know.

Lesbians with one foot out of the closet are tacitly acknowledging that their identities are too inherently negative and flawed to be shared with the whole family. Being grateful for partial and/or conditional acceptance teaches lesbians to be content with crumbs.

Being Out and Grateful

Some lesbians decide to be entirely open with their families, and some families respond without rejection: The woman is not banned from the family, and her partner is invited to family events, like any other in-law. The family may even exchange birthday presents and socialize with the partner's parents—in short, they may have the superficial trappings of normal family life. But rarely are there public displays of affection, such as kissing the partner hello or good-bye, and rarely is the relationship revealed to any children in the family. Family members' casual heterosexist remarks are laughed off or minimized.

While this lesbian is visible in her family, and the family appears to accept her status, the underlying message of this arrangement is that she should be grateful simply for being taken as she is by her family. This attitude reinforces a view of lesbianism as a less valuable life and keeps the power between the lesbian and her family members uneven because she can never thank them sufficiently for their acceptance.

An example of the problems with this arrangement can be found in the experience of Jess, a working-class white lesbian from a large and boisterous family. The weddings of her six older siblings were attended by the entire extended family and preceded by weeks of celebrations. She had come out to her family in her late adolescence. Her siblings and cousins teased her about when she would find "Ms. Right," although her parents remained silent on this topic. They preferred to discuss her work as an increasingly respected electrical contractor. Jess expected that when she did meet the right woman, she would have a commitment ceremony every bit as exuberant as those of her siblings and cousins.

She was shocked, then, when she met and fell deeply in love with Julie: Jess' family, apparently comfortable with her casual liaisons, began to seem skittish at the appearance of the happy young couple, and suggested to Jess in private that she and Julie refrain from holding hands and snuggling up on the couch when visiting. When Jess announced plans for a commitment ceremony at the local Unitarian church where she and Julie worshipped, her mother suddenly mentioned travel plans and told Jess to go ahead without her and Jess' father. Jess was crushed; she told her parents angrily that she could not imagine them being unable to attend any other wedding in the family. Her mother responded: "This isn't really a wedding, dear." While Julie was loved and welcome, she would clearly never be accepted by the family as another in-law.

LESBIAN-CENTERED RELATIONSHIPS TO OUR FAMILIES: A PROPOSAL

In all these portraits, one message emerges clearly: The family, like the Roman paterfamilias of old, decides whether to accept the lesbian into the charmed circle or expose her metaphorically on the hillside, cut off from the family unit. That makes it seem as though acceptance is the best we can hope for.

In a recent issue of the *Washington Blade*, the District of Columbia lesbian and gay newspaper, I came across a political cartoon that expressed perfectly the ideal to which I think lesbians should aspire in our relationships to family. In the first panel, a lesbian couple is proud to be telling their families that they expect great gifts for their celebration of commitment. In the next panel we see the mother of one of the women in front of a four-wheel-drive vehicle with a bow on top, a gift she is proud to be able to give her daughter and her partner. The lesbian couple and their parents have a perfectly normal, almost banal relationship to one another. Each has defined the terms on which to relate with the other.

This ideal was echoed in a recent PFLAG contingent in the Seattle Pride Parade. One young woman marched next to her parents, carrying a sign that said "I love my heterosexual mother and father." While the sign drew chuckles from bystanders, it firmly expressed the notion that the right to accept, to bring family into our lives, is as much in our hands as it is in those of our families of origin.

We need to evaluate what in our families we wish to accept, as well as what we will not. We need to decide how our families, as a group and as individuals, will be welcome in our lives; what norms and standards of behavior will make their presence in our adult families of choice valued and acceptable to us. We can use our positions outside the mainstream to question harmful values there and the ways our families might embody those problems.

In short, lesbians must come to see ourselves as of sufficient value to our families of origin that we retain the right to question harmful patterns of relating, to ask for and expect changes in relational dynamics with other family members. We can ask for an end to silence, abuse, and invalidation of ourselves not only as lesbians but as part of our families. We are *entitled* to be out. We need to overcome the voices of homophobia and heterosexism inside ourselves, and to learn to see our openness with our families of origin as a gift we share with them, rather than as the gift of acceptance they give to us.

This posture seems radical. Many of us struggle with the notion of seeing our lesbian presence in the family as a gift rather than a problem. But the gift we bring is not simply access for our family members to share in the richness and joy, struggles and pains, of our daily lives. It is also the gift of questioning patriarchal norms that are destructive to everyone. Our forthright presence in our families, asking not for acceptance but for a new definition of what is normal and functional in families, enhances the life of any family.

We can also bring to our families the gift of showing courage in the face of oppression, empowering them to overcome oppressions in their own lives. Nadia, a middle-class Latina, comfortably out with her family, turned out to be a major catalyst for change in her mother's life. Seeing Nadia so nonchalantly certain about her own value and worth inspired her mother to challenge the subtle denigration she had long endured from her supervisor at work. She had learned from Nadia that no one had to put up with oppressive treatment, even if it seemed minor and if it were embedded in an otherwise tolerable environment.

But there are emotional risks in embracing and operating from this lesbian-centered model. Some families will not be willing to move beyond patriarchal strictures to value relationship over rules and forms. Some will be more invested in their homophobic beliefs, or in maintaining the illusion of power over their adult offspring, than in having loving, equal, and honest connections with their lesbian daughters, sisters, and nieces. Some will feel torn between loyalty to culture and love for their daughters.

Del Martin and Phyllis Lyon

Heated debates over lesbians and gays in the military, in federal administrative posts, and in employment discrimination suits have put some politically involved parents on the spot. Their lesbian daughters have kept silent about their private lives in order to protect their parents' public image. But some parents are forced to choose between what is right for their children and what is expedient for the political party.

Robert Mosbacher, former secretary of commerce and a top official in George Bush's reelection campaign, accepted his daughter's lesbianism and respected her long-term relationship. Rather, the tension between father and daughter is over political differences. She is a Democrat, and the mean-spirited turn of the 1992 Republican Convention prompted forty-three-year-old Dee Mosbacher to speak out. "This is war," she told us. "My father can separate the personal from the political, but I can't." When national leaders make bigoted and homophobic comments, she said, it is dehumanizing and can have serious repercussions for perceived lesbians and gays.

Bill Byrne, chair of the Cobb County Commission in Georgia, was instrumental in passing a resolution proclaiming gay life incompatible with community standards. His twenty-four-year-old lesbian daughter, Shannon, couldn't change his mind. She watched the controversy over the resolution simmer for nearly a year, then decided to jump into the fray. In a highly publicized press conference, she came out as a lesbian and announced that she would join the effort to have the resolution rescinded. Her father had told her that she would be discriminated against by society. At the end of her press conference, Shannon paused for a moment and smiled. "Thanks, Dad," she said, "for making it happen."

In another incident, Jesse Helms, during the Senate debate over the appointment of a new undersecretary of Housing and Urban Development, called Roberta Achtenberg "that damned lesbian." This prompted Claiborne Pell, a veteran senator from Rhode Island, to announce that his forty-year-old daughter, Julia, was president of the Rhode Island Alliance for Gay and Lesbian Civil Rights, adding: "I would certainly not want to see her barred from government service because of her sexual orientation."

We hope that more lesbian daughters whose antigay fathers are in positions of power will come out publicly, and that more fathers will speak up to defend their lesbian daughters.

However, these risks are not absent from the other patterns of relationships I have described. The risks of being unknown, of being distanced from our families when we want to be close, of invalidating our lives when we want to celebrate them—all are present in the more common strategies for relating to our families. In those patterns, in which heterosexism and homophobia are the defining principles of the relationship, such risks are assumed, by both lesbians and our family members, to be part of the necessary price of being lesbian, a penalty for living outside the patriarchal definitions.

In a lesbian-centered model, these risks are cause for rage and grief rather than resignation. More important, these risks are seen as the fault not of the lesbian but of the resistance of patriarchal cultures to change.

In other words, we have little to lose and much to gain by developing a lesbian-centered stance in our relationships to our families. As our great poet Adrienne Rich has noted, lying, whether by words or by silences, leads to a disconnection from who we are; no one should be asked to pay the price of a lost and disconnected self. Our grief at losing relationships that are highly dependent upon conditionality, disempowerment, and devaluation is often the culmination of the grief that we, consciously or not, feel at not being at home in our families. Consciously choosing to risk losing something that may harm us and our families, in exchange for a clearly empowering and pro-lesbian relationship, should be a step we do not hesitate to take.

Sometimes our families of origin will not be able to let us in; some families are just too broken or dangerous. To believe that we can effect change by refusing to maintain the status quo may require faith in the revolutionary potential of women. But to do otherwise will be to resign ourselves to continue to participate in, and be damaged by, the patriarchal culture that we should be seeking to transform.

FURTHER READING

Loulan, JoAnn. *Lesbian Passion: Loving Ourselves and Each Other.* San Francisco: Spinsters/Aunt Lute, 1987. See particularly the chapters called "Healing the Child Within" and "Lesbian Self-Esteem."

Luepnitz, Deborah Anna. *The Family Interpreted.* New York: Basic Books, 1988.

Pollack, Sandra, and Joanne Vaughn, eds. *Politics of the Heart: A Lesbian Parenting Anthology.* Ithaca, N.Y.: Firebrand Books, 1987. See particularly the chapter by Baba Copper.

Rafkin, Louise. *Different Daughters: A Book by Mothers of Lesbians.* Pittsburgh: Cleis Press, 1987.

Robson, Ruthann. *Lesbian (Out)Law: Survival Under the Rule of Law.* Ithaca, N.Y.: Firebrand Books, 1992.

TWO

FINDING A "WORD FOR MYSELF": THEMES IN LESBIAN COMING-OUT STORIES

Jessica F. Morris, Amy J. Ojerholm, Teri M. Brooks, Dana M. Osowiecki, and Esther D. Rothblum

The beginning of my journey was coming out to myself. All of my life experiences seemed to come together at once, and I knew I'd discovered the core of myself. I finally saw all that I'd been feeling in a new, sexual light, and found the word for myself: lesbian.

—Barber and Holmes, *Testimonies*

Since society holds heterosexuality as the norm and most women grow up assuming that they fit this norm, the process of realizing and naming one's lesbianism is a defining experience. "Coming out" goes on throughout life, as each lesbian makes decisions to share information about her sexual orientation with others, from family members and friends to co-workers and neighbors, even the stranger in the next seat on an airplane.

For many lesbians, the memory of coming out has been crafted into a story that is told and retold and is often the starting point of a friendship or relationship between lesbians. It is not unusual for these stories to become oral histories, passed down from person to person as lesbians learn the details of each other's experience of coming out. As Karla Jay has noted in her article "Coming Out as Process," there are many important reasons to know when a lesbian came out: The age she was is as meaningful as the cultural context at that time.

In an effort to understand coming out, experts have developed a number of stage theories. In her 1979 article "Homosexual Identity Formation: A Theoretical Model," Vivienne Cass develops a six-stage model based on her work as a psychotherapist: Identity Confusion, Identity Comparison, Identity Tolerance, Identity Acceptance, Identity Pride, and Identity Synthesis. The first four stages can be typified by the questions or statements a person in that stage might express: "Who am I?"; "I may be homosexual"; "I probably am a homosexual"; and "I am a homosexual." Stage 5 is characterized by a devaluation of heterosexual values and people as well as by anger and activism. In stage 6, this "us and them" philosophy is rejected, and the final resolution is to see homosexuality as only one aspect of oneself.

This theory, with its assumption of a neat and orderly progression through the same stages for everyone, seems inadequate to account for the experience of coming out today. The stage theories also produce an expectation that women who have moved to a newer place in the process of coming out as lesbians are superior to those who are still at a prior stage or who have "fallen" back into one. Many lesbian activists would take exception to the idea that they have not yet attained the highest level of identity development, especially those lesbians who have never seen themselves as activist and who are considered even less developed by the stage theory. Furthermore, are those women who see their lesbianism as the central, defining characteristic of their lives (including some of the authors of this chapter) doomed never to fully develop their lesbian identity because they continually fail to see lesbianism as only one aspect of themselves?

In 1993, Paula Rust found that sexual identity is fluid throughout one's life and that it commonly changes, in some cases many times, in adulthood. In her sample, lesbians were an average age of 15.4 when they experienced their first homosexual attractions and 17 when they first questioned their heterosexual identity. The average age of first identifying themselves as lesbian was 21.7. Bisexual women reached these milestones in the same sequence but a couple of years later on average. Of those women who identified as lesbian, 41 percent identified themselves as bisexual at some time, whereas 76 percent of the bisexual women had once identified as lesbian.

Sexual identity development is, however, only one aspect of coming out. The disclosure of this identity to others is also of great importance to a lesbian, especially when it involves telling her family of origin. As members of a study group focusing on research about lesbians, we have found that the coming-out models do not capture the richness of lesbian life. Most do not address both *coming* out and *being* out as the separate processes Joseph Harry has described. Furthermore, the traditional models ignore feminism and political identity in general. Instead of developing our own model and thereby imposing a structure on experience, we decided to examine experiences directly and see what sort of structure emerged. We did this by looking for common themes in the published coming-out stories of lesbians. We read a number of anthologies published between 1982 and 1994 containing autobiographical pieces (see Further Reading at the end of this chapter) and identified more than twenty-five different themes, which we grouped into five larger categories. The remainder of the chapter will be devoted to the stories, organized according to these categories: diversity in the lesbian community; the different components of coming out; the reaction of a woman's family of origin; the reception by the lesbian and non-lesbian communities to one's coming out; and the varied emotions experienced by women as they came out.

DIVERSITY IN THE LESBIAN COMMUNITY

There are as many different experiences with coming out as there are lesbians who come out. While scholars and artists generally attempt to discover the common threads within the lesbian experience, we prefer to describe the diversity of the lesbian community. Diversity can be articulated in many ways—across lines of race, social class, age, religion, body size, and ability. The lesbians whose stories we read often discussed the double and triple minority status they experienced as lesbians and as women of color, or as poor lesbians in communities where most women were middle class:

> In this country, lesbianism is a poverty—as is being brown, as is being a woman, as is being just plain poor. The danger lies in ranking the oppressions. The danger lies in failing to acknowledge the specificity of the oppression. The danger lies in attempting to deal with oppression purely from a theoretical base. . . . When the going gets rough, will we abandon our so-called comrades in a flurry of racist/heterosexist/what-have-you panic? To whose camp, then, should the lesbian of color retreat? [Cherríe Moraga, in *The Original Coming Out Stories*]

Many women wrote, sometimes mournfully, of being pressured into making a hierarchy of oppressions. The language and metaphors were sometimes warlike: choosing sides, betraying one's culture. The battles were sometimes metaphorical but often real. Joining a lesbian group on a college campus could automatically disqualify you from participating in a racial or an ethnic student group. As one Indian woman put it:

> I was almost seduced into believing that I could not be an Indian and a lesbian without betraying either the culture of my birth and family, or the culture I had chosen as a lesbian and a feminist. Just as men had silenced me in the solidarity commit-

tees and meetings of the left, so too I found white lesbians talking for me and about me as though I was not present. [Kaushalya Bannerji, in *A Lotus of Another Color*]

For many women of color, coming out jeopardizes not only their sense of self as a member of a racial or an ethnic group but also their place within their family of origin and its cultural identification. The false view that lesbianism is a "white thing" adds a layer of complexity to the nonwhite lesbian's development and her attempts to remain part of her family of origin and ethnic culture. But some women do manage to integrate their lesbian and racial/ethnic identities:

Being a black woman and a lesbian unexpectedly blended, like that famous scene in Ingmar Bergman's film *Persona*. The different faces came together as one, and my desire became part of my heritage, my skin, my perspective, my politics, and my future. [Jewelle Gomez, in *Testimonies*]

There are women who reject their lesbianism, but it is harder to reject one's racial identity, usually a visible characteristic. Some women whose stories we read said that when they walk down the street, people see, for example, their black or Asian identity. When an African-American lesbian is followed by a security guard as she walks through a store, she is no doubt correct in thinking that it isn't her lesbianism that makes the guard suspect her as a shoplifter. Some women resolve this struggle by choosing to identify more strongly with one group than another: "The person who emerged first was the Puerto Rican, followed by the woman, and then by the Lesbian" (Sister Esperanza Fuerte, in *Lesbian Nuns*).

Religion is also an important factor in the coming-out process: "Religious women who happen to be Lesbians live behind two closet doors" (Charlotte A. Doclar, in *Lesbian Nuns*). Organized religions are often gender-segregated, and some lesbians seek out these women-only spaces by, for example, becoming a nun or studying the

Torah. Early in the process of coming out, many lesbians feel a strong pull to be in a community of women, without always understanding the sexual component of this pull.

THE MANY FACETS OF COMING OUT

The coming-out stories we read demonstrate that lesbian identity development occurs in many more than the five or six stages discussed in stage theories. These women commonly describe sensual childhood experiences with other girls or women before their feelings of sexual desire became explicit. The sense of being different came up over and over again in the writings, an idea that is a theme unto itself: "I carried a strong sense that I was different throughout adolescence. I knew I could be happy just being with my girlfriends, and boys seemed unnecessary, even bothersome" (Sarah Holmes, in *Testimonies*).

Some women reported always having had this feeling of being different, even before any sense that they were not heterosexual. Thus, they attributed it to other things, such as ethnic or religious identity. For a number of women the feeling of being different was directly associated with feeling like a boy or preferring boys' clothing, toys, playmates, and games. These feelings were value-neutral for some women; others described them as containing an element of excitement. Either way, feelings of being different commonly developed into a sense of alienation, especially when others also perceived the woman as different and treated her badly.

Eventually, romantic (although not necessarily erotic) feelings for other girls or women developed. One woman describes these romances at a time (1873) when they were socially accepted:

When a Vassar girl takes a shine to another, she straightaway enters upon a regular course of bouquet sendings, interspersed with tinted notes, mysterious packages of "Ridley's Mixed Candies," locks of hair perhaps, and many other tender tokens, until at last the object of her attention is captured, the two become inseparable, and the aggressor is considered by her circle of acquaintances as "smashed." [Anne MacKay, in *Wolf Girls at Vassar*]

For most women, romantic involvement or thoughts lead to sexual exploration. In the stories, the timing of the exploration fell loosely into three categories. First were those women who described sexual exploration with other girls or women outside of any lesbian context—that is, they did not see themselves (or their partners) as lesbian; some did not even know there was such a thing. Some said that they felt more than they thought their partners did: It was more for them than just "practicing for boys." For a second group of women, sexual exploration coincided with their first labeling of themselves as lesbian. And a third group conceived of themselves as lesbians before having any sexual involvement with other women.

No matter when a woman first sees herself as a lesbian, it is an important event. For some, it is a wondrous occasion, as a lifetime of confusion seems to fall into order:

It was then that I realized I loved her. It was so simple. I was not going crazy, I was in love! I remember thinking "of course! How silly of me!" My behavior for the past two months suddenly made perfect sense. I was not frightened by the idea that this meant I must be a lesbian. . . . The idea of loving Sharon made me feel sane and at peace with myself; being a lesbian is infinitely preferable to being dead. [Deidre McCalla, in *The Original Coming Out Stories*]

For others, confronting their lesbianism is an ambivalent experience. Some women look up the word *lesbian* in the dictionary and are horrified or puzzled by what they read. Or perhaps they have an image of lesbians that does not conform to the way they themselves look or behave.

Some of the women in the books we read had difficulty integrating their sense of who they were with their (stereotypical) beliefs about lesbians—thinking, for example, that they couldn't be lesbians because they didn't wear men's clothes, didn't have a "masculine" job, weren't ugly, and didn't hate men. Those who rejected the lesbian label were usually in a temporary phase, but one that could bring on destructive behavior, like excessive drug or alcohol use. Some women, including those in Catholic orders, became celibate; others became sexually involved with men, even getting married and having children.

Among the pieces we read were stories in the Christian fundamentalist magazine *Focus on Family* by women who felt they had been permanently "cured" of their lesbianism:

> I accepted Christ immediately. I was so thrilled, so excited that I had actually experienced the touch of Jesus Christ. Fortunately, I was between lesbian relationships, so God's timing was perfect.

> I looked deep in my heart, and I *knew* I had been living a sinful lifestyle. I wanted out, so I repented and asked God to help me. . . . God *can* change a homosexual's heart. I know because not only have I seen it, I've experienced it.

Whether or not they later reject it, most women who identify as lesbians do so early in life, even if they did not see it that way at the time. One of the exceptions is Phoebe Schock: "I'm one of the gay grandmothers. I spent most of my life trying to do what was expected of me" (*Wolf Girls at Vassar*).

REACTIONS TO COMING OUT: FAMILY

Deciding whether or not to come out to one's family of origin is a major choice for lesbians. Some never do, out of respect for a family's religious or cultural traditions, or out of fear of rejection. The National Lesbian Health Care Survey (NLHCS), examining the experiences of almost two thousand lesbians in 1984, found that 19 percent were not out to anyone in their family of origin, while 27 percent were out to all family members. The other 54 percent were out only to some family members (see also Laura S. Brown's "Are We Family?" in this volume). Those who do come out to family must deal with the consequences, which range across a wide spectrum. Negative responses are unfortunately very common:

> Among some of us young dykes, this was a very important and often-discussed subject: "Does your mother know?" "Oh, God, no! Does yours?" "I think she might suspect." We could talk about it for hours, speculating ways to do it, to Tell, fantasizing situations involving Finding Out and What Would Happen Thereafter. "I could never tell mine. She'd die. It'd kill her." "Mine'd crack up for sure." [Merril, in *The Original Coming Out Stories*]

Some of the harshest responses can come from religiously devout parents, who can clearly articulate their religion's position on homosexuality and often can't integrate their religious convictions with their daughters' lesbianism.

Some women described horrible, painful, even violent reactions from family members, who severed ties with them or harshly criticized them. Other families tolerated the situation, with the expectation that it would simply never be discussed. This often meant that the woman's lover/partner was not welcome in the family's home or, if she was allowed in, was treated as though she were a roommate or platonic friend. Some women described similar reactions when their own children learned of their mother's lesbianism.

Sometimes, the story of a family's response started out sadly and ended up joyously:

Deborah Perkins

"I'm gay. I'm sorry. Please don't hate me."

"I think you're very sick," Mom replied. Then she turned and walked away.

I sat there on her mountain of rejection, calling out, "I'm still your daughter and I love you," and hearing only the echo of my own voice. My heart broke like a pane of glass.

If only I could do it over again, I wouldn't search day after day, trying to find just the right words to ward off her anger and quell her disgust.

"You don't know," I would tell her, "how it feels to discover you're not who you think you are. You don't know what it's like to learn at the age of thirty-two that you've fallen in love with a woman, and nothing in your fundamentalist, heterosexual background has prepared you for that. You don't know how it feels to realize after all those years that you're lesbian.

"You don't know what it's like to sit in a classroom or an office with people who are supposed to be your friends and listen to their sneering comments about 'dykes' and 'faggots.' You don't know what it's like not daring to speak the truth about yourself. You don't know what it's like to have to learn how to lie and how to hide.

"You don't know the fear of being backed into a corner by a man bigger and stronger than you, who is trying to convince you that he can turn you back into a 'real' woman.

"You don't know what it's like to be judged for who you love instead of for who you are. You can't imagine the never-ending ache of wanting to tell your parents the one thing you know will hurt them most of all. And you can't begin to know the depth of that pain when you see the disappointment in their eyes."

If I could go back and do it again, I wouldn't try to find the words that are the easiest to say and the easiest to hear. This time, I would just tell the truth.

Mom, Dad, and I talked for a long time, and we cried a little, too. But they eventually reaffirmed what I'd always known: that they love me very deeply and will always be my staunchest supporters. After much pleading and cajoling, three years later, they marched in my first gay pride parade with me, carrying a sign that said, "WE LOVE OUR LESBIAN DAUGHTER." [Liz O'Lexa, in *Testimonies*]

Families responded both positively and negatively to lesbianism; but some simply denied or ignored the information.

REACTIONS TO COMING OUT: COMMUNITY

It is not the same to come out to heterosexuals as it is to come out to other lesbians. This distinction highlights the importance of the lesbian community in women's coming-out experiences. Before the 1969 Stonewall rebellion, having a safe community of other lesbians was often a life-or-death necessity. The National Lesbian Health Care Survey revealed that 88 percent of women surveyed had come out to all their lesbian and gay male friends, while only 28 percent were out to all their heterosexual friends.

Cultural considerations are also an important reason for situating oneself in the lesbian community: "When I first came out twelve years ago, there were very few South Asian lesbians and gays around. We knew we were around and would travel hundreds of miles to meet" (Pratibha Parmar, in *A Lotus of Another Color*).

Although the lesbian community is a strong force in the life of many lesbians, it is not always perceived as a nurturing bosom into which a newly out woman is welcomed. Some women have difficulty joining the lesbian community because their age, ethnic group, religion, or economic class differs from that of most women in a given community. Others have internalized the homophobic message of the larger society, which can make them close off the lesbian community. When a woman first experiences love for another woman, it is not uncommon for her to grieve the loss of her heterosexual privilege. Often, the burden of this sacrifice is so great that she decides not to make the transition to a lesbian existence.

The Storytellers' Emotions

A final thematic category that took shape as we read these coming-out stories comprises the emotional responses of the authors to their own coming-out experiences. Some common emotions, especially early on, were guilt, shame, and fear: "I was drawn to her but was also very scared. After much anguish, we decided to 'give in' and experiment with being lovers. What followed was a year and a half of a loving, guilt-ridden, closeted relationship" (Adina Abramowitz, in *Twice Blessed*).

Once these women reached the point where their sexual identity was familiar and comfortable to them, they were likely to express more positive emotions—pride, encouragement, hope: "I'd like to say to any other Afro-American woman of color who is out there and struggling with her sexuality and feels there are no role models, there are other black women out there who will appreciate you for everything you are, so go for it!" (Valarie Walker, in *Wolf Girls at Vassar*).

"Becoming" a lesbian is not experienced in a temporal, hierarchical fashion. Most lesbians' accounts of their own coming out and being out describe the process as ongoing.

Coming Out as a Lifelong Process

Sexual identity itself has proved to be a fluctuating status, as Paula Rust has shown through her research with lesbian and bisexual women. Many women assume they are heterosexual, only to come out as lesbian, and perhaps later to see themselves as bisexual. The very labels that we apply to sexual behavior as well as sexual identity are subjectively defined. Researchers, therapists, and anyone interested in the lives of lesbians must begin to examine what lesbianism means to individual women. We can no longer assume that the label *lesbian* means the same thing to everyone. We *know* at this point that it does not.

The stories we read covered an extremely broad range of experiences, many of which were unrelated to the traditional conceptions of coming out. We would like to reiterate that coming out is a dynamic, lifelong process, as illustrated by these quotes: "One day I discovered I was about to be 67. The knowledge that time was running out hit me. What was unfinished in my one chance at life?" (Lenore Thompson, in *Wolf Girls at Vassar*); "At the age of forty, I stopped being a lesbian dropout and re-entered" (Matile Poor, in *The Lesbian Path*); "My coming out story is my life story, which is harder to end than it was to begin. Since coming out is a lifelong process, there's always the possibility of a new beginning" (Liz O'Lexa, in *Testimonies*).

The themes we came across do not cease to be important once a woman has initially come out. This fuller conception of coming out will enhance the knowledge and understanding of lesbian experience in all its beauty, richness, struggle, and complexity. We hope that this new model of coming out as a complex lifelong process will become the backdrop to research on lesbian life and to lesbian lives themselves.

FURTHER READING

Balka, Christine, and Andy Rose, eds. *Twice Blessed: On Being Lesbian or Gay and Jewish.* Boston: Beacon Press, 1989.

Barber, Karen, and Sarah Holmes, eds. *Testimonies: Lesbian Coming Out Stories.* Boston: Alyson Publications, 1994.

Beck, Evelyn Torton, ed. *Nice Jewish Girls: A Lesbian Anthology.* Watertown, Mass.: Persephone Press, 1982.

Cruikshank, Margaret, ed. *The Lesbian Path.* Monterey, Calif.: Angel Press, 1980.

Curb, Rosemary, and Nancy Manahan, eds. *Lesbian Nuns: Breaking Silence*. Tallahassee, Fla.: Naiad Press, 1985.

MacKay, Anne, ed. *Wolf Girls at Vassar: Lesbian and Gay Experiences 1930–1990*. New York: St. Martin's Press, 1993.

"Once Gay, Always Gay?" *Focus on Family* (March 1994).

Penelope, Julia, and Susan J. Wolfe, eds. *The Original Coming Out Stories*. Freedom, Calif.: Crossing Press, 1989.

Ratti, Rakesh, ed. *A Lotus of Another Color: An Unfolding of the South Asian Gay and Lesbian Experiences*. Boston: Alyson Publications, 1993.

Roscoe, Will, ed. *Living the Spirit: A Gay American Indian Anthology*. New York: St. Martin's Press, 1988.

THREE

AT THE CROSSROADS: LESBIAN YOUTH

Joyce Hunter

Teenagers have a hard time in the best of circumstances, but life is tougher with the added burden of being lesbian in a homophobic society. This chapter is based on my many years of work with lesbian, gay, and bisexual adolescents in New York City, first as a counselor at the Student Health Society of Hunter College, then through my work at the Hetrick-Martin Institute (including at a high school for lesbian and gay students), and more recently at the HIV Center for Clinical and Behavioral Studies, where my colleagues and I are examining the coming-out process and its implications for HIV/AIDS among lesbian, gay, and bisexual teenagers.

Lesbian and bisexual youth are as diverse as their heterosexual counterparts, cutting across religious, class, racial, and cultural lines. They grow up in cities, in small towns, and on farms. The majority

The author would like to thank Priscilla Alexander and Jan Baer for their comments and suggestions.

of them make a relatively successful transition to adulthood, but growing up is especially difficult for them.

While most lesbian and bisexual young women can cope with the stress and turmoil of the initial coming-out process, many experience difficulties. Teenage lesbians are in a period of transition between what they were taught about their identity as women (and their place in the world as women) and the emerging awareness of their sexual orientation. As they begin to recognize their difference from their peers, they also recognize that they are members of a stigmatized group. At a time when their heterosexual sisters are receiving acceptance and support from families, teachers, and peers regarding their sexual and emotional feelings, as well as their emerging sexual identities, many young lesbians feel they must hide their attraction to the same sex. As one youth stated in the *National NOW Times*, "Rather than recognize that I am your daughter, your sister, or your friend, society would simply categorize me as a 'man-hating dyke who molests small children.' Many of my friends, who understandably cannot deal with the pressure, decide to remain in the closet."

For lesbian youth growing up in isolated or rural areas of the United States and Canada, where "traditional family values," including conventional sex roles and religious beliefs, are often rooted in religious fundamentalism, it is particularly difficult to find supportive friendships or any accurate information about the lesbian community.

HOMOPHOBIA AND SEXISM

No matter where they live, when young people who think they might be gay experience repeated name calling (directed toward them or others) and see words such as *dyke* or *faggot* scrawled hatefully across school walls and gym lockers, they get a clear message that they are neither accepted nor safe. Many live in fear of being found out, and exposed, before they are ready to come out. The lack of a support system both at home and among their friends can put young lesbians at risk for dropping out of school and engaging in a variety of high-risk behaviors.

SOCIAL DEVELOPMENT

Like all young people, teenage lesbians must master various developmental tasks as they mature: building a sense of identity, self-esteem, and social skills; creating and maintaining friendships; and managing social roles. Acquiring these skills in a hostile environment can be challenging. Trying to establish ordinary friendships while hiding and managing one's lesbian feelings can throw a young woman into crisis, because it will be difficult for her to relate in an honest way when discussing her friends, relationships, and sexuality (for example, she will need to lie about the gender of the person she has a crush on). Being part of a peer group is essential to social development in the teenage years, and isolation of lesbians can be very intense.

During the journey through adolescence, young women experience rapid physical growth and the beginning of menstruation, as well as an awakening sexuality. Adolescence is normally a time of exploration and experimentation, sexually and emotionally. Homosexual teenagers experiment with heterosexuality during this time more than heterosexuals experiment with homosexuality. Lesbians who feel compelled to hide their sexual identity must develop ways to cope. One of these ways is to date boys. Some young lesbians in a discussion group I led said their families would much rather deal with their daughter's unwanted pregnancy, which would at least be a sign of a sexual norm, than with the possibility that she might be lesbian.

Perhaps it is not surprising, then, that some lesbians do become pregnant. Others talk about having a baby as a way of getting in touch with their femininity or creating an important role for themselves. Among young women from lower socioeconomic groups, poverty, unemployment, family problems, and the desire to have someone to take care of have all been shown to be correlated with high levels of teen pregnancy.

In schools, sexuality and health education programs typically censor information, give misinformation, or completely avoid addressing concerns of lesbian youth. Homophobia in the classroom, while it may be subtle at times, can be dangerous. I worked with a young woman who had become pregnant by a gay male friend. When I asked her why she hadn't used birth control, she said that they thought their homosexuality meant she couldn't get pregnant. Lack of information about lesbian identity also fosters anxiety and isolation. One result of this isolation is that a disproportionately high number of lesbians contemplate suicide.

Silence, both at home and in the classroom, affects young lesbians' ability to obtain resources as well, for example, gynecological care. Because most of those I have counseled are hesitant to disclose their homosexuality to health care providers, fearing that their parents will be notified, many give partial information, or even outright misinformation, to medical professionals and therefore receive inappropriate treatment. This mistrust of health care providers follows lesbians into adulthood: Several studies have found lesbians as a group to seek far less preventive medical care, such as Pap smears and mammograms, than heterosexual women, resulting in alarming rates of late detection of cervical and breast cancers.

Some young women attempt to suppress their lesbian orientation despite frequent and persistent homoerotic thoughts, feelings, fantasies, and/or activities. They may bury themselves in school activities and be too "busy" to date, distorting the adolescent experience and missing out on the normal rites of passage: having crushes, dating, developing emotional and physical intimacy and commitment.

Young lesbians of color must grapple not only with their sexual identity but with their racial and ethnic identity as well. They need to integrate all facets of their identities into a complete person in order to achieve a positive self-concept. Wholeness comes from being in a community where they are accepted with all of their identities—racial, ethnic, cultural, and sexual. Between the homophobia of one's community and the racism in the lesbian and gay community, such acceptance is not easy to find. As Barbara Smith put it, "There's nothing to be compared with how you feel when you're cut cold by your own." "But we refuse to make a choice between our cultural identity and sexual identity, between our race and our femaleness," wrote Cherríe Moraga and Gloria Anzaldúa. The issues of racism, sexism, and homophobia need to be continually addressed in all communities. (See Paula Ross's chapter in this volume, "What's Race Got to Do with It?")

RELATIONSHIPS

Despite the gains of the current feminist movement, many girls are still socialized to be dependent and passive. This behavior makes it difficult for them to meet other young people. Depending on their cultural and class background, girls are still taught to wait for Mr. Right, to be nurturing, to put others' needs before their own. They are still told not to be assertive. If they are, they are called "bossy" or "aggressive." In the end, they don't even think about their own needs.

Lesbian teens who meet are often drawn to each other simply because they're both lesbian. They call all their pent-up emotions "love" and settle into an emotionally fused, or "merged," relationship in which they attempt to meet each other's every need—social, emotional, and sexual. They become best friends, lovers, and confidantes and withdraw from other friends. If they begin to have problems and fight, they find they have no one else to talk to. Their self-esteem falls, and they become depressed, which puts them at risk for suicide. In a study done in Maryland by R. Harding, 23 percent of lesbians in late adolescence and early adulthood attempted suicide after the breakup of a relationship.

The situation changes for young women who become socially involved with their lesbian and gay peers and attend lesbian and gay

Kelly Jo Woodside

Due to a probable overdose of Rita Mae Brown novels in high school, when I filled out my roommate fact sheet for Pace University in lower Manhattan, it read suspiciously like a personal ad from the back pages of *The Village Voice:*

> GWF, new to the area, enjoys cappuccino, folk music, and writing poetry, ISO [in search of] kindred spirit to explore the city with. Smoker OK.

It was the first time I had ever admitted my lesbianism on paper.

A naive seventeen-year-old, I easily swallowed the myth of the American university as a mecca of freedom, so I was foolishly indiscriminate in choosing where to spend the next four years of my life. Well, I did have one condition: It would have to be in New York City, which I saw as a shelter for young East Coast queers.

But when I arrived at Pace, reality struck. The first clue that I might have made a mistake came when they broke us down by majors at orientation: Over half of my classmates filed into the main auditorium to be welcomed into the accounting program. So this was a *business* school (read *conservative*).

Discouraged, I went back to my room, where, tearing the last shred of hope from my lonely heart, my roommate had finally moved in.

Jen was nice enough, but, well, not exactly what I'd had in mind. We did go out a couple of times, to bars with some heavy-metal wannabes she picked up in Washington Square. I stopped hanging out with them when I realized the boys wanted to come home with us.

I was too intimidated to hit the bar scene alone. So I lay on my bed memorizing the lyrics to the Indigo Girls' first album and wondering *what* I could have been thinking when I decided on Pace.

But eventually, I began to find friends. Tommy was a fellow Pennsylvanian with a big grin and a stack of Erasure CDs. He had come out not long before I met him, and, like me, he was looking for love. I set him up with my brother.

After a slow start, they hit it off. Because Chris was a three-hour drive away, he called my room just about every day for Tommy, who had no phone in his room.

In the meantime, I was still without luck in my own search for romance. One day, I came back from class while Jen was getting ready to go out.

"Tommy came by," she said.

"Oh?"

"You guys make such a cute couple." She emptied a can of Aquanet on her hair. "There's just one thing I don't understand, though: Why's he always on the phone with your brother?"

I lay down on my bed and picked up my Walkman. This was going to be a long four years.

community events. Because of their excruciating isolation while forming their adult sense of themselves, however, lesbians may have suicidal thoughts whenever they face a profound emotional crisis. Young lesbians need a healthy social environment where they can socialize and be accepted in order to grow up as strong, self-caring adults.

RUNNING AWAY

Members of other cultural groups who are discriminated against can usually turn to their families for comfort and advice, but lesbians rarely have that option. So they often leave home.

Young lesbians run away from home for many of the same reasons that other young women do, including having parents who are emotionally, physically, and/or sexually abusive, or who set up rigid controls that enforce an isolation from friendships outside the family. In many cases, such repression is compounded by alcohol or drug abuse, and young lesbians are often at increased risk for violence at home if their sexual orientation is discovered.

If the young runaway is lucky, she will find a safe environment at a shelter or with a friend or relative. But in many cases she will have little option but to live on the streets, connecting with other runaways and learning how to survive in a hostile world. She may get by with shoplifting and begging, but often, especially if she has already engaged in heterosexual sex, she will wind up having sex with men for a place to sleep and a meal and, eventually, to earn money for survival. Prostitution is hard work and can be emotionally and physically devastating for an individual who does not yet have a solid sense of her own identity and self-worth. An adolescent girl new to the streets is vulnerable to violence, theft, and exploitation and is often unable to recognize trouble before it starts. She may not feel she has a right to get out of a bad situation or may not know how to escape.

Runaway girls often use drugs to help cope, and they are vulnerable to sexually transmitted diseases (STDs) from lovers or clients and AIDS from drug use and unsafe sex—whether they are lesbian, bisexual, or heterosexual. Though the majority of gay street kids in urban areas are boys, there are also a large number of girls. More than 90 percent of teenagers arrested for loitering, or as runaways, are girls, according to Frederique Delacoste and Priscilla Alexander.

One can try to help stabilize the girls' living situations, but who is going to hire a fifteen-year-old? New York State law, for example, forbids a person eighteen or younger from working more than twenty hours a week during the school year. Even at eighteen, these girls may lack education and reading skills. Social service agencies may find a runaway young woman and try to help, but it is much harder to place an adolescent lesbian than a gay boy in foster care.

LESBIAN ADOLESCENTS AND HIV: RISK FACTORS

The incidence of HIV infection has been growing within the adolescent population for over a decade. Adult women have seen the greatest recent growth in the incidence of HIV infection, most through unprotected sex during adolescence.

Preliminary data from a pilot study conducted at the HIV Center for Clinical and Behavioral Studies in New York City suggest that lesbian- and bisexual-identified adolescents are at high risk for several reasons. Fifteen out of twenty adolescent girls who identify as lesbians report having both male and female partners. The male partners are often bisexual or gay friends of theirs. Twenty percent reported having had sex with men in exchange for money and/or drugs. Another study at the HIV Center found that approximately half of gay male adolescents engage in intercourse with girls, and also that they are far less likely to use condoms with their female partners than with their male partners.

These data confirm clinicians' impressions that many lesbian adolescents engage in heterosexual behavior, sometimes with multiple partners, rarely with condoms, and sometimes with the intention of becoming pregnant. If the partners of lesbians are gay boys, then the girls are at high risk for HIV. Alcohol and drug use among lesbian adolescents, which can foster risky sexual behavior, only serves to increase HIV risk.

RECOMMENDATIONS

Despite all the problems discussed in this chapter, the majority of lesbian youth manage successfully to get on with their lives. Many of them need our support along the way.

Lesbian and gay men are the target of negative images. While this situation has been changing, they have been the objects of humor, and rarely have they been allowed to have serious, fulfilling relationships on film. Thus, films and other media, the conveyors of social values, still present a bleak message to young lesbians and gay men: "You'll always be lonely, and you will very likely die because you are gay."

Having positive role models, both peer and adult, is extremely important to their healthy growth. Images of lesbians in the media are rarely positive. Therefore, it is important for those of us who can come out to be visible. I would encourage lesbians who work with adolescents to be open, if it is possible without putting one's job in jeopardy. This will not only provide peer support for other lesbian and gay staff, who may also be afraid to come out, but will provide badly needed role models for our youth.

Other important interventions include developing lesbian support groups and placing positive books about lesbianism in the schools, youth community centers, and public libraries, despite the threat of fundamentalist opposition. Books, which can be read privately, are a major way of de-isolating lesbian youth, particularly if they do not have access to the lesbian community at large.

We also need to establish programs for lesbian youth in our communities. In the past, the lesbian and gay community has been reluctant to set up programs for homosexual youth or to advocate for them in other community settings, because of the myth that lesbians and gay men are child molesters. But if we want to help our youth, then we must conquer the fear of that baseless accusation. Other professionals (school social workers, youth workers) also fear that if they help lesbian youth they will be seen as promoting homosexuality. Their fears keep many teachers and counselors in the closet, and it is important to find ways for them to be supportive to lesbian youth without necessarily coming out.

Another important venue for reaching out to lesbian adolescents is through the health and sexuality education programs in the schools. Despite the difficulty of convincing anxious school boards to include gay-positive materials and information in the curricula, we must continue the fight. The recent decision of the publisher Holt, Rinehart, and Winston to pull its 700-page high school health text out of the huge Texas textbook market rather than remove positive information about sexuality, including homosexuality, is encouraging in that regard. We must continue to sensitize health and sexuality educators to lesbian issues.

Since many girls—lesbian, bisexual, and straight—will become mothers, positive reinforcement of women who raise children without the traditional social support provided to heterosexual married women, and other parenting issues, should be put before them.

HIV/AIDS prevention must be integrated into the school curriculum, and must be culturally sensitive not only to different racial, ethnic, cultural, and religious communities but to the lesbian and gay communities as well. Peer educators have been very effective in reaching out to other teenagers and should be involved in the development and implementation of such curricula on the local level. The young people who are most at risk must be involved in finding solutions.

With all they have to overcome, most lesbian youth grow up with their self-esteem intact. Those whom I have been privileged to know through my work have taught me a great deal about courage, honesty, and the will to survive.

FURTHER READING

Berzon, Betty, ed. *Positively Gay.* Millbrae, Calif.: Celestial Arts, 1979.

Brown, Rita Mae. *Rubyfruit Jungle.* Plainfield, Vt.: Daughters, Inc., 1973.

Fricke, Aaron. *Reflections of a Rock Lobster: A Story About Growing Up Gay.* Boston: Alyson Publications, 1983.

Guy, Rosa. *The Friends.* New York: Bantam Pathfinder Editions, 1973.

———-. *Ruby.* New York: Viking, 1976.

Hautzig, Deborah. *Hey, Dollface.* New York: Bantam Books, 1980.

Heron, Ann, ed. *One Teenager in 10: Testimony by Gay and Lesbian Youth.* Boston: Alyson Publications, 1983.

Klein, Norma. *Now That I Know.* New York: Bantam Books, 1988.

Miller, Isabel. *Patience and Sarah.* Greenwich, Conn.: Fawcett Crest, 1973.

Scoppettone, Sandra. *Trying Hard to Hear You.* New York: Harper & Row, 1974.

FOUR

LESBIAN BABY BOOMERS AT MIDLIFE

Esther D. Rothblum, Beth Mintz,
D. Brookes Cowan, and Cheryl Haller

We are lesbians of a transitional generation, having come of age in the period between Stonewall and the more progressive—or, at least, lesbian-visible—1990s. In 1969, when the police raided the Stonewall Inn, we were in our teens and twenties. Now we embrace midlife in a time when the public is much more aware of lesbian and gay issues.

We are also part of the baby-boom generation. And just as schools, colleges, the military, and the workplace accommodated our numbers as we grew up, the nation, and we as individuals, is preparing for our old age and retirement. Popular magazines have printed many articles about aging baby boomers who had children late in life and are now raising them while trying to care for elderly parents and in-laws. Aging men, we are told, lose their sexual potency and become more focused on family than on career, while women cope with the relative scarcity of men their age. But in all the discussion of midlife crisis and acceptance of personal limitations, where are the articles about lesbian baby boomers? How do our concerns differ from those of heterosexual women?

AFFIRMING LESBIANISM AND AFFIRMING AGING

Midlife is clutter, distillation, ache and triumph.
—Carmen de Monteflores, "Time's Gifts"

For white women, becoming a lesbian means learning to live as a minority. As females in a male-dominated society, both lesbian and straight women are oppressed, although sexism is usually less apparent to young heterosexual women. As Gloria Steinem has noted, this is the age when women have the most social power, since we are at the peak of our physical and sexual attractiveness. At least for able-bodied, middle-class white women, then, ageism may be the first recognized experience of oppression.

Women who are members of other groups, however, have faced oppression throughout life. And researcher Richard Friend argues that the experiences of lesbians and gay men with stigmatization and discrimination can be translated into skills that help them cope with ageism. Similarly, Nanette Gartrell, a psychiatrist, suggests that since lesbians must actively choose their lifestyle, they develop more adaptive skills than do heterosexuals, who come to terms with their sexual orientation more passively.

These observations suggest that lesbians as a group are better prepared than straight women for aging. The dominant culture does not share this view of contented aging among lesbians, however, often perceiving them (if perceiving them at all) as lonely in their old age, and this idea is reinforced by the invisibility of older lesbians in the media. When older women are portrayed, it is usually as wife or grandmother, roles that are more common to straight than lesbian identity. It is not surprising, therefore, that lesbians who are closeted or isolated from lesbian communities internalize this homophobia. Friend argues that lesbians and gay men who have formed a positive identity age more successfully than those who have spent their lives "passing" as heterosexual.

Those of us in the generation since Stonewall are sandwiched between the older lesbians, who are often very closeted, and young women who have felt free to experiment with same-gender relationships since high school. We are the bridge that connects the generations before and after us, and tend to be less easily categorized. Depending on our particular situations, we are more or less closeted, more or less politically active, more or less involved in lesbian communities, and more or less homophobic than they are. Our generation transformed lesbian communities from mostly social circles to cultural institutions. The researcher John Grube has referred to pre- and post-Stonewall gay men as "natives" versus "settlers," and these terms also apply to lesbians.

APPEARANCE NORMS IN THE LESBIAN COMMUNITY

> We all, lesbian or not, are daily bombarded subtly and not so subtly by the swindle, the intense brainwashing of patriarchal media constructions in which anything other than a twelve-year-old face and body on a woman is unacceptable, offensive, shameful, pitiable and blameworthy.
>
> —Robin Posin, "Ripening"

The changes in physical appearance wrought by age tend to be of great concern to heterosexual women. How does aging affect lesbians' concerns about physical attractiveness? Many studies have suggested that lesbians and straight women may be more alike than different when it comes to attitudes and behavior. In *American Couples*, Philip Blumstein and Pepper Schwartz found that gender-role socialization was the most important predictor of attitudes toward a variety of issues in both gay and straight couples—and this may be true for physical appearance. After all, all young women are socialized to value their appearance. For those who become lesbians, whether or not they are out, their occupational and social roles will be influenced by the privilege that accompanies female attractiveness. It is well known that women (both lesbians and heterosexual) diet more and experience more dissatisfaction with their bodies than do gay or heterosexual men. Thus the changes in physical appearance (particularly weight gain) that accompany women's aging may affect lesbians and straight women in similar ways.

Research has also indicated that women's physical appearance is particularly important for attractiveness to men. Pamela Brand, Esther Rothblum, and Laura Solomon found in a study that heterosexual women and gay men (two groups sexually involved with men) were more preoccupied with their weight, and reported lower ideal weights, than lesbians and heterosexual men.

The similarities between heterosexual women and gay men have also been demonstrated in studies of personal ads, where these two groups are most likely to describe their own physical appearance. Lesbians, however, are more likely to describe their personality characteristics, suggesting that they do not focus on appearance in the same way. Thus, the physical changes that accompany aging may have fewer consequences for lesbians than for heterosexual women in the arena of personal relationships. (The study by Pamela Brand and her colleagues confirmed this; there was no relationship between lesbians' weight and whether or not they were in a partnered relationship.)

Finally, lesbian communities may be more tolerant of diversity in appearance. The dominant culture holds negative stereotypes about the appearance of lesbians, and lesbians, like heterosexual women, tend to be more liked when they look most conventionally feminine. The psychologist Laura S. Brown has argued that lesbians are aware of the parallels between oppression against lesbians and oppression based on appearance. Lesbian communities also use appearance cues to determine who is lesbian, and these cues have changed over time. The Stonewall generation grew up when butch and femme roles were mandated for lesbians. Baby boomers reached adulthood in the age of androgyny, when both lesbians and heterosexual women

Lauren Crux

My friends and I, who are in midlife, are talking about growing older. We're reading everything we can find on menopause. We make jokes about our memories and our absentmindedness: "Where did I park my car?" and "Why is the lettuce in the freezer?" Many of us wear bifocals and still have trouble reading the small print. We have more aches and pains. We fear serious illness. We have parents who are ill or dying. Most of us want to work less and play more.

We also wonder who we are, *really*, in this new world of sliding sexual identities. Are we still lesbians, or are we now passé if we are not *queer* (claiming a deviant sexuality that undermines the paradigm of "straight or gay") or bisexual, or transgendered, or other varieties of sex radicals? Has "lesbian chic" done us in? What does it mean not to be cutting edge anymore? Some of us just shake our heads at the new politics, the new language. Some of us feel threatened. Some find change intriguing and challenging.

•   •   •

In Santa Barbara I see three silver-haired lesbians, walking and laughing together, heading toward their Westfalia van. And I see a moment in my future. I amble up and do car talk as a way to meet them. "So, do you like your van?" I am drawn to these women, to the lines, the edges, the years of stories I saw in their faces. I have questions about what the future might hold for me.

"Well, the dogs and I have traveled all across the country in it," the owner answers in a faint German accent. She turns her round, well-weathered face toward me. Her green eyes spark as she looks me up and down and says, "I don't suppose you are old enough for me to invite you to travel with me, are you?" Then she steps closer, peers directly into my face: "No, I don't suppose you are." We laugh. I touch her arm and say: "No, I don't suppose I am." I walk away, smiling. A strong, happy dyke in her late sixties has just come on to me, a strong, happy dyke in my forties. And I see that aging as a lesbian can be fun, filled with possibilities for adventure, friendship, and—yes!—lust.

dressed in flannel shirts and jeans, and had short hair. At midlife, we marvel at the fashions of "baby dykes" who wear the gender-bending outfits of the queer nation generation.

FAMILIES OF ORIGIN

At midlife, our lovers are also granted a particular status. Sometimes this is just because she too is older and people take her seriously. Sometimes it's because the relationship has been going on for years and the family sees her as one of its own. Sometimes it's because we have been alone for so long that when we start seeing someone, our families are happy that we are connected again. Perhaps it's also because most people stop thinking of middle-aged people as sexual objects. Sex isn't the first thing that straight people think of when they see us as a couple.

—JoAnn Loulan, "Now When I Was Your Age"

For lesbians who are out to their parents, midlife may be a time of increasing comfort and decreasing tensions, as their lesbianism can no longer be considered a "phase" that will be outgrown. Theoretically, it should be easier to come out to parents at midlife than at adolescence, when the lesbian is still living at home and financially dependent on her parents. Data from the National Lesbian Health Care Survey indicates that the post-Stonewall generation was more likely to be out to family members than were lesbians who were older or younger, but even among these women, 19 percent of the almost two thousand respondents were not out to any family member and only 27 percent were out to their entire family.

One woman's experience illustrates how coming out to family can be a vehicle for confronting one's own internalized heterosexism. Since reaching forty, Jane had worked to confront what she called the biggest stumbling block to her acceptance of self as a lesbian: "profound internalized homophobia." She began by coming out to her brother, who greeted her tearful admission with powerful silence. He warned Jane not to tell their elderly parents and then explained that he would not tell his wife or his children, so he didn't want her to leave any incriminating messages on his answering machine. He asked one question only: "Are you with someone?" to which she replied yes. "People should not be alone," he stated, and after that indirect message of support, they never spoke of it again.

Although the details vary from family to family, many lesbians have had similar experiences, and it is not surprising that we usually find our major source of social support among friends, followed by partner, family of origin, and co-workers (see Kurdek and Schmitt). In moving away from family in order to keep the secret, lesbians may visit infrequently and have superficial communication with their families.

FRIENDSHIP NETWORKS AND SOCIAL SUPPORT

It's important just to know there's a support system, especially for a lot of brothers and sisters who are on the reserves and very isolated, who are afraid to come out. If they do come out, now they'll have some place to go.
—Leota Lone Dog, "Coming Out as a Native American"

Even the briefest observation of lesbian communities demonstrates how important our ex-lovers continue to be to us. Carol Becker has described this phenomenon in her book *Lesbian Ex-Lovers*, and so has Anndee Hochman in her short story "Extending Family," about a lesbian whose partner's ex-lover moves next door with her current lover. Lesbians seem to remain friends with ex-lovers more often than heterosexual ex-husbands and ex-wives do, which helps maintain the size and stability of the lesbian community and broaden lesbian friendship networks. Even a very closeted lesbian can draw on ex-lovers for support; they may be practically the only people who know that she is a lesbian.

Finally, lesbian communities do not seem as stratified by age as the dominant culture, since lesbians of all ages participate in various lesbian social and political events. One of the authors of this essay once lived in a communal household with four lesbians who ranged in age from early twenties to fifties. We viewed ourselves as peers, not as women spanning two generations.

Social support takes on a different importance as we age and come to terms with our physical, psychological, and financial limits. For many lesbians, having forgone traditional marriage and conventional family as a primary source of support, entering middle age brings a renewed sense of the importance of friends. Lesbian baby boomers are thinking about old age in terms of the "old dykes' home," trying to conceptualize retirement living characterized by mutual support and companionship. Ironically, the typical heterosexual woman outlives her partner and faces the same need for community membership as do lesbians, but she has no large community to turn to.

PARTNER RELATIONSHIPS

My (our) bodies growing older (breast losing elasticity, joints creaking a bit) is fascinating and a source of tenderness for both of us, engendering fantasies about growing old together, starting a sex-positive nursing home for dykes, etc.
—Respondent in a study of lesbian sex at menopause

As the post-Stonewall generation, we have made our way through a myriad of types of relationships as we aged. If we knew other lesbians while we were children and adolescents, they were probably in butch/femme relationships that mirrored the rigid gender roles of heterosexual marriages of the time. During the so-called sexual revolution, monogamy was frowned upon in many lesbian communities, and lesbians had multiple short-term sexual encounters. These days, middle-aged lesbians strive for long-term relationships.

Paula Martinae

On my calendar for July 30, 1994, my fortieth birthday, I wrote simply: "Uh-oh."

Turning forty does seem like a mishap, an "uh-oh." How was it possible to go from childhood to adulthood in what felt like forty minutes? I can't stay up late anymore, and I ache and groan more than I used to. When I'm with twenty-somethings, I sound like an old fogy: "Well, back in '76 . . . "

Of course, forty isn't old, and I'm happier now than in 1976, when I was just graduating from college. Forty is the start of something big: the rest of my life.

But my parents see it differently. To them, I'm the "poor career girl" who couldn't find the right man, so she became a lesbian. They wanted to throw a birthday party for me in my hometown and invite all our relatives—a sweet idea, until I realized they expected me to come without my lover. My mother often forgets Katie's name and refers to her as "the other girl."

I see them once a year, but my parents' hold is like a vise grip, a persistent voice that says, "What have you got to show for your life?" I find myself looking at friends with kids and thinking,

"They're *really* adults." Or belittling myself for not owning an apartment. Or a car. Or even a remote-control TV. Subconsciously, I'm still defining adulthood the way my parents do.

That summer I turned forty, my lover's sister called to invite us to her daughter's high school graduation, which was taking place the same weekend as the celebration of Stonewall 25 in New York. When Katie explained our plans, her sister's silence said, "You're choosing a *parade* over your niece's graduation?" Then we both began to have doubts. Maybe a high school graduation *was* more important than displaying lesbian pride; maybe we weren't acting like adults.

When I told this to a friend, she said wisely, "But *we're* the adults. *We* define what adulthood means." It seemed so simple, but it was something I had been forgetting.

Turning forty meant writing a letter to my parents—the longest since I came out to them in 1984—redefining myself. Your daughter is an adult in a good, committed relationship. She doesn't have children, but she has a family. She can't afford to buy a house, but her rent is cheap. Be happy for her.

Increasing numbers of lesbians are making the decision to become parents, not just rearing the children of one partner's former marriage but bearing or adopting children as a couple. Moreover, lesbians are rearing children later in life than their heterosexual sisters. Aside from the high costs of child rearing and adoption and the relatively lower income of women compared to men, this is no doubt happening because of the lack of norms and role models to define modern lesbian life. Thus, unlike heterosexual women, who often simply assumed they would parent, many lesbian baby boomers assumed the opposite but changed their minds as they aged. This certainly characterizes the women in one local "dykes with tykes" support group, where an assortment of forty-something women marvel about finally deciding to become mothers.

Many heterosexual women turn forty as their children begin to move out; many lesbians are just beginning a family at this age. Although there has been little research on how the lesbian baby boom affects lesbians' aging process, the demographics suggest that middle-aged lesbians may be more likely than heterosexual women to be caring for both aging parents and young children as the "sandwich generation."

Most important rituals for straight women focus on partnered relationships (the high school prom, dating, engagement, marriage, divorce) or childbearing. Some lesbians create rituals around their partnered relationships, such as commitment ceremonies or long-term anniversaries. We are proud to witness such rituals, even while many in the community may deride them for imitating the heteropatriarchy. While our society has few ceremonies for biological markers, anthropology has described the significance of rites of passage such as aging ceremonies among women elders. Rituals of this sort, unrelated to marriage and childbearing, may hold more significance for lesbians and allow us to celebrate the vibrant life course lesbianism offers.

One issue that confronts long-term couples as they age is the death of a partner, and some research has described how lesbians fare better than heterosexual women after the disruption of a relationship due to a breakup or death. Lesbians have had to be financially independent and are rarely covered by their partner's health insurance. Heterosexual widows are thus more likely to be economically disadvantaged than are lesbians, many of whom have been in the labor force throughout their adult years. Also important in this regard is the less coupled nature of lesbian social and cultural events, which still welcome participation after the death of a partner. Very closeted and isolated lesbians may limit their socializing to a few couples, and in this respect may experience a social marginalization similar to that experienced by heterosexual widows. This pattern is especially likely when lesbians are not out to families of origin, who therefore cannot acknowledge their loss.

THE WORKPLACE

We do not follow the traditional woman's developmental line of turning, in our mid-forties, toward career and work fulfillment after having raised our children who have now left the nest. Even those lesbians who have raised children have been involved simultaneously in work. Nor do we follow the traditional male line of development which leads men to seek deeper relationships and greater involvement with family after two decades of establishing themselves as workers. . . . The patriarchal dichotomy between work and relations, or, for that matter, the rest of life, does not hold for lesbians.
—Barbara Sang, Joyce Warshow, and Adrienne Smith,
Introduction to *Lesbians at Midlife*

Baby-boomer lesbians reached young adulthood during the current feminist movement, which made available job and career opportunities that had generally been blocked to women of earlier generations. Lillian Faderman has written about the importance of economic opportunities for women in the establishing of lesbian communities; without them, some women feel forced to marry for financial security.

As a result of the political climate of the late 1960s and 1970s, some lesbians who came of age in those years pursued alternative or low-paying jobs. Some were unemployed or underemployed while very active in grassroots politics. Recently, a friend of ours involved in the fight for partner health benefits remarked: "Ten years ago, who needed health insurance? And who had a partner?" As her comment indicates, lesbian baby boomers in recent years have looked for jobs with more stability, income, and employee benefits.

At the same time, some middle-class lesbians maximized their career chances early on. Being unmarried and often geographically mobile, they reached career markers at very early ages. In this respect, these lesbians are similar to men—even down to experiencing midlife crises. We recall the story of a colleague who raced through college, graduate school, and a postdoctoral fellowship, and ended up an assistant professor at twenty-seven, an associate professor at thirty-four, and a full professor at thirty-eight. She was not in the first cohort of women in academia—the ones who were harassed and denied tenure. She was mentored by her father and then by male professors, and had no trouble fitting into the system. By all accounts, she was an academic success story, so successful in fact that by age twenty-nine, she had a major midlife crisis, having done all the things she wanted to do in life and not knowing what to do with the remaining years.

Of course, some lesbians have followed paths similar to those of heterosexual women. Some are pursuing new directions now that their children are older. Others grew up assuming that they would marry and have children, making their own work lives secondary to their aspirations for their families. For this group, coming out may leave them psychologically on hold, since they were not socialized for alternatives to marriage. Carol Thompson has written about grief and loss issues facing lesbians who come out and realize they will

Sandra Butler

As I approached my fifty-fifth birthday, I found myself filled with regrets. While I was, for the most part, satisfied with the choices I had made in my life, each inevitably carried some loss. A direction unexplored. A possibility never known. Time that had been lost to my failures of courage, my uneasiness with ambiguity, my fear of judgment, my need for love.

I wanted to find a way to mark the losses and the regrets, as well as the deeply satisfying public and private life I had led. I needed to look back with regret, pride, and kindness and to look forward with enthusiasm and optimism.

My partner, Ellyn, planned a ritual centered on the symbol of the double five, representing the dual visions of hindsight and foresight. She called together our community. The lesbians and the heterosexuals. The mothers, the sisters, and the daughters. We began my birthday ceremony outdoors at dusk, at the ending of the day and of a period of my life. Each participant recalled a loss, a disappointment, a place or a time in her life when she could have been braver, stronger, or more whole. Each wrote her regrets on a Post-it note, read it aloud, and then attached her note to one of five helium balloons in the center of our circle. As the sound of the last voice faded into the stillness of the night air, I released the balloons and we all watched them carry off our losses, growing ever smaller and more distant.

After a moment of silence, we all rose and went indoors, forming a second circle for the second number five, representing my future, filled with light, blessings, wishes for the coming year. I was given a mazel tov bag, used to envelop the glass that is shattered in a traditional Jewish wedding ceremony, a bag to contain good luck. First one, then another loved one gave me a symbol to place in my bag to carry their wishes into my future. There was an eagle feather, a bird's nest, a perfectly rounded stone, and a paper clip to hold it all together. Ellyn gave me a small wooden house to represent the home we were to purchase three months later. Along with it, she offered a ring with three triangles, each encompassing the others. The inner triangle represented me; the second, surrounding it, our union as a couple; and the third, enveloping both, our community.

On my fifty-fifth birthday, my life, my partnership, and my community were, like the triangles on my ring, embedded in one another. All I had been and would become was held in the circle of the ring and the circle of women.

never have the societal approval that is part of heterosexual privilege, or the rituals accompanying it.

Finally, lesbian friendships cut across social class as well as age, which, among other things, affects how people view their work lives. Kathleen Newman's book, *Falling from Grace*, focuses on downward social mobility, on what happens when middle-class people lose their jobs and cannot replace them. One of the individuals interviewed was a gay man, and he was the only respondent whose loss of job did not affect his social network. Therefore, he maintained an important source of stability during an extremely stressful period. We find the same to be true of lesbians.

THE DIVERSITY OF LESBIANS AT MIDLIFE

I am wiser now and more reckless.
—Lauren Crux, "The Ripening of Our Bodies,
the Deepening of Our Spirits,"

As the post-Stonewall generation turns fifty, other issues will come to the fore. As Sarah Pearlman has said: "Early mid-life may be the theory, but late mid-life is the practice." We are well aware, for example, that older lesbians have experienced significant ageism, including from younger lesbians, but the baby boomers have not yet had to face this themselves.

We are also aware that while many of us do not feel old, turning fifty is considered old in countries with high rates of malnutrition and disease. Muriel Miguel describes feeling as though she were at midlife since she was twenty-five; growing up, she saw members of her Native American community die before age forty. Also, gender differences are particularly marked for this generation: At the same time that lesbian baby boomers are turning fifty, the AIDS epidemic is killing young and middle-aged gay men.

There is a world of diversity in the post-Stonewall generation. Those of us who live in rural, conservative, Bible Belt communities may lead lives not too different from those of lesbians in the 1940s and 1950s. Lesbians in Boston or San Francisco, in contrast, may be part of the mainstream and out to everyone. There may be more similarities between lesbians and heterosexual women of similar political backgrounds in this generation than there are between lesbians with different politics, religion, and other factors.

More than any other factor, whether or not lesbians are out determines to what degree they will be integrated into or isolated from a supportive community. Growing up, many of us thought we were the only lesbian in the world. As a culture, we were socialized to devalue women and to hate lesbians. Coming out, in all its complexities—self-realization, sexual relationships, self-revelation, becoming part of a lesbian community—involved many small and large acts of courage. Our generation was at the forefront of the recent feminist movement, political activism, and current lesbian culture, and we should take pride in our legacy. In the words of Arianne Haley in a letter to *Ms.* magazine: "When all other women have given up hope; when all other women have silenced our voices; we will still be there, wearing our pink triangles and working for the equality of all women. Lesbians were at the start of the movement. Lesbians will be there to the end. We may be your worst nightmare, but we are also your future."

FURTHER READING

Bradford, Judith, Caitlin Ryan, and Esther Rothblum. "National Lesbian Health Care Survey: Implications for Mental Health Care." *Journal of Consulting and Clinical Psychology* (April 1994).

Doress-Worters, Paula. *The New Ourselves, Growing Older: Women Aging with Knowledge and Power.* New York: Simon & Schuster, 1994.

Duberman, Martin. *Stonewall.* New York: Penguin Books, 1993.

Faderman, Lillian. *Odd Girls and Twilight Lovers: A History of Lesbian Life in Twentieth-Century America.* New York: Columbia University Press, 1991.

Friend, Richard. "The Individual and Social Psychology of Aging: Clinical Implications for Lesbians and Gay Men." *Journal of Homosexuality* (Fall 1987).

Kurdek, Larry, and J. Patrick Schmitt. "Perceived Emotional Support from Family and Friends in Members of Homosexual, Married, and Heterosexual Cohabiting Couples." *Journal of Homosexuality* (Fall 1987).

Lynch, Lee, and Akia Woods, eds. *Lesbians Off the Rag.* Norwich, Vt.: New Victoria, in press.

Pearlman, Sarah. "Late Mid-life Astonishment: Disruptions to Identity and Self-esteem." In Nancy Davis, Ellen Cole, and Esther Rothblum, eds. *Faces of Women and Aging.* New York: Haworth Press, 1993.

Sang, Barbara, Joyce Warshow, and Adrienne Smith, eds. *Lesbians at Midlife: The Creative Transition.* San Francisco: Spinsters Book Company, 1991.

Thompson, Carol. "Lesbian Grief and Loss Issues in the Coming Out Process," *Women and Therapy* (Spring/Summer 1992).

FIVE

WE NEVER PROMISED YOU
ROLE MODELS

Jeanne Adleman

I was born in 1919 and am seventy-five as I write. I offer here what I have learned since 1980, when I converted from being bisexual by temperament and heterosexual by (what seemed my) choice to being lesbian by choice and committed to other lesbians and lesbianism. *Converted* is the word I use to describe how one, after considerable fear, longing, concern, and reflection, abandons a long-standing and well-developed self-identification for a lesbian identity. The gay and lesbian term for this process is "coming out," a code phrase with one set of meanings for insiders and a very different meaning for most others, who tend to assume it means coming out of hiding.

Invited to write on lesbian aging, in a nonacademic mode, I sought among my friends and acquaintances lesbians whose diversity of past and current life experience would challenge ageist stereotyping (whether negative or positive) and instead illuminate at least some lesbians' lives after sixty. To the extent possible, I have done this in their own words.

The thirteen lesbians I interviewed for this chapter, born between

1905 and 1934, are among my most important teachers. Thanks to much consciousness raising, we are out about age. Many of us have taken on the practice of adding our year of birth in parentheses after our name when we write or are written about, as part of our anti-ageism politics. We are not, however, immune to internalized ageism; one friend who sometimes took part in anti-ageism activities lied about her own age even to friends—as we learned only after her death.

Among the old lesbians I interviewed are some I know in the San Francisco Bay Area, where I live and work. Some I met at professional meetings. I make my living as a feminist therapist, but no one mentioned here has ever been my therapy client. Most have asked me to use their own names; those who didn't chose their own pseudonyms, presented within quotation marks at their first use.

TIME AND PLACE IN PERSONAL HISTORIES

Among the factors that have a significant impact on our lives, even into old age, two of the most important are when and where we first knew ourselves as lesbians. "Charity" (1928) and "Doris" (1927) fell in love in college, and are still together forty-six years later. As students, they were warned against their relationship, and the dean even threatened them. After graduating, they constructed their lives so as to isolate themselves from anyone who might betray them and ruin their careers. Charity has written movingly about living a hidden life while struggling against feelings of shame.

Charity is now in the process of gradually retiring. Charity and Doris live in a small, conservative southeastern city where they are still not publicly known as lesbians. But they are no longer isolated and are happy to have friends who acknowledge their relationship.

At the time I interviewed her, Betty (1918) was finding it difficult "to be single after more than ten years with Silvia—such an exceptional person," who died in 1993 at the age of eighty-five. Betty has suffered an unusual amount of loss in her life. She was married to a gay man for four years ("We were both trying to be straight," she says), and then raised a daughter who, as a young adult, committed suicide. At forty-one, Betty developed breast cancer, and her left breast was removed. Asked how she sustained herself through all this, plus subsequent illnesses and operations, she says, "I believe we're all born with a certain amount of inner strength, but I must have been given a little bit extra. I've always just taken life as it comes. And I've had a couple of good therapists!"

Silvia and Betty met in a group Betty had started for lesbians over fifty, and the relationship "took off quickly. There was a lot of sexual intensity in our first year, but it was never the mainstay of our relationship," Betty says. "Intimacy and the depth of our friendship and companionability deepened when we stopped being sexual. Sex was not what worked for us."

Christine Burton (1905) graduated from high school at sixteen and went directly into full-time work. A lifelong lesbian, she says she "overcame the despair, disorder, and confusion" of her earlier years when, at the age of sixty-six, she "discovered feminism, identified patriarchy as the root source of my pain, and began to experience hope."

She adds, "In my early seventies, I learned of a lesbian contact service and mailed in my check and listing. I identified myself as over sixty." In return she received an envelope containing her check and self-description, with a note saying, "Unless you have made a mistake in your age, we cannot accept your listing. Nobody is looking for anyone over fifty."

Christine determined then to start a service especially for "lesbian women fifty and over, and the women who love them." In 1985, she founded Golden Threads (see Resources) with a handful of women who listed themselves anonymously; now there are hundreds of members at any given time. The Golden Threads motto is: "You're never too old to love and be loved."

Unlike Christine, many lesbians had negative experiences with feminist organizations and theory. Aiming to discredit the women's liberation movements, the establishment tended to label all feminists as lesbians. Frightened, and in misguided defense, many feminists became hostile to lesbians. As a result, numerous lesbians involved in women's movement organizations remained as closeted within feminism as in their work settings, families, or anywhere else. But it was the women's movement that, over time, would bring many women who had never thought of themselves as lesbians to new levels of respect and affection for other women, and eventually to love and sexual involvement.

Kate (1922) became a lesbian and a feminist at the same time, when she fell in love with a woman and joined "a group of graduate students eager to challenge and combat patriarchal institutions." Now she thinks that if she had found the right woman under other circumstances, she would have become a lesbian independent of feminism.

Doreen (1928) was not actively involved in the early years of the women's movement, but later worked on projects and "began to hear stories—for example, in the National Organization for Women—from several women who had left what they considered good marriages to be with a woman because, they said, women offered not only good sex but also companionship. All of this had an effect on me in my bad marriage and gave me the courage, later when I fell in love with a woman, to leave my husband."

As for me, I had been in love with one or two women earlier in my life, but affirmed myself as a lesbian only after years of working alongside lesbians in women's movement organizations. It was at a time when I was not in love with any one woman, just with women, just with lesbians. It was also at a time and in a place (the 1970s in San Francisco) where lesbians were highly visible and admired by many feminists. It took me five years of uncertainty to believe I could be *good enough* to be a lesbian, could equal the qualities I saw in others. I was helped by recognizing that the particular group of lesbians and nonlesbians I worked with shared progressive political commitments around, for example, race and class. I believe a key element in such work is understanding that *not* mentioning race when referring to whites supports those whites who take for granted that their race is the ordinary, normal one. The lesbians introduced in this chapter so far are white.

SOME RACIAL DIFFERENCES

The differences between lesbians of color and white lesbians reach a profound depth too important to ignore but too complex to clarify fully here. And those differences last into old age. Some white lesbians breezily try to explain away their perception that lesbians of color distance themselves from primarily white lesbian projects, events, and organizations. "The Black community is so homophobic," is what I still often hear, as if there is such a thing as *a* Black community; as if the thought of a single white community would make sense to the speaker; and as if white communities are not homophobic!

Lesbians of color protect themselves in their own ways from the unconscious arrogance that white supremacy has conferred upon white women: from the unintended, unwanted, and usually unrecognized comments and behavior of well-intentioned white lesbians. Perhaps more important, they may also want to protect themselves against a degree of rejection by their home communities based not so much on homophobia as on disappointment or anger that they are becoming too close to white people.

Of the three lesbians of color I interviewed for this chapter, one is single, one is in a biracial relationship, and one is partnered with another African-American woman. "Grear" (1934) says that who she is today "comes from having borne the mark of oppression. I started working when I was very young, mostly in some kind of service work, including domestic work. I grew up with a tremendous amount of anger at having to do the work I did, especially so young, feeling so unprotected and unseen. Once I got my professional degree, I was able to turn my back on domestic service, only recognizing it as a viable alternative in difficult times." She now rents a pleasant apartment in Berkeley, and is still active in her professional life. "I'm comfortable," she says. "I don't have many needs, or a desire to be rich."

Getting to this point in her life, Grear says, "means being freed up not to have to pick at myself as much as I used to—the kind of intellectual and emotional grooming work of the developing years. Picking at myself to make sure my intelligence, productivity, and creativity were not overlooked by others. I am also more selective about when, for example, I do or do not argue with someone to prove my point. I can hear an opinion and, even if I disagree, let it go. I no longer have to have the last word."

Grear is surprised and pleased that she is still sexually active, sexually "up." She says she always thought women sort of "topped off, sexually, like men. I like the freedom of it, being able to flirt and play—not worrying about what others think, just forging ahead."

Evie (1921) and Janny (1923) met as political activists on a committee to help refugees from Franco Spain. Evie, looking back on their early years in San Francisco, says they were young and talented; they wrote songs and performed together for various causes they believed in, and truly enjoyed their lives. (Janny adds, "We did everything together.") Evie identifies herself as Black; Janny is white.

Their relationship dates back to 1949. It was difficult enough then to be an interracial couple, and being lesbians made it even harder for them to be accepted. Janny told me that she was thrown out of the Communist Party because she wouldn't give up the relationship. "This was heartbreaking for me," Janny says, "and that's when I started drinking—in 1953. I got sober in 1982," she adds, "and now I'm productive again, but I feel I wasted too many years."

Evie says they didn't know any gay people when they were young, but when they took up bowling they eventually made gay friends. "When I retired," she says, "all I wanted to do was nothing. When that got boring, and also for exercise, I went back to bowling. Janny can't physically bowl anymore, but I still can." She sums things up with, "I am lucky to have had a companion all these years, and that we care very much for each other and have nice friends."

Shaba (1934) began her relationship with Lillie (1939) in 1968 and, except for a break between them for four or five years, they have been together ever since. Both are African American. During much of the relationship each had grandchildren living with them, whom they felt obliged to raise. Now that that phase has finally passed, they can "renew our acquaintance, really get to know one another again," Shaba says. She appreciates the comfort and the "language" Lillie brings to the relationship. "Knowing each other more than twenty years, we can be ourselves with each other." Years ago they had "done vows" in a personal way, but at this writing they are thinking of redoing them "with more of a ritual and with many friends present." Shaba has bought land in New Mexico where they plan to retire together. Not certain their resources will remain adequate, she hopes they will operate a small business together there.

FINANCES: COMFORT, ADEQUACY, OR ANXIETY?

Economic status is of nearly overriding importance in determining the satisfactions and stresses in lesbian old age (as, indeed, in anyone's). I do not personally know any old lesbians who are destitute, but I am sure they exist. I define *destitution* as the situation from which mere poverty looks good. The federally defined poverty line, a statistical average, is the same all over the United States, but its applicability varies. It may be adequate in areas where the cost of living is low, but terribly inadequate in parts of the country where rent and living expenses are high. Do we have to leave where we want to be, where we are productive and have friends, in order to get by as we grow older? Most of us who do not own our homes or other major assets manage by working more years than we had planned and by holding on to our dreams.

Rusty (1923) lives alone in a one-bedroom apartment in the Tenderloin district of San Francisco, an area she describes as being "colorful on good days" but most of the time "a sewer. . . . I'm still dreaming of having a home of my own some day," she says. Rusty worked as a machinist or mechanic most of her life, for thirty-one years in the navy. "They brought me back from Vietnam more dead than alive, when I was forty-seven. A year or two later, my medical discharge came through. I can live on my pension and Social Security by being very, very careful. I save for things I want, and also work when I can. For the past few years, I worked in a laundromat near my apartment: fifteen hours a day, seven days a week, at minimum wage. I was able to eat out occasionally and buy certain things that make me happy, like a good TV and stereo, and a good leather jacket on sale." Rusty, like the other women still to be introduced in this chapter, is white.

Doreen and her partner, Bev (1919), also speak of managing carefully, but the resources they manage are very different from Rusty's. Bev and Doreen met through Golden Threads and have been together for four years. Doreen had had a painful marriage for twenty-seven years and raised six children before falling in love with a woman and beginning an eleven-year relationship. When it ended, she remained single for several years. In contrast, Bev had lived many years with one partner, very quietly and very closeted, until the partner's death after a lengthy illness. Having come out to herself in 1941 and finally retired in 1989, Bev found herself free to be as out as she wished.

Doreen sold her house to move to Bev's in a prosperous section of Berkeley. Both have worked most of their adult lives, Bev as a university librarian and Doreen as an elementary-school and community-college teacher. "We watch our finances and we're careful," Doreen says as Bev nods, "but we do just about anything we want to do, including travel." They plan to be together the rest of their lives, and consider one way to do so is by keeping up their sexual connection. "You don't have to be old not to have sex," Doreen says, "but sex is important to both of us and we really enjoy our sex life."

CHILDREN IN OUR LIVES—OR NOT

How different are Charity, Doris, Betty, Christine, Grear, Evie, Janny, Shaba, Lillie, Rusty, Kate, Doreen, and Bev from women over sixty who are not lesbians? Is it true that lesbians, who may never have depended on men for their income, have been better able to plan for their late years? I find myself unable to answer these questions, possibly because I have not been a lesbian all my life, and possibly because the question is so complex. Maybe my feminist commitment keeps me attuned to the common ground between lesbians and other women, so that I am more likely to seek out similarities than differences. On a personal level, I cannot think of any woman my age, lesbian or not, who has not done her best to provide for her independence one way or another.

More interesting to me is the issue of differences *among* lesbians sixty and over. One obvious difference is between those who have raised children and those who have not. Ongoing connections with *and* disconnections from one's children—and even grandchildren—have an impact on a lesbian's life well into old age. Even among those of us who have raised children and still have loving relationships with them, there are differences. Some of us take great joy in frequent visits with our children and grandchildren. Others, like me, deeply love them but want to keep our lives more separate.

It is sometimes assumed that having children provides a security against very old age, that parents know they will always have somewhere to go if they can no longer take care of themselves. This may be true as a last resort against being homeless on the streets, but I know few old mothers, lesbian or not, who look forward to living with their adult children. It seems increasingly clear to me that there are an enormous number of possible permutations between old lesbians and children: Some lesbians co-mothered with partners over a lifetime; some created extremely important and ongoing relationships with nieces or nephews; some have given birth to a child but voluntarily or involuntarily relinquished raising that child; and some have been rejected by their children because we were or became lesbians. Yet many of us have been fortunate enough to experience loving acceptance.

OLD AGES

There is also a difference among old lesbians that derives from the diverse ages of "old," and the different ways we age socially, psychologically, and physiologically. Old is both a biological/physiological state of development and a social-cultural construct. Before I got to *be* old, if I thought about old age at all I assumed it began at sixty-five, when Social Security and Medicare ordinarily came due. I first heard of sixty as old when I participated in organizing the First West Coast Old Lesbian Conference in 1987. Until then, I neither knew nor cared that gerontologists and bureaucrats had made sixty the defining age. Thanks largely to the strong leadership of Barbara Macdonald in the organizing committee, we agreed to accept sixty as the beginning of old age. We wanted to celebrate our age and lesbianism, to teach against ageism, and especially to refute the lie that it is shameful to be old.

Nevertheless, all lesbians sixty and over are not the same, nor do we age at the same rates or in the same ways. There really is no one old age; there are old ages. Rates of physiological aging are profoundly affected by differences in levels of health, frequency and severity of illness, susceptibility to accidents, availability of care during healing, and other factors. Even those of us who age in good health should probably expect certain changes. For example, I am not in ill health if my visual acuity decreases or I experience hearing loss or I have to rely on a dentist to replace teeth that have worn out. Some of us who are in relatively good health after sixty are not always respectful of others who are aging differently.

Shevy Healey

It wasn't until my seventieth year that I finally realized a lifelong dream: traveling around the country in a recreational vehicle (RV). Luckily my new partner, Ruth, had a similar dream. Since the lease on our apartment was up, we put our stuff in storage and off we rolled, two white Jewish lesbians in their seventies with a sixteen-pound cat. We drove a three-quarter-ton Chevy truck and pulled a 26-foot fifth-wheel trailer.

Neither one of us had ever pulled a fifth wheel. We barely knew how to stay firmly on the highway, let alone how to back up this monster. What we had going for us was our love of adventure and each other, and our willingness to give it a try.

Although we planned to be gone only one year, we were on the road for almost two— traveling through four provinces in Canada and thirty-seven states in the United States.

As members of the steering committee of Old Lesbians Organizing for Change, we were particularly interested in meeting with other old lesbians. In twenty-two months we met with some twenty-four groups, talking about our travel adventures, as well as our experiences of sexism, heterosexism, and ageism across this land. We participated in some fantastic lesbian potlucks, and we heard some amazing stories of the (extra)ordinary lives of old lesbians.

Everywhere we heard about the dual experience of being old. On the one hand, our new friends felt a sense of greater personal freedom: no more nine to five, no more everyday contact with homophobia on the job. On the other hand, they experienced a narrowing of options, as society's unremitting and overwhelming ageism struck home. So while many old lesbians dare as never before to seek out the lesbian community, start a new relationship, or try a new life, we all also feel the brunt of the ageism of a community and a society that tells us we are over the hill, unimportant, and ugly.

We have finally settled down long enough to establish a home base in Arizona. What makes our seventies so grand is our good health and our ongoing desire to keep trottin', keep learnin', keep doin'. Our own ageist expectations of what our old age would be like left us unprepared for the reality of our aging: a time when our lives are very much in process—sometimes scary, irritating, and frustrating, yet always full, rich, poignant. Our most fervent wish is for *more time*, so that with luck and good health, we can keep on travelin'.

PARTNER AGE DIFFERENCE

A particular aspect of lesbian age difference sometimes occurs between partners. A majority of the couples I know are fairly close in age, not more than five or six years' difference between them, especially but not exclusively those who have been together twenty or thirty years or more. But Mary and Ginny began their relationship when Mary (1915) was seventy and Ginny (1936) was forty-nine. Pat (1926) and Magge (1943) are one of the most contented couples I know.

At a recent psychology conference, I attended a workshop titled "Lesbians in Relationships with Significant Age Differences." For a long time, almost the only concern the mainly young and midlife participants voiced was fear of taking care of a partner in her late years. Then I pointed out that older partners have no monopoly on sickness, surgery, convalescence, or even death. We who are older also risk becoming caretakers of younger partners, who may experience health problems we ourselves have long ago surmounted. Moreover, even age-similar partners risk future caregiving in times of need.

Reflecting during that workshop, I realized I was still influenced by the ending of a tremendously significant relationship I had had with a woman fifteen years my junior. *I* had thought of us as con-temporaries until I learned that she did not. I do not always think that was why we lasted only two years together, but sometimes I do. Maybe I don't want to be that much older than a lover again. If so, that would be internalized ageism on my part, as if assuming that no younger woman would ever want to stay with me. But writing in this chapter about coupled friends who are contented with signifi-cant age differences leads me to reconsider. What is wrong with *reciprocal* caregiving as a loving act? (See Jeannine DeLombard's "Who Cares?: Lesbians As Caregivers.")

Clarke (1921) has been experiencing a postretirement surge of freedom. "During the last twenty years, people I have loved and cared for were very ill. They are no longer alive, and though I may feel sad for them, I do feel freer." Clarke taught for thirty-five years, until the age of seventy. She liked teaching, but the last several years of it felt very pressured, so retirement came as a relief. She went to the 1993 March on Washington with Old Lesbians Organizing for Change (OLOC). "I was thrilled to march with all the beautiful old dykes," she said. She sees herself as being "more out in every way as a *person*" than she had been in the past, "and as a lesbian I am a member of a minority group where I feel pride and a readiness to speak up for everything I think is right." She credits her freedom also to having some financial security.

"Be happy!" she says. "This is a good world for me and my friends, with a lot of love and caring." She adds: "It is important to be *out* every day, to everyone and in every way. Spread the love around. It's wonderful when people 'click' and think of you in an entirely different way. You're a lesbian!"

Along with when and where we first knew ourselves as lesbian, when and where we can be lesbians joyfully and publicly is also important. Our current relative freedom is not accidental, but the result of years of struggle for equality and recognition.

OLD IS NOT A ROLE

I have frequently heard a longing expressed by midlife and younger lesbians for "role models"—as if each will not have to become old in her own way if she lives long enough, and as if being old were a role. There seems to be a temptation to "heroicize" the lives of old dykes, which to some old lesbians may feel like a long-awaited recognition of their struggles against oppression. But each time someone is seen as a role model, she is simultaneously being stereotyped. Once on the heroic pedestal, her imperfect traits become invisible. She is no longer a whole person whose life includes sadness, physical distress, impatience, anger, rage, loneliness, or possibly unbearable stress, intermingled with the wisdom, love, compassion, courage, reflectiveness, and other qualities that go with the status of role model.

Old lesbians have a stake in presenting our lives as satisfying. It helps us to understand our lives as worthwhile and to keep thinking of new satisfactions that may lie just ahead. In this chapter, I have offered some of the ways we may present ourselves, but certainly not the fullness of any of us. And if we were to respond to younger lesbians with reports of any physical or financial difficulties, or with our fears, how long would it be before their eyes glazed over? Before they felt embarrassed or impatient? Would we still be role models for them?

When I try to describe or explain myself, or a period in my life, I unconsciously or consciously select only some things. What I select depends on the context of the person I am speaking with or writing for, or who is asking me questions. It is impossible to condense one's whole self into a single facet, or even a few facets. Interviews, whether formal or informal, are the product of the interviewee's state of mind, body, and emotions at the moment; of the interviewer's direction of questions; of the writer's purposeful selection of what has been provided by the subject; and of an editor's purpose in making changes.

So if you meet an old lesbian and appreciate certain things about her, don't look at her with shining eyes and tell her what a role model she is for you. Surely you mean it as a compliment, but it is not *her* reason for being. Just tell her the specific things you appreciate about her. If you can say truthfully that you enjoy being with her, tell her that. You could ask her if she has room in her life for another friend. Be prepared to take "Sure" for an answer or, "No, I really don't," or even another question: "What does friendship mean to you?" Some of us feel we do not have time enough in our lives to maintain and enrich the depth of the friendships we already have; others will always make time for new friends who are not too demanding.

BOTTOM LINES

The farther along we are in age, the more likely it is that we give consideration to the manner and timing of our death. Barbara

Macdonald has written, in the updated edition of *Look Me in the Eye:* "Today, gradually, sometimes not easily, I begin to understand that my body is still in charge of my life process and has always been. It is still taking good care of me, but it has always had two jobs: to make sure that I live and to make sure that I die."

Janny, who planned carefully for retirement with Evie, danced and sang in pleasure at finally being free to be completely out. Her careful planning, however, had not included the physical problems, including cancer, that have arisen since retirement. After the initial freedom to take part in everything that mattered to her, she now feels isolated by illness and must plan carefully how to apportion her limited energy. Nevertheless, she says she is happy, and I believe her.

Kate, too, has had cancer, and is happy to have passed the five-year survival point. Her concerns are not financial but center on "the slowed-down body that houses the eager and ambitious person I still am."

Rusty says she never expected to live this long, but did expect that, for as long as she would live, "things would be better than they are, financially and healthwise." She still hopes to fulfill some of her old dreams, but also expresses herself as satisfied with her present life.

None of the old lesbians I interviewed mentioned anything about circumstances under which they would not want to go on living, but this chapter is incomplete without a consideration of that issue. Shevy Healey (1922) has written a most insightful essay in which she writes of having heard many people speak directly or indirectly of not wanting to go on living *if*... She acknowledges that at seventy she cannot know how she will feel at seventy-five or eighty or ninety: "I don't know now what my bottom line is."

I, too, have said firmly when younger, "I wouldn't want to go on living if...," and have finished the sentence with one or another stipulation at various times. But, like Shevy's, my bottom line has shifted with time and experience. I witnessed my aunt's recovery from a massive stroke at seventy that left her voiceless and immobile except that she could voluntarily blink her eyelids and move her left wrist. I thought, I would not want to live. But I am glad I never said it aloud, because eventually—with skilled rehabilitation, tremendous effort, and a very expensive support system, and despite two subsequent heart attacks—my aunt recovered a high degree of speech and a fair amount of mobility, though not enough to live independently (at which point I again thought I would not want to live under comparable conditions). She also remembered everything she had overheard and understood in the hospital when no one quite believed she would ever recover anything at all. Life became ever more precious to her and she lived to be eighty-five, a rewarding companion all the way.

For years I thought I wouldn't want to live if my mental capacities were seriously diminished, but while my mother aged to ninety, I observed that as her mind weakened, she became softer, sweeter, and less critical. She seemed unable to recall the many bitter experiences of her life; apparently unconsciously, she sanitized her memories to a uniform pleasantness. When all memory was gone she lived completely in the present, finding something every day of her last three years in a nursing home to light her up with pleasure.

I am coming to agree with May Sarton's comment in *Endgame: A Journal of the Seventy-ninth Year:* "[A friend's suicide] has made me more determined than ever to cast aside my fantasies of suicide as a way out of the constant chronic pain. In the first place I don't know how to do it, but somehow or other I feel one must have one's death, one must not make one's own death." She adds, though: "It's easy to say that if one is not in too great agony."

I support the campaign for death with dignity only a little less than I continue to support the right to *live* with dignity. I've made a will and a medical directive (a living will), and I have set up powers of attorney both for general and for health matters, in the event I am unable to speak for myself at a critical juncture. But so long as I can think and speak for myself, well, I will either find my bottom line in due time or stop trying to control things and surrender.

I am only seventy-five and mostly enjoying my life. Having taken care of those practicalities, I can shrug off the questions most of the time. Maybe that is true of the other old lesbians I know, and that is why we don't talk about it much. When someone asks me what I want more of in my life, I answer, "dancing." Of course I might also want more hours in the day, but I prefer to ask for what is possible. Ambitious to accomplish all I have not yet accomplished, do I continue to live with the stress of incessant effortfulness, stress that feels overwhelming at times? Or do I try to de-stress by relinquishing some of my ambitions and learning to take life easier? So far, all I seem able to do is accept living with the tension, pulled in both directions at once.

FURTHER READING

Adelman, Marcy, ed. *Long Time Passing: Lives of Older Lesbians*. Boston: Alyson Publications, 1986.

Adleman, Jeanne, R. Berger, Malcolm Boyd, et al. *Lambda Gray: A Practical, Emotional, and Spiritual Guide for Gays and Lesbians Who Are Growing Older*. North Hollywood: Newcastle Publishers, 1993.

Copper, Baba. "Voices: On Becoming Old Women." In *Women and Aging*. Edited by Jo Alexander et al. Corvallis, Oreg.: CALYX, 1986.

Davis, Nancy D., Ellen Cole, and Esther Rothblum, eds. *Faces of Women and Aging*. Binghamton, N.Y.: Harrington Park Press/Haworth, 1993.

Healey, Shevy. "The Common Agenda Between Old Women, Disabled Women and All Women." In *Women with Disabilities: Found Voices*. Edited by Mary E. Willmuth and Lillian Holcomb. Binghamton, N.Y.: Harrington Park Press/Haworth, 1993.

Macdonald, Barbara, and Cynthia Rich. *Look Me in the Eye: Old Women, Aging and Ageism*. San Francisco: Spinsters Book Company, 1991.

Martin, Del, and Phyllis Lyon. *Lesbian/Woman*. Volcano, Calif.: Volcano Press, 1991.

Mikels, Elaine. *Just Lucky, I Guess: From Closet Lesbian to Radical Dyke*. Santa Fe: Desert Crones Press, 1993.

Old Lesbians/Dykes. Sinister Wisdom, no. 53 (1994). Available from
Sinister Wisdom, P.O. Box 3252, Berkeley, CA 94703 ($5 + $1.50
postage and handling).

RESOURCES

Gay and Lesbian Outreach to Elders (GLOE)
1853 Market Street
San Francisco, CA 94103

Golden Threads
P.O. Box 60475
Northampton, MA 01060–0475

Old Lesbians Organizing for Change (OLOC)
P.O. Box 980422
Houston, TX 77098
A facilitator's handbook on Confronting Ageism is available for $15.

Senior Action in a Gay Environment (SAGE)
208 West 13th Street
New York, NY 10011

PART TWO

RELATING TO EACH OTHER

SIX

LESBIAN COUPLES

Beverly A. Greene

Lesbians encounter unique challenges in relationships with partners who have the same gender socialization, in a culture in which they are degraded, attacked, minimized, and held in contempt. While all intimate relationships are fraught with difficulties, both internal and external, it is a wonder that lesbian relationships survive at all.

For many lesbians, simply exposing their sexual orientation or their relationship may pose real risks to their safety, job security, or even child custody. The heterosexist and homophobic climate plays a decisive role in many of the internal (personal) and external (environmental) barriers to intimacy in lesbian couples and in the challenge of finding partners. Lesbians of color face the additional challenge of racism both within and outside the lesbian community.

THE SEARCH FOR A PARTNER: EXTERNAL BARRIERS

The fact that many lesbians cannot be open about who they are determines how they go about finding one another. To begin with, lesbians face a smaller pool of potential partners than heterosexual women do. For lesbians of color and other subgroups of lesbians who wish to limit their potential partners to women like themselves, the pool is even smaller. In small communities, lesbians may share the same limited number of partners. As one woman reported, "everyone has been lovers with almost everyone else." Some lesbians find that openly approaching women outside the lesbian community or lesbian-identified establishments may be risky, undesirable, and time-consuming. As one woman lamented, "You waste all kinds of time just trying to figure out first if she is even a lesbian or not."

Many lesbians look to lesbian social clubs and establishments to meet other women. Depending on where they live, however, there may be few such places. Even in large urban communities like New York City, there are far fewer lesbian social establishments than heterosexual venues. Many of these establishments are bars or clubs, and thus undesirable to women who struggle to maintain their sobriety. Women with small or limited incomes often cannot afford social clubs. And lesbians who have children or careers may have limited time for this kind of socializing.

Gender-role socialization also plays a part. Women are still socialized to wait for someone else to initiate sexual relationships. (See "Procrasti-dating" in this volume.) One woman I interviewed for an article on African-American lesbians described the dilemma this way: "With two women, you could wait forever for someone to make the first move." Furthermore, many women feel guilty about having sex without being in a committed relationship. Pressured by the difficulty in finding a partner, some women may find themselves entering or committing to relationships prematurely. As one woman explained: "It's so difficult meeting women that when you finally meet someone, you're not so picky. . . . You don't know when someone else will come along. . . . It's not like straight women who have lots of choices."

Because it is unsafe, in varying degrees, to be out, the issues of how and where lesbians may safely meet, where they may go

Mary Meigs

Advice to young lesbians: Stop worrying about aging! No watershed marks old age. At seventy-one, I was one of eight cast members, seven over sixty-five, of *The Company of Strangers*, a semidocumentary made by the National Film Board of Canada. In the film, our rented bus breaks down, and we find an abandoned house. In the process of fending for ourselves, we become friends. The film's success has made friends for us all over the world; it inspired a fan letter to me from a woman in Australia who had seen the film and read my first book. Her letter initiated a correspondence that quickly developed into an epistolary love affair. She invited me to visit her, and I went to Australia for two months. The relationship between us was exactly as we'd imagined it would be. We felt like our much younger selves in love, with the added delight of being old and, it seemed, wise.

Eventually we discovered our differences. In Australia, my artistic side was camouflaged by my readiness to share Kate's comfortable habits. But when she visited me in Canada, with the belief that I'd adopted her habits, she found that I'd gone back to my own.

By the time we are old, we have chosen shapes for ourselves; mine is the shape of a lesbian painter-writer who found freedom in coming out and who needs a disciplined work schedule and lots of time alone. Kate is relaxed and hedonistic; she is ready to sacrifice her creative life to the work of friendship. We have different perceptions of the ways time can be wasted. For many years, she was a teacher for whom coming out meant danger. She still lives in the ambiguous no-woman's-land where a lesbian can be both out and in. She is a good writer with no confidence in herself. She has discovered that changing my life in the name of love means less to me than writing a book about our love story. My book is also a threat to her because I am taking control of her secret. I believe that we old lesbians have earned the right to consecrate our energies to the best uses of ourselves. If it happens that these best uses are so different for each of us that they are unnegotiable, that is less important to me than the old-age miracle of our love story.

together openly as a couple, and whom they can tell, even among their closest associates, about their relationship can all create excessive stress for both partners. Homophobia may also make some lesbians arbitrarily idealize or devalue their relationships. One woman confidently pronounced her belief that lesbian relationships are simply "superior" to heterosexual relationships because "women know how to treat one another well." Others express the belief that lesbian relationships do not last. This belief may be a function in part of the invisibility of large numbers of lasting lesbian relationships, and in part the result of lesbian relationships being consistently devalued and ignored in the broader culture. It may also express a woman's personal conviction that relationships—or, more specifically, her own relationships—cannot last, and so become a self-fulfilling prophecy. Some partners cling to each other, banding against the oppressor, in ways that can become stifling to the relationship and interfere with intimacy. Lesbians in isolated environments, surrounded by few friends, peers, or other couples, may be most vulnerable to this tendency, and may come to rely unrealistically on each other and on the relationship.

A woman's tendency to idealize people who are like her and devalue people who are not like her can reflect a particular stage of lesbian identity development. However, it may also represent a woman's own deeply rooted sense of self-hate, or in this case internalized homophobia. In any case such a stance, when generalized to other aspects of a lesbian's life, actually makes it harder for her to develop relationships or get support from the outside world by restricting the range of people by whom she will allow herself to be supported and understood. For instance, there may be a self-fulfilling fear of being unable to obtain support or of being unworthy of it.

Homophobia also creates internal barriers to intimacy. Some of us internalize our culture's negative stereotypes of lesbians, which might be manifested in feelings of guilt or shame about our sexuality or sexual desire. The result may be inhibited sexual desire, choices of unlikely or unavailable partners, and successive short-term relationships, as well as avoiding potentially intimate relationships altogether. Some women become sexually promiscuous in order to stop any one relationship from becoming too important. Internalized homophobia may also lead a lesbian to sabotage intimate relationships.

Clearly, individual dynamics and personalities must be understood in evaluating the success or failure of any relationship, as they often serve as the loom on which these disparate threads are woven. And we must avoid the trap of using the homophobic culture as an excuse for behavior that is really rooted in personal feelings about a partner or a relationship.

SPECIAL ISSUES FOR LESBIANS OF COLOR

The positive cultural mirroring that women of color usually receive during development, especially through their families, helps to buffer the demeaning messages and images of themselves created and maintained by the dominant culture. Those who do not receive positive cultural mirroring are at risk for internalizing society's racism.

Lesbians of color also learn a range of negative stereotypes about alternative sexual orientations long before they know that they are lesbian themselves. With the exception of Native Americans, other ethnic groups often have either no words in their language for lesbian or they have only degrading words and names. The internalization of pernicious attitudes about lesbians, learned from loved and trusted figures, complicates their process of lesbian identity development and self-acceptance in ways that are not as complex for their white counterparts.

Regardless of the specific group to which they belong, lesbian women of color must manage the dominant culture's racism, sexism, and heterosexism. They must also manage the sexism, heterosexism, and internalized racism of their own ethnic group. With the exception of large cities, most minority communities are not large enough to maintain a distinct or formal lesbian community of their own. This and other factors may make it even more difficult for lesbians

Tee A. Corinne

Breaking up has never come easily for me, and the memories of those wrenchings are like waking nightmares. Often I would know a liaison or an affair had spent its creative energy, but would hold on, digging my nails in, wailing. Therapy would be tried or couples counseling or discussions with friends. I wouldn't want to leave. Then a corner would be turned someplace deep inside and I would say, "Now. I have to get out now."

Is it related to being an artist? Often my lovers have also been my inspiration, their images lingering in my imagination, igniting my passion, driving me to make picture after picture. I have wanted to secure them to me, to celebrate their outward form as an external announcement of my tumultuous feelings, erupting, contained only by the aesthetic that ultimately represents their form.

Sometimes I have been attracted by danger, more often by intellectual stimulation. Yet always there has been a visual component, the way one moved at twilight, the sooty, shaded eyes, the clearly defined mouth, the curve of cheekbone or thigh or mons.

Breaking up included letting go of ownership in the present and dreams of the future. What were left were memories that would haunt or deteriorate in time, and the pictures I had taken or made of the beloved, a different kind of ownership, complex and sometimes disputed.

Occasionally, still, an old lover will return in a dream or appear in the charcoal musings of my hand against the paper, a little out of focus, a smile touching the corners of those oh-so-sensuous lips. Sadness follows.

More often I remember the breaking away with relief, as of a difficult task accomplished with great force and an expenditure of energy I hardly knew I had. Always the result has been a clarifying of my path in life, the line of demarcation drawing the artist forward, separating her/me from the little deaths of conformity, the comfortable languor of domesticity, or the cruel combustion of a love not fully realized, not returned in kind.

And yet I am grateful to each, discrete, melodious, pheromonal, coming into my imagination with inspiration, a gathering of muses who, through memory, fuel and refuel my art, surely my deepest love.

of color to find partners and may place more importance on interactions with members of the mainstream lesbian community. However, lesbians of color commonly report discriminatory treatment in lesbian bars, clubs, and social and political gatherings and from individuals within the lesbian community. Some are surprised by this phenomenon, expecting that the discrimination against lesbians by the dominant culture automatically makes us more sensitive to issues of discrimination and exclusion.

Many lesbians of color report feeling an intense sense of conflicting loyalties to these two communities, each of which seems to require that they conceal or minimize important aspects of their identities to be accepted. This feeling may give them a sense of never being part of any group completely and leave them feeling isolated and vulnerable. If they get together with other lesbians of color, there may be a tendency to idealize the group and expect to be liked and understood in ways that may not always be realistic. This only serves to make them feel even more alone and disappointed.

RELATIONSHIP ISSUES FOR LESBIANS OF COLOR

While lesbian women of color may be accustomed to their families' support in their struggles with racism, and perhaps sexism, they cannot assume that family members will support their romantic relationships or console them when a relationship fails. On seeking professional assistance, they may find few, if any, therapists who are culturally literate in treating lesbians of color, who have training in addressing the many nuances of nontraditional relationships, or who understand the dynamic interactions of both these dimensions.

Significantly larger numbers of lesbians of color than white lesbians may have relationships with women who are not members of the same ethnic group, in part because there are simply more white lesbians to choose from. While heterosexuals in interracial relationships certainly face challenges and often lack the support of either their families or the community, for lesbians of color this is one more challenge in a process already fraught with difficulty.

An interracial lesbian couple may be more publicly visible as a couple than two women of the same ethnic group would be. They may become frequent targets of homophobic harassment and violence, suddenly forcing racism upon the white partner who has probably never had to confront it before and may have no coping mechanisms to address it. A white partner may also feel guilty about her membership in the privileged group. She may attempt to compensate for the racism her partner faces in the world, but this will ultimately leave her feeling angry and frustrated with both herself and her partner. Neither the lesbian of color nor her white partner may realistically presume that the white partner is free of racism because of her political beliefs or even her mere presence in an interracial relationship. The lesbian of color in such a relationship may also need to be aware of her own feelings of jealousy or resentment of her lover's privileged status in the dominant culture and in the lesbian community. Both partners may be perceived by members of their respective ethnic groups as lacking in loyalty, and both may harbor feelings of shame about their involvement with a person who is not of the same culture or race. All these factors complicate the relationship and intensify the complex web of loyalties and estrangements for lesbians of color. While racial issues and cultural differences may contribute to realistic challenges to lesbian relationships, couples must be careful not to blame them for problems that have more complex personal origins within the relationship.

Some lesbians of color say they feel more hurt in the wake of failed relationships with other lesbians of color than in breakups with white lesbians: "There is something about being rejected by one of your own that is much more painful than being rejected by a white woman. . . . When it comes from a sister, that's really awful."

Some lesbians of color may be appropriately sensitive to what Vickie Sears calls "pony stealing" and Merilee Clunis and Dorsey Green describe as "ethnic chasing." These terms are used to describe

Jean Swallow

I had been praying for a lifetime partner when my friend Marian insisted I fly to Seattle for her fortieth birthday. She wanted me to attend an aikido workout with her (I had been promising to do so for more than fourteen years) and to play another hand of bridge with her.

I can't remember the first time Marian and I played bridge. We are not serious players, and perhaps we are not very good. But we don't table-talk, and we don't get angry with each other, and mostly we win. When I fulfill an impossible bid no one in her right mind would have made, and she grins at me, I feel as though we have succeeded in doing the impossible. My parents no longer play bridge because they fought so much over it.

Though Marian and I have been friends for many years, there have been times when we disappointed each other. So what? It doesn't mean we aren't friends. She taught me that—and about a million other things from her Quaker heart.

What I like best about our friendship is the way we never yell at each other

about how we play bridge. If something goes wrong, we spread our cards out afterward, study them together, and try to figure out how we might have played better. This is how we go through our lives, too.

When we first met, in San Francisco, we used to have lunch together every day. We started out discussing how to play our hands, and ranged out from there. When she moved to Seattle, I refused to stop the discussion. When I moved here, too, to live with the woman I married, a woman Marian introduced me to at that birthday bridge game, I moved at least in part because I knew I would be able to play bridge with Marian again.

Somerset Maugham, that wonderful British queen, once wrote, "To have learnt to play a good game of bridge is the safest insurance against the tedium of old age." I have a sure feeling my old age will not be tedious. Or lonely. I plan to be playing bridge with Marian. Or at least discussing our hands and how we could play them. Because we're friends. And family. And that's how we love each other.

white women who seek out lesbians of color as partners to assuage their own guilt about being white, to compensate for their lack of a strong ethnic or personal identity, or to serve as proof of liberal attitudes. The stereotypes of lesbians of color as less sexually inhibited than their white counterparts may also be behind such behavior. An ethnic chaser may seek, often unconsciously, to gain from proximity to a lesbian of color whatever she perceives to be lacking in herself. As these attempts at self-repair are doomed to fail, the white partner may respond by feeling angry, resentful, and somehow betrayed by her partner.

Lesbians are an extremely diverse group, and that diversity is reflected within their relationships. The challenges to lesbian couples may make their relationships more difficult, but may just as easily lead them to develop creative survival strategies. Taking place as they do in an atmosphere that explicitly impedes their success, it is amazing how many lesbian couples have transcended the challenges confronting them.

FURTHER READING

Clunis, Merilee, and Dorsey Green. *Lesbian Couples.* Seattle: Seal Press, 1988.

Greene, Beverly A. "Ethnic Minority Lesbians and Gay Men: Mental Health and Treatment Issues." *Journal of Consulting and Clinical Psychology* (April 1994). For copies, write to Prof. Beverly Greene, Department of Psychology, St. John's University, Jamaica, NY 11439.

———. "Lesbian Women of Color." In *Women of Color: Integrating Ethnic and Gender Identities in Psychotherapy.* Edited by Lillian Comas-Diaz and Beverly Greene. New York: Guilford, 1994.

SEVEN

PROCRASTI-DATING

Jacqueline Lapidus

My teen years were so painful that I swore I'd never go back there again. This was in the 1950s, when sitting home without a date on a Saturday night felt like a living death. Girls of my generation believed that if you dialed a boy's phone number, your finger would blacken and drop off.

It never occurred to me that I might be in love with these girls who said I was "too intense" or "expected too much" and who canceled plans with me if they had a date. I thought I was hurting because I wanted dates. Dating was something I didn't do very often. I never knew what to say to a guy on a date. It was easier just to have sex—or get married.

Now here we are in the nineties. I've been divorced and out as a lesbian for more than eighteen years. I'm old enough to be somebody's grandmother, and just because I'm single I'm supposed to have the social life of a seventeen-year-old? Spare me! I'd only go out with another mature lesbian, which makes two of us who think that if either one calls the other for a date, our fingers will blacken and drop off before we can use them otherwise.

People ask, have you tried the personals? Of course—haven't we all? I described myself as a vintage car: 1941 model, high mileage, good body, some rust. In reply I got ten letters. Most of them I ruled out immediately: too young, too far away, smokers, spelling errors. The one I answered described the writer as a well-worn, interesting book with the final chapter missing. We met for a drink. She was intelligent, courageous, creative, and friendly—but, alas, the strings of my heart just didn't go zing. Neither did hers. Shortly thereafter, she got involved with somebody else.

I get around my cultural conditioning by pure denial. I don't date; I do things with my friends.

For example, when I lived in Provincetown, I used to go out with "Dee." In the winter we'd meet in the Holiday Inn lounge for free movies and popcorn. In the summer we'd go to the Pied Piper and dance for two hours without stopping or dropping. Some folks might call that dating, but not me. I didn't even kiss her goodnight (hugs don't count). Besides, she's straight.

For two years, while I was in graduate school, I always had something to do on Saturday nights: 200 pages to read for Monday, and usually a paper to write. Thank God I wasn't dating—I didn't have time to pee, let alone go anywhere. Members of my lesbian network tried to encourage me.

"Haven't you met anyone at school yet?"

"Of course I have! Lots of wonderful, brilliant people."

"I mean, anyone *cute*."

Well, yes, but she was half my age, straight, and engaged to be married. The night she came over to work on a paper we were writing together, she had such a bad case of the flu she couldn't drive home. She slept in my study wearing two layers of flannel pajamas. It was no date, but we got an A.

When my roommate's chorus gave a concert, I asked "Lou" to go with me. That wasn't a date either, because after the concert we went out to dinner with my roommate. When we got home, my roommate said to me, "What an interesting woman!" She sounded so enthusiastic that I invited Lou to our New Year's Eve party. In February Lou called me: "Do you think it would be okay to ask her out?" By July they were involved; a year later they moved in together. I had made a successful match and shot myself in the foot. Now that they've bought a house, they invite me over for dinner now and then. Not a date. Not even close. Mind you, their idea of dating was camping in the rain, or going to the Harvard-Yale game on the coldest day in November. Thanks, but no thanks.

My downstairs neighbor, who's even shyer than I am, went to a DOB (Daughters of Bilitis) rap on dating. At the end of the rap, all the participants put their names in a hat and agreed to go out on a date with the person whose name they drew. Mary Charlotte and a woman I'll call "Bee" drew each other. When Mary Charlotte got back from the date, my roommate and I were waiting up for her.

"How was it?" "Did you like her?" "Did she like you?" "Are you going to see her again?"

"Yes."

They lasted four years. Of course, they didn't have to worry about dating all that time. They went to bed on the third date, and that was that. Eventually Mary Charlotte decided she really didn't want to be part of a couple. She started taking crafts classes and spending more time with her friends.

A couple of months later, Mary Charlotte and I went to a swing dance together, to hear my new roommate play in the band. We didn't dance—we just wrote "Band Groupie" on our name tags, giggled, applauded, and cheered. This was certainly not a date.

I hang out with "Nan," watching TV, celebrating holidays, swimming at our favorite lesbian beach. But is it dating? Not when you've got a chaperone of kindergarten age.

A friend named Gloria, just breaking up with her partner, was terrified of being home alone with nothing to do on weekends. I invited her to join me for dinner and a concert downtown. We got dressed up. She picked me up in her pickup truck.

"Sounds like a date to me," commented Mary Charlotte.

"No, it wasn't."

"Why not?"

"We aren't even thinking of getting involved" (translation: having sex).

And a good thing, too, because Glo and her ex-ex have patched up their relationship.

The previous weekend, as Mary Charlotte quickly reminded me, I had gone to hear a terrific jazz pianist with a lesbian friend whose name I won't mention because ever since she asked me to a big family party last year, everyone thinks we're doing it already. After the show we went out for a drink and a dance or two. Then we came back to my place. We got undressed. We got into my bed. Then we rolled over, snuggled up tush to tush, and fell asleep. Next morning we fooled around for a while, just for the fun of it, but we stopped before we *did* anything.

"Well, you *were* thinking of having sex with her, weren't you?"

Okay, Mary Charlotte. It looked like a date, it talked like a date, it felt like a date. But we're such good friends we don't wanna mess things up.

The way I see it, lesbian dating is the art of buying entertainment in public places for the purpose of postponing sex with someone you're attracted to, in order to avoid splitting a premature mortgage with someone you can't live with. Getting to know and love other women by sharing work, political activity, or sports for five or ten years seems a lot less complicated to me. If you think you can convince me otherwise and you're a short, single LF 45–55, fit, intell, nonsmkg prof into Bach & beaches, contact the editor of this book. She's got my number.

EIGHT

LESBIAN MARRIAGE CEREMONIES: I DO

Kitty Tsui

Aformer girlfriend kept asking me to marry her. My excuse was that since nothing could top a wedding like Trinity and Desirée's, we could not get married. The truth of the matter was, I wasn't ready for commitment. I wasn't ready for responsibility. I wasn't ready for monogamy. The sex was great, but, heck, I wasn't even in love!

Even so, Trinity and Desirée's wedding would have been hard to top.

Trinity and I had met in 1987, when a group of us was organizing the first Asian Pacific Lesbian Retreat. She was also working on a slide show about the history of the Asian Pacific lesbian movement. I was at once struck by her energy, her enthusiasm, and her political commitment. We became fast friends and comrades in political activism.

In October 1987, we went to the National March on Washington for Lesbian and Gay Rights, taking our program, *Asian/Pacific Lesbians: Our Identities, Our Movements* (a combination of her slide show and my performance pieces) from San Francisco to Chicago,

New York, and then Washington, D.C. One of the biggest events at the march was The Wedding: two thousand same-sex couples in a mass ceremony under an arch of balloons in front of the Internal Revenue Building.

Desirée had recently moved to San Francisco from Hawaii, and it was obvious to anyone who saw Trin and Des together that they were deeply in love. Soon after, they announced that they were getting married. When Trin asked me to be her "best dyke," I was overjoyed.

According to Hawaiian Japanese tradition, a bride is to make one thousand gold cranes for good luck. For weeks, friends spent hours helping to fold the origami cranes, all one thousand of them.

The ceremony took place the Saturday before Gay Day 1988, in Golden Gate Park, in front of family and friends. Trin's parents and many of her twelve siblings and their spouses attended. Her mother made the wedding dresses that both brides wore that day—a Filipino dress with traditional butterfly sleeves for Trin and a *holoku,* a formal Hawaiian gown, for Des.

As Trin's best dyke, I walked her down the aisle (actually a dirt path) to meet Des, who was escorted down another path by her best dyke. Ku'umeaaloha, their good friend and matchmaker, performed the ceremony and blessed the union with a Hawaiian wedding chant. The bride and bride wore *na liepo'o,* ceremonial head leis, and the bridal party and family members of both brides all wore leis. The stage was bedecked with flowers specially flown in from Hawaii.

After the ceremony, there was a wild procession from the park to the Castro. A flaming red Mustang convertible was decorated with the Chinese symbol for double happiness. Cans and shoes were tied to the back bumper and messages sprayed on the windows with shaving cream. Later that evening, there was a banquet for a hundred and twenty of their friends at a Thai restaurant. Guests danced to Hawaiian music provided by Des's friends from Hawaii and Top 40 tunes from Trinity's brother's band.

The next morning, San Francisco's official Gay Day, dawned clear and sunny. I rode with Trin and Des in the parade. They sat in the back of the convertible holding a sign that announced "Just Married!" I showered the brides with confetti and sparkles all along the route. It was truly memorable.

Four years later, on Gay Day 1992, Judy, my lover, and I got married in Chicago, her hometown. The house was filled with flowers: orchids, irises, peonies, and roses. We had prepared vows and alternately spoke each line. Then we exchanged rings and kissed. We were married in the sanctuary of our bedroom in our birthday suits. My old vizsla, Meggie, was the witness. Later, much later, we went to the parade.

Passionate love between women is as old as time. It has existed in all cultures, in all periods of time, whether recorded or unrecorded. The relationships between women have many names: Boston marriages, romantic friendships, devoted companions, special friends, sworn sisters, kindred spirits. We are called and call ourselves many other names: invert, deviant, pervert, homosexual, sapphist, amazon, diesel dyke, bulldagger, kiki, butch, fluff, femme, switch, dyke, queer, lesbian.

There were goddesses, spirit-women, seers, healers, prophets, witches, women warriors. There were women who passed as men; lesbian cross-dressers; lesbian shamans who were tribal leaders; *hwame*, daughters of Doublewoman. There was women-marriage in some Native American tribal cultures; *koskalaka* among the Lakota; medicine women in some African tribes; butch-femme marriages between black lesbians in Harlem in the 1920s. In China there were *dui shi*, "paired eating" ladies of the Han court; female transvestism in wealthy households; partnerships between actresses in same-sex opera troupes; and the marriage resisters of the Golden Orchid Associations in Guangdong Province in southern China.

If the existence of women-loving-women is not a contemporary phenomenon, the emergence of lesbian commitment ceremonies is. Marriage is an institution that existed in many cultures before civilization had tools to record its history. In the United States, marriage is fundamentally a matter of law. In 1923, the Supreme Court stated that the liberty guaranteed by the Bill of Rights includes the right to marry, provided, of course, that the interested parties are a man and a woman.

Marriage is a heterosexual institution, a permanent and exclusive union between a man and a woman for the purpose of procreation. The formalization of that union creates a set of moral, legal, and economic responsibilities to protect and perpetuate the basic family unit. The marriage contract formalized male domination over woman as property and bearer of his progeny. As such, it is one of the traditions that is central to our oppression as lesbians.

Why, then, are so many lesbians getting married? There are announcements (frequently accompanied by photographs) in gay newspapers, magazine articles, and even books on lesbian commitment ceremonies. In Chicago, Jan Dee, a successful jeweler, advertises herself as The Ringleader. And everyone knows she is not talking about pinkie rings, navel rings, or organized crime.

In the seventies and eighties, if a lesbian announced she was getting married, we would have frowned with disapproval and dismissed her with disgust. Back to men! Now, not only is it fashionable, but we smile in approval.

As feminists, we have long fought against the patriarchal tradition of ownership. We abhor the notion of taking a man's name, keeping a man's house, having a man's child. So how can lesbians embrace the tradition of marriage?

When a man and a woman get married, the relationship is recognized by the church, the state, and society. In addition, there are entitlements such as health insurance coverage. The sharing of Social Security benefits, veterans' benefits, pension plan payments, and inheritance (barring a prenuptial agreement) is automatic. There are legal protections for hospital visitation privileges, survivorship benefits, and housing rights. There is also the ability to invoke immunity from testifying against a spouse. A foreigner who marries a citizen is usually entitled to residency in the United States and can obtain a foreign visa and apply for priority citizenship.

At the state level, there are benefits that include adoption and foster-care advantages, custody and visitation rights for nonbiological parents, and divorce protections. In addition, buying health, home, and car insurance may be easier, and the heterosexual couple may qualify for privileges given only to family members at institutions such as health clubs and museums.

These privileges of marriage have always been restricted to those the law wishes to recognize. In 1958, for example, two residents of Virginia—Mildred Jeter, a Negro female, and Richard Loving, a white male—were married in the nation's capital. When they returned home, they were indicted with violating the state's ban on interracial marriages. The laws were not overturned in all fifty states until 1967, when the U.S. Supreme Court decision on *Loving v. Virginia* was handed down.

But interracial marriage does not threaten the fundamental institution of marriage. A same-sex marriage challenges the very concept of family; it threatens the pillars of morality at the cornerstones of society.

Thomas Stoddard, an attorney and former executive director of Lambda Legal Defense and Education Fund, in his essay "Why Gay People Should Seek the Right to Marry," argues for our right to marry. He asserts that by denying lesbians and gay men this right, society deems us both incapable and unworthy of sustaining meaningful relationships, though we may share the same bed, bank account, and children: "Marriage may be unattractive and even oppressive as it is currently structured and practiced, but enlarging the concept to embrace same-sex couples would necessarily transform it into something new. . . . Extending the right to marry to gay people—that is, abolishing the traditional gender requirements of marriage—can be one of the means, perhaps the principal one, through which the institution divests itself of the sexist trappings of the past."

A marriage ceremony is a rite of passage. If we as women can take back the night, we can surely take back symbols, rituals, and traditions, and transform them for our own use. Some couples get married under the *chuppah*. Some use crystals, candles, chants, poems, prayer wheels, stones, shells, sea water, songs, beads, bells, blankets, bowls, feathers, and flowers in their ceremonies. There are Protestant, Catholic, Jewish, and Quaker traditions. And there are Native American, African, Buddhist, Wicca, Pagan, and other nonreligious ceremonies.

Perhaps to best understand the current popularity of lesbian marriage ceremonies, we need to look back at the politics of an earlier time. In the 1950s, groups of lesbians were just becoming political after a repressive period involving the purging of homosexuals from the military and the post–World War II witch-hunts. Taking cautious steps in finding themselves, they discovered like-minded women and began to forge a social identity. In 1955, during the McCarthy years, the Daughters of Bilitis (DOB), the country's first lesbian organization, started in San Francisco with four lesbian couples. Fourteen years later, a group of working-class gays including drag queens, leathermen, Third World gay men, and butch lesbians, started the modern gay and lesbian liberation movement in response to a raid on the Stonewall Inn, a gay bar in Greenwich Village.

This riot, though widely credited as the spark that ignited the gay rights movement, was not the first show of discontent. In 1967, several hundred people rallied on Sunset Boulevard after a police crackdown on gay bars in Los Angeles. The sixties saw the rise of the militant black power movement and the antiwar movement. This militant political activity, coupled with momentum from the civil rights movement, inspired students, women, gays, and the radical left to organize in earnest.

The liberal air of the posthippie sixties and the sexual revolution of the seventies led to the birth of a new, permissive sexuality. A radical faction in the feminist movement proclaimed that not only could women take power by organizing together, but they could keep their power within the clan by devoting all their energies, including sexual energy, to other women.

In the unconventional seventies, monogamy was rejected as a patriarchal convention. Experimentation was encouraged, sexual freedom was embraced, having multiple partners was the norm. In this postcountercultural, antiestablishment milieu, the last thing a lesbian wanted was marriage.

It was not until after the Stonewall rebellion that lesbian marriage ceremonies came into the open. Another factor was the Metropolitan Community Church. Founded in 1968 in Los Angeles by the Reverend Troy D. Perry, this was the first religious organization to include union ceremonies for same-sex couples.

On June 12, 1970, Reverend Perry married Neva Joy Heckman and Judith Ann Belew in their Los Angeles home. The two women exchanged rings and spoke their vows. It was described in *Lesbian/Woman* as "the first religious marriage in the nation designed to bind two persons of the same sex together legally." The rite was performed under a California statute that allows a common-law union to be formalized by a religious service and a church certificate of marriage to be issued, but the courts ruled it invalid as the statute specifies "man and woman."

As of this writing, the only countries to recognize same-sex marriages are Denmark, Norway, Hungary, and Sweden. In the United States, three same-sex couples unsuccessfully challenged the marriage statutes in three states in the 1970s.

By the 1990s, monogamy had swung back into fashion, and three cases made their way sluggishly through the U.S. court system. On May 1, 1991, two lesbian couples and a gay male couple filed suit against the state of Hawaii for the right to marry. In 1993, the state Supreme Court ruled that the policy against granting marriage licenses to same-sex couples was "presumed to be unconstitutional" sexual discrimination. A year later, Hawaii Governor John Waihee signed into law a ban on same-sex marriages. Developments are pending.

Despite these legal obstacles, lesbians see many reasons to get married. For Trinity Ordoña, a Filipino American, and Desirée Thompson, who is of Japanese, Chinese, native Hawaiian, and German ancestry, it was a decision based on cultural values. In talking about their future, Trin, who is working on her doctorate in the history of human consciousness, and Des, a letter carrier, realized that they had much in common: family ties, cultural compatibility, a commitment to work at the relationship, and a desire for a home and children.

Soon after they moved in together, they attended a seminar on lesbian parenting that cemented their desire to have children. Trin said that they would have to get married. "As a Filipino, to have children, you have to be married. I got raised that way. When you bring a child into the world, and promise to do the best for each other, that's a commitment. People I know who make a commitment and have children, a house, who are committed to helping each other with their careers, get married."

Even though their marriage is not recognized by the law, it is recognized by their culture and their families. Two months after their wedding, they flew to San Diego to attend the wedding of Trin's brother. In Filipino culture, marriage is not just to a person but to a family, as Trin explained: "When my brother played our wedding song, Des and I got up and danced. We had no doubts. No one blinked an eye. There was no hubbub. When you get married, you marry the family. I am part of that family. If my sister-in-law has to accept it, [her] family has to also."

For Bay Area residents Akemi and Amy, both teachers in the public school system, acceptance by their families played a large part in their decision to get married. They wanted children, and they wanted their families to recognize the importance of their relationship.

Akemi pointed out: "Amy and I could live together for the rest of our lives and they'd accept it, but I wanted my family to under-

E. J. Graff

Almost against my will, one day I knew we were going to stand up in front of the people we love and commit ourselves to each other. Of course, it's ridiculous to say it was against my will. I decided. Marilyn, being distinctly private, wanted just to exchange rings. But it was a private suburban life that had strangled my childhood and my parents, so I recoiled. There are many ways to root love among others, but something inside me insisted on a ritual moment in full community view.

But each time I told someone, sweat ruined my shirt. For months I bolted awake after two hours' sleep, every cell on full alert as I planned to brave cultural taboos. First was that of the Western world. Some irrational cluster of brain cells, trained by a lifetime of being hated, fully expected the het world—represented by my family and friends—to spit when I declared my love for a woman.

Equally powerful was the lesbian/feminist community's distaste for anything that hinted at heterosexuality. Marilyn, happily sentimental, openly called it a *wedding*, a word I hated. Over and over I explained that I was not contracting my love with the state, or subordinating my life to another's. I was sharing my love with my community—emotionally explosive enough, thank you, without adding the political history embedded in the word *wedding*.

It took a while to write a ceremony that meant enough, but not too much. We would say a few Jewish prayers, recite four favorite poems, exchange rings, speak our declarations, and, of course, kiss.

All of which we did, a semicircle of family's and friends' eyes on us like lamps.

How can I explain what came next? In that backyard in (yes) June, we kissed madly, actually forgetting about our friends' neighbors. Marilyn forgot to eat or drink. I would have kissed the letter carrier had he walked through. My jokester brother cried so hard he could barely complete his sentences. My stepfather, who once squirmed at hearing I was queer, announced his pride in me and my friends. My mother charmed my friends and kissed us both. To poke fun at our earnestness, we played Mendelssohn's wedding march as we brought out a cake topped with two brides.

How corny it sounds! But it was, in my life, the single perfect day.

stand what it meant, and to see it as equal to as if I had a straight marriage."

Amy agreed, adding: "Akemi is the one I want to spend my life with. Having a ceremony was a symbolic way of doing this. We did it as a way of showing commitment to ourselves and to family and friends."

Akemi, a *sansei* (third-generation Japanese American) born in Oakland, and Amy, a *happa* (one of mixed heritage) born in Japan, had a public ceremony attended by 131 people. Both their families are supportive, though in a silent and subdued way that is not culturally atypical. Only Akemi's brother and a cousin actually verbalized their congratulations to the couple.

Some see lesbian marriage as the ultimate declaration of love, a statement of a lasting union, a deeper level of commitment, a rite of celebration as life partners, a validation of a bond, a formal announcement of eternal love. Others see it as a political act, another step out of the closet, a leap from invisibility, a public affirmation, an in-your-face statement. Some get married for family and community support. Others do it to strengthen their partnership. For some it is crazy and courageous. Others do it from a longing for security, stability, safety.

Jo and Michele, both white, did it because they fell in love. They met through a personal ad in a local gay paper and moved in together soon after. Eight months later, they got married while on vacation. They wanted to involve elements from other cultures in their ceremony, so they borrowed the idea of a wedding vase from the Native American tradition and a wedding blanket from the African tradition. They also exchanged eighteen-karat gold rings.

When Michele started a new job as vice president of planning and strategic development at a Catholic hospital in the Chicago area, her parents cautioned her about wearing the ring. "It's going to raise questions," they warned.

Michele laughed. "The fact that nuns wear wedding bands is a more bizarre concept!"

Jo, an associate director of campus housing at the University of

Illinois at Chicago, is out at her job. Michele, who had always been out at work, laments that she is back in the closet: "I didn't know how I'd react to going back into the closet. I hate it! I've come out to my staff, and I intend to come out to everyone else."

Jo does her part to spice things up by sending elaborate floral arrangements to Michele at her office. Michele says: "I make jokes about it. Just because they come in and see these flowers doesn't mean I have to come out to them then and there. I want to be in control of the situation."

For lesbian couples, marriage, like pregnancy, seldom happens by accident or necessity. Some, like Trin and Des, plan the wedding for months. For others, it happens spontaneously. Maddy and Dior followed the Nike ad: They just did it.

Maddy, who is white, is in law enforcement, and Dior, a Filipina, is a health care worker. They met at an AIDS walk. Afterward, they went out for lunch, then for dinner, then talked all night. Two months later, they bought a condo and moved in together. They also had a private ceremony, witnessed only by their cats. Dior said: "It was another level of commitment, and something we both wanted. Getting married was a way of validating the relationship."

Maddy agreed: "Okay, so it's not valid in the eyes of the law, we get no benefits. But to us it's a confirmation of who we are, two women who are in love and who are committed to each other for life. That's what's important."

Unlike Jo and Michele, Dior and Maddy can't be open about their relationship.

"Because of what she does, Maddy can't be out either about her sexual orientation or about me," Dior explained. "That's just the way it is. We didn't do rings. We wear special bracelets. And for me as a person of color, I'm much more concerned about my day-to-day survival in the world than about the recognition of our marriage. I'm more concerned about the racism in the lesbian and gay community. I'm also an immigrant, so that raises other issues. Of course, if it were legal, I'd be a citizen, just like that."

Many times, the desire to have children plays a part in wanting to formalize the relationship with a ceremony.

Sue and Jennifer met in October 1989 when Sue was coaching a rugby team. Jennifer was the new player from out of town.

They got married in 1993 in a sorority house at Wellesley College, Jennifer's alma mater, surrounded by "a cast of thousands."

Sue legally changed her surname from Dragoon to Levi the day after she got married. She explained: "We wanted to have a family name because we want a baby." Jennifer Hertz became Jennifer Levi two years later. They had considered taking the name of the street where they first lived together, as well as names of famous women. Nothing sounded right. They wanted a Jewish name and thought of Cohen, a common name. Suddenly Jennifer said, "I'm not from the tribe of Cohen, I'm from the tribe of Levi."

For Sue, a schoolteacher, the wedding was wonderful: "It was a spiritual and community experience. The legal aspect is secondary. It was an incredible coming out. I could spend time with relatives not talking about the relationship, though Jennifer would be there. The invitation was very in-your-face, with *lesbian* in the text. . . . Going to Crate and Barrel and registering. . . . Telling the hairdresser, 'Oh, I'm getting married!'"

For some, having a marriage ceremony is a political act.

Eleanor Soto and Yvonne Yarbro-Bejarano were married on March 17, 1990, in the living room of Trin and Des's home in the heart of the Castro.

In Becky Butler's *Ceremonies of the Heart,* Eleanor said: "Having a same-sex wedding is a political move; people can somehow ignore your relationship with another woman, but when you really say that you want to make this commitment, it zings a lot of people's reality recorders."

Relationships that are both long-term and monogamous are often hard to find in the lesbian community and perceived to be difficult, so the act also had a strong political significance for Yvonne, also quoted in Butler's book: "One thing we wanted to do was create and make public a perception of lasting commitment among lesbians. In that way, getting married is an important part of building lesbian community. We weren't imitating an oppressive and sexist heterosexual institution; we were demanding the same rights and privileges of heterosexual couples. Our goal is not to imitate it but to transform it in progressive ways. If people continue to do this, maybe one day we'll also have the legal and economic privileges that go along with heterosexual marriage. I see getting married as part of the gay and lesbian movement. It really does make a difference. That difference was brought home to me very personally and powerfully as I saw how it brought things up for my family, sometimes in a very painful way."

For Dior also, getting married was serious business: "For me, as a person of color, the statement 'the personal is the political' is not just rhetoric. I can't be out at my job, but I am out to my family. And that's important. It's a cultural thing. They may not like the fact that Maddy and I are together, but they respect it. Of course, they would rather Maddy be a man. But she's not! And they know I'm happy. That's what counts."

Until lesbians are granted full civil rights, it will continue to be a political act for a woman to love another woman. By having a ceremony and making it public, Akemi and Amy demanded attention. Akemi said: "I know that it is a political act, but that's not why we did it. But I see it being political, just like coming out is political."

Amy agreed: "Our motive was more on a personal level, but on another level, it is a political act because it's not legal and we don't gain benefits. It's a statement that we are doing this, something outside society's norm. We are together as a gay couple." For Akemi and Amy, as for many lesbians, the ceremony is not just a celebration of the beginning of a relationship; it is a celebration of the continuation of a commitment. Unlike many straight couples, who get married early in a relationship, many lesbian couples get married when they have already been together for a few years.

But what happens when the relationship ends? How do lesbians get divorced? Nikki Carlton feels that most lesbians don't take their union strongly enough to dissolve it publicly when it is over: "If the intent is to remain together in a long-lasting relationship, they should honor the time they did have by having closure."

Nikki, a self-professed "computer monkey," took the bond seriously. She and her wife, Deborah Wallin, lived together for nine years. They were joined in holy union at the MCC church in Salt Lake City, two and a half years after they met. They got married because they were in love and planned to have children and wanted some measure of protection. Nikki explained: "There was a news item about a [same-sex] couple who had had a child. When they separated, the other was given visitation because they had a holy union with the intent to have a child."

Nikki and Deborah never bore a child, but they did raise fifteen foster children together. When the relationship ended, the couple signed and filed papers of dissolution at the MCC church in Glendale, California, where they had relocated.

For some lesbians who have few joint possessions and no legal ties, separation may be easier than for heterosexual couples, who can be encumbered for months by divorce proceedings.

Unlike gay men, most lesbians have never been big on casual sex, and with the specter of AIDS, lesbians have come to see monogamy in an increasingly favorable light. In all probability, this renewed commitment to monogamy has translated into an increasing number of marriage ceremonies.

In the 1990s, lesbians have been thrust by the media and popular culture into the spotlight as the new epitome of chic. Is the preponderance of ceremonies the outgrowth of that new visibility?

Nikki says: "Being a lesbian today is now chic, and we're the slowest-growing group of people getting AIDS. People are sleeping around less than they used to. And with the violence in the world, people tend to stick together more. It's a safe harbor."

Are times really changing, and is society ready to give us equal rights? If gay marriage is legalized, the state will have taken a big step toward legitimizing our lives.

"Society is changing," Jo explains. "I think that if we had a ceremony, my mom would have given me away. She would have participated. Ten years ago, she wouldn't have been able to say the 'L' word."

Michele adds: "There's a whole societal acceptance that's happening. People are more out, there's not this shroud of secrecy. Maybe this rush to get married is to demonstrate that though we are of the same sex, it means the same thing."

As lesbians who demand our right to love, we must also demand the right to marry, a ceremony blessed by the church (if that is our wish), acknowledged by society, and protected by law. The civil rights, black power, antiwar, and women's liberation movements have taught us that social change comes only when people organize and fight for it. At the opening ceremonies of the 1990 Gay Games in Vancouver, Canada, I heard the comedian Robin Tyler tell the crowd of 17,000 gay and lesbian people: "We're not talking about our lifestyles. We're talking about our lives."

I hope that one day soon, Trin and Des, Akemi and Amy, Jo and Michele, Maddy and Dior, Sue and Jennifer, Eleanor and Yvonne, Nikki and the woman in her future, Judy and I, and other lesbian couples will be able to go to the county clerk's office and obtain a marriage license. I do.

FURTHER READING

Berzon, Betty. *Permanent Partners.* New York: Dutton, 1988.

Butler, Becky. *Ceremonies of the Heart.* Seattle: Seal Press, 1990.

Faderman, Lillian. *Surpassing the Love of Men.* New York: Morrow, 1981.

———. *Odd Girls and Twilight Lovers.* New York: Columbia University Press, 1991.

Hinsch, Bert. *Passions of the Cut Sleeve.* Berkeley: University of California Press, 1990.

Martin, Del, and Phyllis Lyon. *Lesbian/Woman.* Volcano, Calif.: Volcano Press, 1991.

Roscoe, Will. *Living the Spirit.* New York: St. Martin's Press, 1988.

Sherman, Suzanne. *Lesbian and Gay Marriage.* Philadelphia: Temple University Press, 1992.

Tessina, Tess. *Gay Relationships for Men and Women.* New York: Putnam, 1989.

NINE

OUR RELATIONSHIPS AND THEIR LAWS

Ruthann Robson

W e call each other lovers, friends, sisters, compañeras. We are coupled or not, sexual or not, cohabitating or not. But whatever we are, we are usually not legal. The traditional stance of the American legal system toward lesbian relationships is absolute nonrecognition: lesbian lovers who have shared one night together, or a decade and a child, or thirty years and a home, are all strangers to each other in the legal sense.

The effect of being a "legal stranger" can have numerous impacts because the law exalts other relationships. At times, lesbian relationships suffer by comparison: A lesbian couple in which one lover works for pay and the other does not may be excluded from tax, insurance, and other economic benefits that are guaranteed to a married couple. At other times, the nonlegal status of our relationships can leave us uncertain about how to resolve conflicts between us without resorting to legal recourses such as divorce. Sometimes lesbian relationships suffer more directly: A member of a lesbian couple who becomes incapacitated can be controlled by a person with a legally recognized relationship, such as the father who may not believe she is a lesbian, the brother who may have abused her, or the husband she may not have seen for twenty years but never divorced.

Lesbians have vigorously challenged the legal system's refusal to recognize our relationships. One of the most devastating—and galvanizing—cases has been that of Sharon Kowalski and Karen Thompson in Minnesota. In November 1983, Sharon was in a car accident and suffered extensive physical and neurologic injuries limiting, among other things, her ability to communicate. Before the accident, she had been living with her lover in a house they were buying together. But, despite the fact that she and Karen had exchanged rings and considered their relationship a "life partnership similar to a marriage," they were legally strangers. In the legal controversy over who would be responsible for her care, the rule of law gave first preference to Sharon's parents, who did not believe that their daughter was a lesbian or could be involved in a lesbian relationship with anyone. As Sharon's legal guardians, her parents could control her finances and medical treatment choices, as well as where Sharon could live and who could visit her. The prospect of not being allowed even to visit her lover prompted Karen to bring an action in court. In one of the many court papers filed in the litigation, a doctor testifying in behalf of Sharon's parents stated that "visits by Karen Thompson would expose Sharon Kowalski to a high risk of sexual abuse."

Such explicit homophobia made many lesbian lovers realize that they were only a car accident away from Karen and Sharon's situation. Lesbian, as well as gay, bisexual, feminist, and disability activists focused considerable energies on the litigation. In eight years of court proceedings, Karen Thompson won many battles, including the right to visit her lover. Finally, a court ordered that she be appointed guardian.

But the judge refused to name Karen Thompson as guardian, even though Sharon's parents eventually withdrew their claim. He expressed concerns that Sharon's parents still objected to Karen as guardian (in part on the basis of her lesbianism), that Karen had been involved with at least one other woman in the years since Sharon's accident, and that Karen invaded Sharon's privacy by revealing her sexual orientation to her parents and by taking her to lesbian and gay gatherings. Rather than naming Karen as guardian, the judge named a supposedly neutral third party, a legal stranger but not Sharon's lesbian lover. Lesbian love acknowledged can be just as dangerous as lesbian love unacknowledged.

But eventually the acknowledgment of their committed lesbian relationship prevailed. The appellate court reversed the trial judge's decision, relying on the uncontroverted medical testimony that Sharon Kowalski had sufficient capacity to choose her guardian and had consistently chosen Karen Thompson. The court also noted that Karen Thompson was "the only person willing to take care of Sharon Kowalski outside of an institution." In a phrase that the lesbian and gay press reiterated in tones of victory, the appellate court also confirmed the trial court's finding that Sharon and Karen were a "family of affinity which should be accorded respect." This respect, however, is somewhat mitigated by the court's commonsense approach in preventing Sharon from becoming financially dependent on the state for institutional care.

Prompted at least in part by Karen Thompson's protracted litigation, lesbian (and gay) legal reformers have developed strategies to make the rules of law more hospitable to our needs. These strategies include both working within the rules of law as they presently exist and trying to change the rules. For example, if Sharon Kowalski had had a durable power of attorney, she could have named Karen Thompson her guardian in the event of her incapacitation. And if lesbian marriage was legalized, Karen Thompson would have been recognized as next of kin.

Such strategies are aimed at more than improving lesbian daily survival—the law operates on a symbolic level as well. The law's symbolism regarding our relationships is often confusing, contradictory, and pernicious. When we think about lesbian relationships, we often evoke family images in a way that blends the intimate and the legal. We infuse this blending with our own stereotypes, experiences, and anxieties. Furthermore, real political differences have surfaced in the controversies surrounding the extent to which lesbians should demand legal recognition of our relationships. The debate has devolved into basically two camps. On one side are those who recommend treating lesbian relations "just like" heterosexual ones, advocating that marriage be extended to same-gender couples and, until that change occurs, advocating various reforms, including domestic partnership policies. On the other side are those who insist that lesbian relations are "different" from traditional heterosexual ones, thus seeking broader reforms that would not link economic or other benefits to relationships. In a practical context, lesbians in the "just-like" camp argue that it is unfair for a married spouse to be able to obtain health insurance or other benefits for her partner while a lesbian (denied the legal state of marriage) cannot, while lesbians in the other camp argue that what is unfair is that anyone's health insurance benefits depend upon maintaining a relationship with someone employed by a corporation that provides health benefits. In the political context, lesbians in the first camp are often derided as assimilationists, naive Pollyannas who believe that the institution of marriage and the hegemony of heterosexism will be dismantled the day lesbians are legally allowed to marry. Lesbians in the other camp are also derided, portrayed as politically correct separatists who believe that monogamy, coupledom, and home ownership are bad for us.

The challenge is making the law serve lesbian relationships instead of having lesbian relationships serve the law. Meeting such a challenge requires constant adapting to changing social conditions but also attention to our specific and particular relationships. I began my own research and thinking about the legal impact upon lesbian relationships within the context of a specific relationship. My lover and I had long conversations that sometimes seemed like arguments. At times, we used our relationship as a specific example, but we both attempted not to make our relationship universal, typical, or even exemplary. Some of these arguments drew on our own past relationships or on our perceptions of relationships of friends, acquaintances, and even characters in novels. One result of these discussions is that I came to understand that each lesbian relationship is unique and fluctuating. Similarities are often merely superficial, which makes devising legal rules—meant to be "generally applicable"—difficult.

Another result of those arguments was that we wrote a law review article on the subject, dividing conclusions about legal rules applicable to lesbian relationships into three parts: legal tools to prevent laws that would otherwise operate, contracts, and marriagelike arrangements. I continue to rely upon the three-part division because it puts lesbians, rather than law, at the center. It also makes distinctions between using law within our relationships and using law with regard to nonlesbians.

LEGAL TOOLS OF PREVENTION

The legal strategy most often advised, and the one Karen Thompson recommends in her book as well as in her many public speeches, is a document called a durable power of attorney. A durable power of attorney is nothing more than a piece of paper that conforms to some formalities (witnesses, for example) and authorizes one person to act for another. Traditional powers of attorney generally terminate when the principal—the person who makes the power of attorney—becomes incapacitated. Durable powers of attorney generally *begin* when the principal becomes incapacitated and authorize one person to make all types of financial decisions and generally act as an "attorney in fact" for the other. Medical durable powers of attorney can authorize one person to make all types of medical decisions and generally act as a guardian for the other.

All durable powers of attorney are creatures of regional statutes, so each of us is governed by the laws in the state, province, or country in which we live. It is perfectly permissible for a statute to limit powers of attorney to people related by blood or marriage. A law may also mandate separate documents for financial and medical decisions, or require specific formalities such as witnesses or notaries. There are several books directed at American lesbians and gay men that discuss durable powers of attorney, even including advice and forms (see Further Reading at the end of this chapter). Additionally, many statutes themselves provide forms.

It is important to remember that any desired practical effects of powers of attorney are only possibilities, not certainties. As is the case with wills leaving property after one's death, powers of attorney are subject to legal challenges by disgruntled family members. There are many legal theories that support such challenges, including the popular claim that one lover has exerted "undue influence" or fraud upon the other. Such challenges are no longer as successful as they once were.

Thus, while the existence of a durable power of attorney might have eliminated the Kowalski litigation, it is no guarantee as a preventive or even an outcome determinant. A lack of absolute certainty always applies to legal documents, but for lesbians this lack of certainty is compounded. Nevertheless, durable powers of attorney (and similar documents, such as wills) are valuable tools that allow one to carve a niche in the legal edifice. They are not tools that can, in Audre Lorde's apt phrase, "dismantle the master's house." But they can possibly improve the lot of those of us who are (temporarily) living within it. They are not always available and not always foolproof, but they can override the laws honoring "family" that would otherwise operate.

However practical the rules for durable powers of attorney may be, they should also be evaluated from a lesbian-centered perspective. From this perspective, powers of attorney and similar tools seem unobjectionable. These tools are not confined to coupledom as conceptualized by the law; in fact, a woman might just as easily name a trusted friend to make her medical decisions rather than a lover. Further, unless distorted, these tools have little impact upon the relationship. We might be flattered or impressed at being named as someone's attorney in fact, and a mutual naming may indicate commitment and trust. Nevertheless, the purpose of these tool-type documents is outer-directed; they seek to prevent third parties from taking advantage of the rule of law that privileges nonlesbian relationships. The documents themselves do not give one person any rights against the other and they do not define the relationship. Legal documents that do give us rights against each other and attempt to define the relationship, as is the case with relationship contracts, pose different problems.

CONTRACTS OF LOVE

An amazing array of lesbians who agree on little else agree that relationship contracts are great ideas. They rightly point out that an explicit written agreement can prevent a lot of nasty arguing in a courtroom or household about who promised what when. Yet despite their good points, I think relationship contracts can pose problems.

A contract, whether written or oral, states the obligations of and benefits to the people who enter into it. As such, it gives each person rights that are legally enforceable against the other person(s) involved, even if the person never intended such a result. There are numerous cases where courts have decided that written, oral, or implied agreements were legally enforceable contracts, despite one person's protests that he or she never intended to enter into a contract. Given this possibility, the most sensible choice might be to execute a formal written document that would be the relationship contract. Yet creating a relationship contract means resorting to the rule of law, even if the agreement is never litigated. The rule of law then becomes part of the relationship.

A contract is a legal creation, and by using it as an expression of a lesbian relationship, we define our relationship in the terms of legal ideology. We become domesticated when the rule of law is our lesbian "common sense," when we start to relate to each other as bargaining parties. Although Pat Califia (in *Sapphistry*, a book of lesbian sexuality stressing pluralism and nonconformity) has proposed that rather than issuing ultimatums, we should think of forming a relationship as the "process of negotiating a contract," her solution may not be any better than its alternative if lesbianism is about something other than bargaining to trade this for that: I'll love you if you love me; I'll do the dishes if you take out the garbage. Such agreements may seem ridiculous or fair, but when they are conceptualized as contractual agreements, they rely upon the rule of law, one meant to enforce the (free-) market economy. Do we really want to express our love, our commitment, or our daily tasks in the terms set by the rule of law? The difficulty we have in imagining anything different is attributable to our domestication. Having a contract has become part of our common sense. It forecloses the development of a lesbian sensibility that might be different.

When we enter into a relationship contract, we are participating in a very specific legal ideology. This ideology is derived from "original contracts" such as those between Man and the State. There are two underlying myths in this process: the myths of freedom and equality.

Applied to lesbian relationship contracts, the myths that support contract ideology obscure realities of lesbian existence. First, it is too easy to assume that lesbians entering a relationship contract have freely chosen to do so. I have indulged this assumption myself. But if freedom is more than not being coerced—as in the classic legal example of someone holding a gun to someone's head—this may not be true. If we listen to those who tell us that relationship contracts are good, and perhaps the views of our own lovers, making a relationship contract can be more like acquiescence than free choice. Further, if we consider the emphasis on relationship(s) in many lesbian cultures, combined with heterosexuality's tangible exaltation of coupledom (bridal showers, weddings, marriage certificates, anniversaries), it is possible that our longing for a relationship or for a tangible indication of our relationship is not truly "freely" chosen. Legal theorists disputing the freedom of choice in employment contracts often argue eloquently that workers have little choice about the jobs they take, the wages they are paid, and the conditions under which they work, given the market economy. We might say the same of the relationship ethic.

For example, Janice and Maria (a fictional couple) may find themselves in a relationship because of the pressures to name their enjoyment of each other's company. Their friends, especially their coupled friends, may assume that Janice and Maria are a couple and begin to discuss them as such (talking the relationship into existence) and to invite them as a couple. Even if Janice and Maria individually have doubts about whether each desires a "relationship," expressing these doubts is often interpreted as disregard for the other person. If Janice says, "It isn't that I don't like you; it's just that I'm not sure I want a relationship," this rings hollow in Maria's ears. The dominant cultural message is that if Janice likes Maria *enough*—and certainly if Janice loves Maria—Janice will desire a "relationship" with Maria. The details of the relationship may be subject to negotiation. The fact of it presumably rests upon the intensity of our emotions.

Deciding upon the details of the relationship raises the second, and I think more troubling, myth: the myth of equality. The assumption that the contracting parties are equal may never be more powerful than at the beginning stages of a relationship, the very time at which a relationship contract is advised. At this stage there are romantic illusions, and if we believe even half of what we've been told about the "merging" of lesbian couples, there is a tendency to subordinate individuality. The assumption of equality obscures not only the differences that may develop during an extended relationship, but also the very real social, cultural, racial, economic, religious, political, physical, and emotional differences among lesbians. Such differences may have an impact on the way we think about contracts.

For example, if Janice is an African-American lesbian, her own great-grandmother could have been the object bargained for in a contract signed by slavers. And if Maria is a lower-class lesbian, she might be unaccustomed to asking for things. For both Janice and Maria, however, there is a great deal of ambivalence that cannot simply be factored in an equation for contract equality. Janice, whose ancestors have been excluded from the right to contract, may feel empowered by the ability to contract. And Maria, who feels that she is now bargaining rather than asking, may feel empowered by the ability to contract. Just as the property acts in the nineteenth century empowered many married women by allowing them for the first time to enter into contracts, entering into a lesbian relationship contract can empower lesbians, both on a practical survival level and on a political/personal level.

What all these advantages and disadvantages of relationship contracts suggest is that any absolute position either favoring or rejecting lesbian relationship contracts is simplistic. The potential for domestication and the potential for concrete benefits and empowerment are both important considerations. Each lesbian must make the choice about relationship contracts for herself. While the choice we make is important, it is more important that we make our choices after considering the possibilities. The goal is to use the law without being used by it, to put our lesbian selves rather than the rule of law at the center of the decision. We must put the contract in its place, rather than assume positions within the contract.

STATE APPROVAL

The marriage contract is the ultimate institution of coupledom. In it, the state sets the terms and conditions, and the parties have relatively little freedom to bargain. The state can also change the terms of this contract: Think of the women who married in the 1950s and became good (house)wives in accordance with the prevailing rules of law, only to be divorced in the 1980s and become poor in accordance with the new prevailing rules of law. The state also polices the borders of this contract by defining who can get in, as well as if and how people who are in can get out. For lesbians, the state's police power has been relatively uniform. If a lesbian marries a man, his claim of her lesbianism may be enough to get an annulment, a judicial declaration that the marriage never existed. If a lesbian seeks to marry another lesbian, this marriage is void. The rule that lesbians cannot participate in the marriage contract with other lesbians is an edifice that is displaying some cracks, however. Recent changes in some Scandinavian countries extend marriage to same-sex couples, while still prohibiting their adoption of children. At least one American court, in Hawaii, has ruled that same-sex couples may be entitled to marry. And many varieties of quasi-marriage, often known as domestic partnership, are being recognized.

The restrictions on same-sex marriage are thought by many to parallel the restrictions on interracial marriage. At one time, many states enforced laws prohibiting "nonwhite" persons from marrying "white" persons. These miscegenation laws were not declared unconstitutional by the U.S. Supreme Court until 1967. Lesbians and gay men who have litigated their right to marry have relied upon this case to challenge laws that prohibit same-sex marriages. The courts that have considered this claim have generally decided that laws limiting the state-created contract of marriage to opposite-sex couples are constitutionally valid. The courts have found no violation of equality doctrine because "homosexuals" are not a class entitled to heightened protection; therefore the state laws are rational. Litigants who raise the possibility of gender as well as sexual-orientation discrimination are told that there is no gender discrimination because women cannot marry women and men cannot marry men; there would be gender discrimination only, for example, if men could marry men but women could not marry women. (One exception has been the well-publicized decision in Hawaii in which a state court did find there was "sex" discrimination in prohibiting same-sex marriage, but the impact of this decision remains uncertain.) The courts have also found no violation of the fundamental right to marriage because it is defined as one man and one woman, according to the courts' own "common sense."

For lesbians in coupled relationships, state-sanctioned marriage could have numerous benefits. There are economic benefits such as certain tax considerations, Social Security, workers' compensation, health insurance coverage, automatic inheritance of pensions, and other private employer benefits, immigration preference, and inclusion in housing regulations. Furthermore, if a lesbian couple were legally married, there would be little need to provide for one's lover through other means (such as wills or powers of attorney) because the operative laws would favor the lesbian spouse. There might also be many practical disadvantages for a married lesbian couple, depending on their circumstances, including increased tax liability, decreased financial aid, including public assistance, and the costs of any divorce or resultant support obligations such as alimony.

The practical advantages and disadvantages are only part of what is at stake in considerations about lesbian marriage. Even when discussions about the practical consequences of marriage seem to occupy center stage, the debate implicates deeper political positions, which are further complicated by other considerations such as race, class, age, and ability, making a consensus stance on lesbian marriage as unlikely as agreement on other political divisions within our communities.

While the desirability of marriage is being debated and its legal future seems far from certain, other avenues to obtain practical benefits for some lesbians are being pursued. At one time, adoption—one lesbian partner adopting her lover—was an option, but this tactic has been generally discredited both by courts and lesbians because the legal relationship created is one that must replicate parent and child. A much more popular and recent avenue is domestic partnership. This strategy is available as a result of ordinances in some cities and municipalities and by benefits provided by some employers, notably, universities and large or progressive corporations. Attempts to institute statewide domestic partnership laws have so far been unsuccessful, although this is certainly a possibility. As presently administered, a domestic partnership is usually certified by an affidavit from both partners and entitles them to certain benefits, most typically health insurance or other spouse-of-employee benefits such as leave, pension, or family housing. Such affidavits typically require a sworn affirmation that the relationship meets criteria associated with traditional marriage: There must be exclusivity ("I swear this is my one and only domestic partner"), economic interdependency (joint bank accounts), and shared living quarters, sometimes for a mandated period of time.

Another way to achieve some of the benefits of marriage has been specific litigation to have a regulation or policy referring to a spouse or family member be interpreted to include a lesbian (or gay male) partner. Such litigation has had mixed success. For example, it has helped forestall an eviction based on a regulation that allowed only surviving "family members" to remain in a rent-stabilized apartment after the named tenant's death. In this case, the court held that the gay male lover was equivalent to a family member of the deceased tenant. But the same strategy was not successful in allowing a gay male lover not named as a beneficiary in a will to claim the share he would have been entitled to if he had been a spouse who was disinherited. In this case, the court would not extend the statute prohibiting a husband from disinheriting his wife (or vice versa) outside the marriage context. In both cases, however, the criterion employed is that of a traditional heterosexual marriage, including economic interdependency, cohabitation, and exclusivity of the relationship.

The recent invention of the "domestic partnership" to accommodate lesbian relationships to legal considerations makes it clear that the law is in a tremendous flux. The general trend seems to be toward more and more legal recognition, and regulation, of our relationships. Whether this will ultimately serve the interests of lesbians in our myriad relationships with each other remains as much of a question as what we as lesbians ultimately want. The debates over what "family" means for lesbians—and what we want it to mean, if anything—will persist as long as family remains a legal category. Our relationships have endured under their laws for centuries. We must now decide whether we can make their laws serve our relationships or whether their relationships will become our laws.

FURTHER READING

Curry, H., and D. Clifford. *A Legal Guide for Lesbian and Gay Couples,* 5th ed. Berkeley: NOLO Press, 1989.

Leonard, Art. *Sexuality and the Law: An Encyclopedia of Major Legal Cases.* New York: Garland, 1993. (See chapter on family.)

Robson, Ruthann. *Lesbian (Out)Law: Survival Under the Rule of Law.* Ithaca, N.Y.: Firebrand Books, 1992.

Rubenstein, William, ed. *Lesbians, Gay Men, and the Law.* New York: New Press, 1993. (See chapter on relationships.)

Thompson, Karen, and Julie Andrzejewski. *Why Can't Sharon Kowalski Come Home?* San Francisco: Spinsters Ink, 1988.

Weston, Kath. *Families We Choose.* New York: Columbia University Press, 1991.

TEN

WHAT'S RACE GOT TO DO WITH IT?

Paula Ross

We are standing around a campfire at a Girl Scout camp in the Santa Cruz mountains, and the talk turns to travel. Peg, a red-haired Irish-American woman, enthusiastically recounts her recent trip to Australia.

My lover, consumed with a tenacious strain of wanderlust, asks her what she thinks it would be like for the two of us to travel there as a couple. I, of course, know what my lover means and listen in fascinated horror and weary amusement to Peg's response, which, if she weren't quite so butch, could almost be mistaken for gushing.

"Oh," she says, "Sydney is very liberal. There are women's bars and bookstores. And just in general, I was treated real well. And I look pretty dykey." She laughs. Everyone else laughs.

I keep my black girl's mouth firmly shut. Peg has addressed none of her comments to me, and it's unclear whether this is because she and my lover are both butch, because they are both white, or some complicated combination of the two. In any event, this discussion is between them. And it's just one in a long line of incidents my white lover and I face every day, though obviously from two very different sides of the same fence.

In order to love each other, we spend a lot of time in uncomfortable territory, territory for which there are few maps and to which neither of us is native. In order to love me, she must relinquish, or at least examine, the presumed privilege that accompanies her white skin and upper-class background. In order to love her, and myself, I must resist the temptation to make it easier. Tonight, in this group of lesbians where I am the only woman of color, these emotional currents pass wordlessly between us. I move closer into the circle of her arms. A baby screech owl is testing its squawks somewhere in the clearing, beyond the campfire light.

Nothing if not persistent, my lover says, "No, I mean what would it be like for us as an interracial couple?" Even in the uncertain light of the campfire, I can see the realization fall upon Peg, the instant white girl guilt, the rallying to rectify, to make amends, the scrambling to retrieve the politically correct consciousness she hopes can save her in my lover's eyes, in mine. I feel a deep sorrow for Peg and an enormous rage.

There is rarely a time when I can attend to my self as lesbian apart from my self as black, a diasporic offspring, one of the millions of Africa's daughters dispersed by imperialism, greed, and an overweening appetite for colonization. I stand around this campfire with fifteen other lesbians. We are all erotically and sexually connected to other women. My lover's butch and my femme identities are not questioned for an instant. But even here, I cannot forget about race. They can forget—perhaps at their own peril, but they do have the option.

In the wider world outside my female, feminist, and lesbian one, I encounter racism daily. From the moment I enter her store, the Japanese shopkeeper follows me, not even bothering to disguise her assumptions that unless she keeps me under unblinking surveillance, I will rip her off without a moment's hesitation. My *Mexicana* colleague and I drive seven hours to interview representatives from an organization that has applied for a grant. On our arrival, I watch the almost imperceptible narrowing of the eyes of the white executive director and board members. We are not what they expected. The waiter or waitress automatically takes the orders of the white members of our party first, then looks slightly surprised that I am still sitting there, clearly expecting to eat.

I know that I am in the heart of the dominant paradigm. There is nothing about me in these places that makes me acceptable, with the possible exception of my class and the privileges it has allowed me: access to education and other resources. I am one of those "presentable" people of color. I don't, in the opinion of well-meaning but woefully out of touch and insensitive white people, act like other blacks. To be fair, I've been told this by some black people as well. Regardless of who says it, I want to kill.

But despite my automatic and often unconscious scanning of the racial terrain, when I'm among lesbians I confess that part of me lets down my guard. Because all lesbians, regardless of color, ethnicity, or race, break a fundamental precept simply by having female sexual partners: We displace maleness as the center of our worlds, create new points of reference, elevate our own and other women's desires to positions of honor. And we do this at the risk of psychic or literal obliteration. Almost unbidden, the fact of these shared experiences raises my own expectations. And those expectations transcend realities of racial, ethnic, class, and other divisions and differences that would ordinarily put me on alert. I desperately want this to make a difference, to provide some measure of relief from twenty-four-hour guard duty.

Can it be that even here, among women for whom other women are at the center, I cannot find rest from what sometimes feels like an incurable case of "race fatigue"? (I first encountered this term in Helen Lee and Cameron Bailey's "Evidence: Race and Canadian Cinema," *Take One, Film in Canada*, no. 5, Summer 1994.) An entrancing saboteur, race fatigue paints shimmering mirages on the horizon, offers the illusion of safety and respite and the possibility of wholeness. It is as dangerous and as deserving of trust as a chimera.

All of this has whipped through my brain in the time it has taken Peg to recover her equilibrium. She stares into the fire, poking it with a long stick. Thoughtfully, her voice more subdued, she offers, "Well, I was traveling with a group of young CCC [California Conservation Corps] members and two of them were African American and three were Chicano." She stops for a moment. The baby screech owl's practice squawks run high above our heads, echoing among the tops of the trees. Peg begins again, and I can almost see her casting back in her mind's eye, trying to reconstruct the world from the eyes of young men of color traveling in a country where the indigenous people have been ravaged and colonized with a fervor that rivals that of the white boys who played out their games here. "It didn't seem to me that they were treated any differently than any of the rest of us."

The baby screech owl has flown to another part of the clearing; it's starting to sound a little hoarse. And I can tell that Peg desperately wants to believe that what she's just told us is true. And then she adds, a tone of defeat leaking through, "Of course, that's from a white person's perspective." For a fraction of a second, the world shifts; the possibility that other realities might rival that of Eurocentric presumptions of centrality hovers in the air above the campfire's flames. The baby screech owl flies off, a partially consumed log falls apart into incandescent red embers, a new conversation starts up, and the possibility disappears like smoke.

Currents of intolerance and racism flow unimpeded through the contours of the lesbian nation. But despite the destruction they cause, girls still gotta find other girls, walks are still taken on the beach, the political correctness of sex toys is still debated, demands for increased funding for breast cancer research and women and HIV heat up, and the most commonly asked question by straight folks, right after the but-what-do-you-do-in-bed query, is, But how do you know she's a lesbian?

When I was in high school in Detroit in the 1960s, my best friend, Lexie, and I dreamed about going to New York and becoming bohemians. We were enamored with the whole image of late-night poetry readings, black turtlenecks and heavy black tights, and the studied indifference of some tortured but terribly talented young man who, for reasons that would not become clear to me for several years, remained conveniently faceless.

Hiding beneath these faintly avant-garde but basically harmless images was one I never shared with Lexie. It sprang from a brief but disturbing encounter with one of those pulp novels in which an innocent, young, blonde small town girl is taken up and temporarily seduced by the "unnatural desires" of an older, knowing, and clearly depraved denizen of the City. This forbidden reading matter made the rounds among our little circle of friends, appearing mysteriously and disappearing with just as little explanation. We were each allowed to take it home overnight, swearing to return it to school the next morning to be passed to the next eagerly guilty consumer.

I have always been a quick reader, but I made my way slowly though this book. Lexie had already read it. Ordinarily, we would have spent hours rehashing the plot, borrowing details to add to our New York fantasy. In this case, however, neither of us ever mentioned the book.

I learned three things from that experience. First, the lives of women who were "that way" were depressing and tragic and could only lead to death or worse. Second, those kinds of women were known as "lesbians" or "lezzies." And finally, I had to bury immediately the sense of recognition I'd felt, even among the all-white, degraded world described in the story. The fact that there were no characters even remotely resembling me or anyone I knew made this seem an easier task than it would turn out to be. And while my white counterparts in other parts of the country's heartland may have found no one resembling themselves either, they had one less hurdle to leap in order to recognize and identify with the erotic charge, that of race. Not only did knowledge that women loved women in "that way" unlock my own lesbian desire, but apparently I was the only black girl for whom this was true.

Thirty years later, I am not alone in the same way, but the leadership and the citizenry of the lesbian nation is still presumed to be white, young, middle class, able-bodied, slender, and Christian. What was de rigueur for white lesbians in the 1970s—overalls, plaid shirts, Birkenstock sandals, or work boots—gave way to the more assimilated, "we're just like everybody else" dress-for-success drag in the 1980s, at least among a certain class of lesbians. I think of how the lesbian nation of the 1970s desperately wanted all women to be alike and how some of us didn't fit. Incongruent with the media portrayal of The Lesbian, we were determined to expand the limits of her silhouette.

I came out during the 1970s, at the height of the (white) lesbian-as-androgynous period. But because I am black, I was allowed (and claimed) much more latitude than white women around me. While my friend Connie was hounded and guilt-tripped about her long hair and dangling earrings, I blithely wore whatever I wanted: overalls, dresses, long, slender skirts and soft, fuzzy sweaters, Redwing boots, and high-heeled T-straps. Under the flannel shirts I wore (while chopping wood for the stove I used to heat my house) were sexy, lacy bras.

It gave me enormous delight to watch the look of horror on the faces of the lesbian fashion police when I appeared in my more femme ensembles. They dared not say a word for fear of being accused of racism. After all, in that small Pacific Northwest city, where people of color were barely a two-digit figure in the census and there were even fewer lesbians of color, what did they know about what black lesbians were supposed to wear or look like? Still, isolated in this world of whiteness, I felt the pressure, even though I outwardly defied it.

As a lesbian of African descent, I sometimes feel as if I am at the bottom of an enormous funnel. At the top, covering the wide mouth, are the white, straight men of the world. Their weight is felt by everyone below them. For many white women, there is a reluctance to acknowledge, much less relinquish, the positions they hold above women of color on the tiers of privilege. And for white lesbians, there is an assumption that the tyranny of sexism combined with the tyranny of homophobia exempts them from really having to own their class and/or white skin privilege. For no matter what other differences lay between us—class, culture, religion, physical and mental ability—it always comes down to the question, "What's race got to do with it?" And the answer is, of course, everything.

It is bittersweet, this longing for connection and recognition. In our bones we carry the knowledge that until the world truly shifts, until the tiers of privilege are transformed into an interdependent network, until whiteness and maleness become ordinary rather than the ruling paradigm, we are our only authentic mirrors. Hungry for ourselves and for each other, we always search and are grateful for clues that allow us easily and quickly to identify the sisters, like variable and colored waves, arching and curling across the top of a milk-white sea.

FURTHER READING

Bulkin, Elly, Minnie Bruce Pratt, and Barbara Smith. *Yours in Struggle, Three Feminist Perspectives on Anti-Semitism and Racism.* Ithaca, N.Y.: Firebrand Books, 1984.

Ferguson, Ann. "Is There a Lesbian Culture?" In *Lesbian Philosophies and Cultures.* Edited by Jeffner Allen. Albany: State University of New York Press, 1990.

Lim-Hing, Sharon. *The Very Outside, An Anthology of Writing by Asian and Pacific Islander Lesbian and Bisexual Women.* Toronto: Sister Vision, 1994.

Lorde, Audre. "The Uses of Anger: Women Responding to Racism." In *Sister Outsider, Essays and Speeches.* Freedom, Calif.: Crossing Press, 1984.

Lugones, María. "Playfulness, 'World'-Travelling, and Loving Perception." In *Lesbian Philosophies and Cultures.* Edited by Jeffner Allen. Albany: State University of New York Press, 1990.

Moraga, Cherríe, and Gloria Anzaldúa. *This Bridge Called My Back: Writings by Radical Women of Color.* Latham, N.Y.: Kitchen Table Women of Color Press, 1984.

Porter, Connie. "Beauty and the Beast." In *Minding the Body: Women Writers on Body and Soul.* Edited by Patricia Foster. New York: Anchor, 1994.

Signs: Theorizing Lesbian Experience 18, no. 4 (1993). See esp. essays by Beth Brant, Karin Aguiliar-San Juan, and Jewelle Gomez.

Smith, Barbara. *Home Girls, A Black Feminist Anthology.* Latham, N.Y.: Kitchen Table Women of Color Press, 1983.

Uttal, Lynet. "Inclusion Without Influence: The Continuing Tokenism of Women of Color." In *Making Face, Making Soul, Haciendo Caras, Creative and Critical Perspectives by Women of Color.* Edited by Gloria Anzaldúa. San Francisco: Aunt Lute Foundation, 1990.

ELEVEN

CREATING LESBIAN FAMILIES

Heather Conrad and Kate Colwell

In 1972 two divorced women met in a lesbian bar and within weeks moved in together with their four children to form a family that still endures. In 1976 a woman in a nonmonogamous lesbian relationship became involved with a man who fathered her child. In the mid-1970s there were rumors in the lesbian community of turkey basters and sperm donations from male (usually gay) friends. Before the 1970s the concept of lesbian families didn't exist. Without much information or technology, lesbians began getting pregnant, and quietly the number of lesbian families grew.

Today's lesbian family is likely to consist of two women who have chosen to have children together. The relationship may have even formed around this mutual goal. In some urban areas, know-how and resources for lesbians forming families are plentiful: "Considering Parenthood" workshops, insemination support groups, pregnancy and mothering groups, summer camping trips, ski trips, and special contingents in Gay Pride parades. The "gayby" revolution is on!

While a nuclear family created through intentional pregnancy is probably the most common way lesbian families are formed today, it certainly hasn't always been so and remains only one of many ways to have a family. There are merged families from previous relationships, single lesbians with children, intentional families with co-parents living in several households, foster families, and families by adoption. The diversity of lesbian families makes it difficult to find reliable research on them.

MERGED FAMILIES

In the early 1970s, lesbian families were most commonly formed by the merging of two women and their children from heterosexual marriages or relationships. Sometimes these lesbian mothers had exclusive and open custody of their children, but often women or entire families had to stay in the closet to avoid custody battles with former husbands, parents, or in-laws. Biological mothers who are lesbians can still lose custody of their children in some states, especially if another family member contests the custody. As recently as 1995, Sharon Bottoms was denied custody solely on the basis of her lesbianism. Many lesbians have endured long, painful, and enormously costly custody battles with former husbands only to lose their children in the end.

Others are more fortunate. Bonnie Arthur and Kay Kerridan, who have lived in Penngrove, California, for twenty-two years, raised their four daughters together. Of their former husbands, they said: "They were aware of our relationship and were uneasy with it, but they had liberal attitudes on it and other subjects, and they left us alone. Their parents and our parents were, in the main, supportive of our efforts to provide a good home, and that was wonderful." Currently, it is much more likely for a divorced lesbian to be allowed to maintain custody or share joint custody of her children than it used to be. As Phyllis Chesler points out, the majority of men do not want custody of their children anyway.

The most common merged lesbian family today is established by two women and their children from former lesbian relationships. The children may be biologically related to the women or not, and may live exclusively in the new household or in more than one home if the original co-parents share custody. In the new household, children gain stepparents and sometimes siblings. These modern merged families can be even more complex if the children were conceived with a participating sperm donor. He and his partner, and perhaps his ex-partner, may also be involved.

These situations have advantages as well as problems. Often they parallel the camaraderie and rich resource accessibility of the large extended families of other cultures. Multiple stepparents are like numerous aunts and uncles who deeply love and care for their children. On the negative side, antagonisms between ex-partners, as in any divorce, can create competition and block cooperation. Sometimes these antagonisms escalate to custody battles that end up in the courts.

Co-parenting contracts between lesbians are, unfortunately, not generally considered binding in the courts. As Liz Hendrickson, executive director of the National Center for Lesbian Rights (NCLR), has explained, the legal code in the United States is at least a generation behind the changing customs and mores of the population. Hard-fought civil rights battles by lesbians and gays at the end of the twentieth century won't make their way into legal precedent until the next century. Nonbiological parents are especially at risk for losing rights in a conflict, regardless of contracts they have signed with partners or co-parents. The nonbiological lesbian mother has no legal status and little, if any, social status. The only legal protection available to her is a second-parent adoption, but this mechanism, adapted for lesbians by NCLR, is available in only a few states.

Written agreements between lesbian mothers and male sperm donors who have relinquished their parental rights were also ignored in the courts until the 1990s, when the beginning of a trend toward upholding these agreements began. Agreements that have been upheld had usually been in effect for several years, and the children were old enough to testify that they wanted the original agreement to stand.

The majority of today's lesbian families—whether nuclear families, extended stepparent families, or single-mother families—are able to work out fulfilling parenting relationships with no need for legal action. At forums and workshops on lesbian and gay parenting, the refrain is the same: "Our kids are great! They're worth it all—and more!"

PREGNANCY

Getting pregnant is often the first choice of lesbians who want children, but it can be a complex process.

Choosing a Sperm Donor

Lesbians as a group are known for incessant "processing." The stereotype of the lesbian couple who spends a decade in therapy working through every detail of their life together, from sex to distribution of household tasks, may seem mild compared to the complexity of choosing a sperm donor for their child.

Should they use a known or an unknown donor? Should a known donor be involved or uninvolved with the child, and, if involved, how much? Should they use fresh sperm for a greater chance of getting pregnant or frozen sperm that has been rigorously tested to eliminate the possibility of HIV or other infections? And then come all the issues of physical and personal characteristics. Should the donor look like the nonbiological mother, so the child will be genetically likely to resemble both mothers? How important are height and weight, being gay or straight? For participating donors, what about personality, values, political beliefs? Decision after decision—and *then* comes the actual search for this perfect donor.

Donor or Father

It is remarkable how much controversy and acrimony have been generated around the issue of known versus unknown donors. Articles in the gay press about parenting have elicited scores of angry letters on each side. The basic arguments for an unknown donor cite the legal safety for the lesbian couple (no risk of custody battles) and the emotional safety for the lesbian family (the child will identify the two women as the parents, not an outsider who donated sperm). Arguments against an unknown donor include the theoretical risk that, if his progeny are numerous, half-siblings might unknowingly marry. But most sperm banks limit the number of pregnancies in a given state to about ten from one donor, making intermarriage very unlikely.

The strongest arguments for using a known donor often come from women who were adopted and who feel that to be deprived of knowing one's biological parents is traumatic for children. In addition, there are the arguments that children need male as well as female role models. The fact that insemination tends to produce substantially more male children than female makes this last point especially relevant.

The need for a male role model for children, especially for boys, is promoted with increasing fervor in our society, the more so as men disappear from the family setting. In 1970, 12.9 percent of American families were headed by single mothers. In 1991, that figure was 28.9 percent. In 1994, 33 percent of families with children were headed by a single parent, according to a Census Bureau study. Ten percent of all families with children are headed by women who have never married. Millions of male children are being raised by women alone. (Joan Lester points out in *The Future of White Men* that part of the vast increase in unmarried women having children, which baffled 1990 census takers, was due to the lesbian baby boom.)

Only two-thirds of children today have a father in the home, yet from Dan Quayle to Robert Bly we hear that if a boy doesn't have a male role model he will be hopelessly effeminate or turn into a criminal. The psychologist Olga Silverstein addresses this concern in *The Courage to Raise Good Men:*

> The . . . very notion of a male role model as something a young boy needs in his life if he is to become a man . . . is simply the latest trendy psychological panacea for a host of societal ills. . . .
>
> [B]oys seem to have no trouble arriving at a masculine identity with or without a father around, and it is now believed that they arrive at their sense of themselves as male as early as age eighteen months. . . . They are born male, and from that will follow the gendered and sexual aspects of their masculinity. For better or worse, what they do acquire over time . . . is a social definition of masculinity.

And this social definition must be expanded, as Dr. Jean Baker Miller states in *Toward a Psychology of Women:*

> We have reached the end of the road that is built on the set of traits held out for male identity—advance at any cost, pay any price, drive out all competitors, and kill them if necessary. . . . Full and mutual participation in all of life, that is, in the growth and development of others and oneself, does not have to be a threat to maleness.

One can conclude that having only women as role models is not harmful to children and, in fact, may be especially beneficial to boys and to society.

The issue of the male role model is separate from the fear that the absence of an identifiable father will make a child subject to a painful sense of being different when he or she realizes that most children have fathers. While over thirty studies on lesbian parenting (according to the American Psychological Association) show that children raised by lesbians are every bit as well adjusted as children raised by heterosexuals, in many of these cases the children do have an identifiable father from the mother's heterosexual marriage. The use of alternative insemination in the lesbian community is too new for any long-term studies on children of lesbians conceived this way to have been completed.

Studies that have been done on social stigmatization of children of lesbian and gay families in general show that very few have been harassed by other children, according to an NCLR publication: "More importantly, there are no clinical reports which suggest that harassment or stigmatization has created significant emotional problems for such children."

Finding a Donor

Sometimes the choice of donors can be made on philosophical principle, but often it comes down to pragmatic decisions about what's available. If a sperm bank is used, the donor is always unknown, although a few banks provide the option for the donor to be identified when the child is eighteen. Some lesbians have gay male friends who can be approached as potential donors, and ads in the gay press looking for sperm donors are another popular route. In the San Francisco Bay Area there are social gatherings for potential gay parents where lesbians can meet gay men who want to be donors. Rarely, an obliging male relative of the nonbiological mother can be found, making the child biologically related to both mothers.

If a known donor is used, the legal and emotional issues are complex. In most states, if the sperm passes through the hands of a doctor, the donor loses all parental rights and has no parental obligations (for example, he can't be sued for child support). If the sperm does not go through a doctor, then neither side has any guaranteed legal protection. Many lesbian couples and donors draw up legal agreements to ensure that the donor has no paternal rights or obligations, but these contracts are still being tested in the courts.

A donor's intentions can vary greatly. Some donors freely give sperm out of a philosophical support for gay families or a desire to pass on their genetic inheritance without wanting to raise a child. Sometimes these feelings change once the child is born. Other donors want to be minimally involved in what has been described as an "uncle" role; the child will know that the man is his or her bio-logical father and may see him occasionally, but contact is limited and the donor does not function as a parent. Some lesbians are will-ing to have this or an even less limited parenting relationship with the donor. Their children may live part of the time with the father(s) and part of the time with the mother(s), with financial obligations and decision-making power shared. This relationship can be the most emotionally and legally risky for lesbian mothers but also offers the potential of a rich, extended family for the child.

Some couples choose a gay donor because they feel more comfort-able with gay men than straight men. Some choose a gay donor because if custody issues arise and both parents are gay, the court's decision will not be influenced by homophobia. On the other hand, HIV is a serious fear and obviously the risk is much higher with a gay donor.

Obtaining Sperm

If fresh sperm is used, there needs to be tremendous trust that the donor is either celibate for the number of months it takes to insemi-nate or is HIV-negative and in a totally monogamous relationship. Also, to maximize the chance of fertilization, the donor needs to have abstained from ejaculation for two to three days before donat-ing. When the woman's ovulation can't be predicted exactly, the tim-ing can get extremely complicated to calculate. Fresh sperm has to be used within two hours of ejaculation; one hour is preferable. It has to be kept close to body temperature for that time, often a logis-tical nightmare.

Frozen sperm is much safer and somewhat easier to obtain, but it's much more expensive and yields lower odds of successful insemina-tion. Frozen sperm is usually obtained through a sperm bank. A

Sylvia Blackstone

On our first date, Laura told me she wanted to have a baby.

How strange, I thought.

Six months later, in love and talking about living together, she asked me, "Are you going to leave me when I have a child?"

I smiled. "Who knows the future?"

We rarely referred to this need of hers to reproduce, knowing it would disrupt the excitement of our hot new love.

I've never wanted children. I have never had any desire to be pregnant. Breastfeeding seems unpleasant at best. Why would anyone have children? I imagined some vague reward in producing a tiny version of oneself. But I've always preferred self-replication in the abstract, in art. Maybe it was something about relationship, I thought, the joys of nurturing. But having never had even a pet, I couldn't fathom it. Responsibility, anxiety, constraint, expense, and loss—that's what child rearing signified to me. Loss of freedom, silence, and space: everything I'd come to value deeply. Unthinkable.

For Laura, it was a life dream, nearly an obsession. She put it off in order to finish graduate school, but there was no question that one day she would get pregnant.

In those first days of our relationship, the end of graduate school looked very far away. So we proceeded to enjoy our love, to live together, to develop the most wonderful relationship either of us dreamed possible.

Then suddenly, it was time to face it. We talked, fought, considered and reconsidered, and I decided, well, maybe I could live with it. Who knows the future? I really didn't know what having a child would be like, in the middle of our house, our love, our lives. But maybe I would like it. Anything is possible. It couldn't be worse than having to leave Laura.

The logistics, the father part, were difficult and time-consuming. I was grateful for the delay. After a while, I thought maybe the whole thing would never happen. I was off the hook.

Then one morning, Laura took a test and ecstatically discovered she was pregnant. I was happy for her. She had longed for it so deeply. But by evening I was terribly depressed. I was not off the hook after all. Rather, her greatest joy was my greatest sorrow: the end of our life together.

As the weeks went on, I felt more devastated. To leave would be to lose the best relationship of my life. Yet my identity in no way involved motherhood. Hadn't I spent the better part of my life trying to escape and regroup after my original family experience? Why create a new one now? Several hellish months followed.

Then the baby was born. A healthy, beautiful, exuberant child. Now I'm in love all over again. I feel very lucky.

donor is put through an extensive screening process before being accepted. He must complete a questionnaire about his and his family's health and be interviewed about his reliability and his motives for becoming a donor. Then there is a physical exam and a battery of tests of his blood and sperm. If a potential donor meets all criteria, he is paid for each donation on a prearranged schedule. Most of the sperm is immediately frozen in liquid nitrogen at temperatures much colder than ice and stored in nitrogen tanks. A small amount is tested every few months to determine ongoing freedom from infections, including HIV. The sperm can be transported or stored for several days in dry ice. A woman usually calls the sperm bank on the first day of her menstrual period and orders sperm for just before the estimated time of ovulation. She can then pick it up or have it sent to her at the appropriate time for insemination.

Insemination

When to inseminate is the next hurdle. Women trying to get pregnant usually keep charts of their morning temperatures for several months before inseminating to be sure they're ovulating. Cervical mucous checks (which, like temperature charts, were originally used for birth control) verify the fertile time. When ovulation is expected, a daily check with an ovulation predictor kit should pinpoint ovulation within twenty-four hours. Inseminating right at the time of ovulation gives the greatest chance of achieving pregnancy and the greatest likelihood of a boy baby. Inseminating twenty-four to forty-eight hours before ovulation is more likely to produce a girl, but this timing is much more difficult to pinpoint and thus may decrease the probability of getting pregnant at all.

The nearly mythical days of turkey basters are over. Even home insemination has moved into high-tech, although a spiritual or sexual aspect may be retained. There are multiple variations on how to inseminate at home. Tiny syringes waste less sperm than larger instruments; some couples use a speculum to see exactly where the sperm is to be deposited. There are special cervical caps that hold the sperm next to the cervical opening. Some women prefer to be alone when inseminating; others want help or the symbolic impregnation by their partner. Orgasm can make the sperm travel faster into the uterus, and some couples make insemination a sensual/sexual experience. Others visualize the sperm's pathway and the hoped-for fertilization.

Many lesbian couples start by inseminating at home because of a desire to keep things as natural as possible and because it's the least expensive and least intrusive way to get pregnant. If they don't achieve pregnancy at home, they may seek help from a doctor or sperm bank. Vaginal insemination by a professional isn't much different from home insemination, but what professionals can offer is expert advice, medications, and more sophisticated methods. Intrauterine inseminations deposit the sperm in the uterus, near the fallopian tubes, so that the sperm have less distance to travel. This is theoretically valuable with frozen sperm that may not have as good motility as fresh sperm. Sperm that are to be used for intrauterine inseminations have to be specially washed and centrifuged to avoid potential life-threatening allergic reactions.

Difficulty Getting Pregnant

Community mythology holds that it takes an average of nine months for a lesbian to get pregnant by donor insemination, but good studies have not been done because so many couples impregnate privately. Comparisons of the rates of pregnancy for fresh and frozen sperm and of the various methods of inseminating likewise remain to be studied. In addition, a substantial number of lesbians currently trying to get pregnant are over thirty-five and may have diminished fertility.

For a lesbian or lesbian couple attempting pregnancy, the months of inseminating can take a huge economic and emotional toll. The logistics of predicting ovulation, obtaining sperm, and inseminating at the correct time require daily attention for the first two of every four weeks, and then come two weeks of avoiding anything that might hurt the embryo (alcohol, medications, hot tubs, sushi) and waiting and hoping. The disappointment can be nearly unbearable when all comes to naught and the menstrual flow signals that tender breasts and fatigue were premenstrual symptoms rather than pregnancy. Menstruation signals a monthly loss of a pregnancy, but there's no time to grieve, as it also signals a new cycle of record keeping and arrangements to obtain sperm. A couple's life can be organized around the menstrual cycle, vacations rearranged, work schedules altered from month to month to allow the optimal timing for insemination.

The medical definition of infertility is based on a heterosexual couple having intercourse at the appropriate time of month for twelve months without achieving pregnancy. But many fertile women take more than a year to conceive, and infertility workups can be tedious, expensive, and painful. Therefore, many doctors and most insurance companies are reluctant to start a workup or treatment for infertility until at least a year has passed. This definition of infertility obviously does not apply to lesbians, and a year of inseminating can easily cost several thousand dollars. There are thus financial as well as emotional pressures on lesbians to seek medical assistance in achieving pregnancy as quickly as possible. Techniques of hormonal manipulation that were developed for in vitro fertilization can help a woman produce multiple eggs every month, thus increasing her chance of pregnancy. For a lesbian couple using frozen sperm, these techniques level the playing field and give a woman with normal or marginal fertility a reasonable chance of achieving pregnancy. However, many insurance companies will not pay for infertility treatment or donor insemination, so the costs of more cycles with lower technology have to be balanced against the possibility of getting pregnant sooner at greater cost.

Having difficulty getting pregnant can put a huge strain on a couple's relationship. The grief and sense of betrayal by her body that are felt by the inseminating woman cannot be equally shared by her partner, no matter how involved or caring the partner is. The non-inseminating partner may mourn the loss of pregnancy but also may resent the amount of the couple's resources (emotional and economic) that are going into the effort. She may feel that her needs have become secondary in the relationship, and this inequality can be very stressful.

It can be very helpful for a couple going through long, hard months of trying to get pregnant to join a support group with other lesbian couples who are inseminating. Couples can share information about new techniques and medications and also support each other through the grief and the stresses. Seeing that others share the same stresses depersonalizes the friction between partners, and an outside source of emotional comfort can take some of the pressure off the noninseminating partner.

A unique possibility exists for overcoming infertility within a lesbian couple. If one woman is unable to become pregnant, her partner can try, assuming she is also of childbearing age. Many couples hold this possibility in reserve, and some successfully have children this way. But it's not without risk to the relationship, as the infertile woman deals with her grief and jealousy.

ADOPTION AND FOSTER CARE

While pregnancy is the most common way for contemporary lesbians to create family, some lesbians prefer adoption for personal or philosophical reasons. In other cases, lesbians do not try to get pregnant even though they would like to. For example, pregnancy is often not a viable option for single lesbians in small communities where social censure is extreme. And away from urban hubs, there are not always the necessary resources and support for lesbians to get pregnant. For other lesbians, age or health problems can preclude pregnancy. Foster care or adoption then become options.

But some states have specific rules that prohibit gays and lesbians from becoming foster or adoptive parents. These bans can force a lesbian into the closet so that she can adopt as a "single woman." Other lesbians go through private arrangements to eliminate the control a public agency exerts over the process. Fortunately, in some states there is more widespread acceptance of lesbian parenting, and lesbian couples need not be in the closet when planning to adopt a baby. Yet often these adoptions can be finalized by only one of the mothers because the lesbian relationship is not recognized by the courts.

In a few locales, lesbians can openly adopt a child as a couple, although it depends on a friendly judge rather than on guaranteed rights for lesbians. Mindy Spatt and her partner, Laurie Nobilette, spent over a year adopting their daughter, Michaela, who has lived with them since birth. Near the end of the process, Mindy said, "My lover and I are lucky to live in San Francisco, where our adoption is likely to be approved by a judge despite a negative recommendation from the California Department of Social Services. DSS will not recommend adoption if the adoptive parents are unmarried. This means, in DSS's eyes, our homosexuality is more determinative than our parenting skills, the stability of our home, and the wishes of the baby's birthmother. It's ironic, because statistics show that not having a father actually greatly decreases the likelihood that our daughter will be abused."

Obstacles for lesbian couples wishing to adopt may be different from those for straight couples, but the three major methods of adoption are the same: public agency adoption, private adoption, and international adoption. Each method has its pros and cons.

Public agency adoptions are often the least expensive but the most fraught with obstacles for gay people. The potential parent(s) go through a course provided by the agency and then undergo a lengthy evaluation of their suitability. But most public agencies, like DSS, have a policy of not accepting gay or lesbian parents. If a lesbian couple *is* approved, there are other risks. Children available through public agencies may be newborns whose mothers are unable to care for them; these are often drug-exposed children who may be disabled or infected with the AIDS virus. Some are older foster children who have been removed from their biological parents because of abuse or neglect. And even after a child is placed in a lesbian household, the adoption is subject to court approval, like any other adoption.

Private adoptions can be a faster method for a lesbian to find a child, but they can be expensive and there are no guarantees. After the adopting lesbian(s) are "chosen" by a pregnant woman, they may provide months of financial, logistical, and emotional support to her with the expectation of receiving her child. The birthmother, however, retains the right to change her mind after the birth, so these adoptions can be fraught with emotional and financial peril. A lesbian couple is likely to be even more vulnerable than a heterosexual couple if the birthmother later petitions to regain custody. Private adoption has been successful for a great many couples, however, including gays and lesbians.

International adoptions are the most expensive but the most sure method of obtaining a child for the lesbian who is willing to present herself as a single woman. A prolonged episode in the closet while undergoing intensive personal scrutiny, however, is a heavy emotional burden. International adoptions require at least one trip to another country to pick up the child, whose health and physical and emotional history may be uncertain. While there are many happy stories of international adoptions, there are ones of supposedly healthy children who turn out to have cerebral palsy, AIDS, or other debilitating diseases.

All three adoption methods raise questions with which each individual or couple has to struggle. What are the ethical implications of being a childless person who, by accidents of race or class, has the resources to provide for a child, thus being able to procure a child from a pregnant woman who may not have the education or job skills that would enable her to keep her own child? Is it a favor to the child to bring him or her into a family with more resources, or is it better to assist the birthmother to raise her child herself? If a child is adopted from another country or is of a different race than the adopting parent(s), how can the adopting parent(s) honor the child's origins, teach him or her about a culture they may not be familiar with? Won't a child feel "different" having been adopted? Isn't it too much of a burden to ask a child to have gay parents on top of being of a different race than his or her parents? Some of these questions are not substantially different from those facing all adoptive couples, but lesbian parents know what it is to feel different and, in many cases, have a progressive political awareness that may make these issues painful to reconcile.

Foster care is another way for lesbians to create family. For some, foster care provides a way to nurture and relate to children for weeks or months without the total commitment of lifelong parenting. For others, it's a definite entree into adoption, a way to find a child, get to know him or her, and prove one's suitability as a parent before committing to adopt the child. These children are rarely newborns, and older children often come with a background of neglect, abandonment, or abuse, which complicates their relationship with their new parents. It can take a great deal of emotional skill to provide loving foster care.

LESBIAN FAMILY RELATIONSHIPS

The differences that emerge in a lesbian couple when one woman is a biological mother and the other is not can add to the stress that parenting brings to all couples. Sometimes both women are equally desirous of being mothers and plan to share the parenting role equally. But starting with insemination, through pregnancy and breastfeeding, the biological reality is that the emotional states, physical strain, pain, and workload of caring for an infant are different for the biological mother than for the nonbiological one. Resentments and jealousies can arise, and often come as a surprise to those lesbians who were counting on a fifty-fifty experience. Egalitarianism may be easier to achieve in the case of adoption and foster care. But lesbian couples must be flexible and willing to let go of a few cherished notions in order to stay harmonious.

The expectation of equality can also be a problem in cases where the choice to have children is not entirely mutual. If one partner is less interested in child rearing (usually the nonbiological mother), she may be less willing to devote the enormous energy and time it takes at the expense of her own interests. Yet because lesbians often expect to divide work equally, the couple may feel compelled to split the domestic work even when they are not equally motivated. This arrangement may lead to resentment, rebellion, or even guilt on the part of the less involved mother. In turn, the more involved mother may feel guilty for making her own major interest—child rearing—the central focus of the relationship, and also resentful because her guilt may make her overcompensate and do more of the work. This imbalance can affect power dynamics adversely because the partner who ends up doing most of the work often assumes more authority in the household. And usually the other partner will resist. This problem is unique to lesbian relationships, for the most part, because in heterosexual relationships it is often assumed that the wife will do more domestic and child-rearing work while the husband maintains principal authority in the home. Only when partners expect total equality in a relationship do they assume that the degree of work one does earns an equivalent degree of power. It can take frequent negotiating for these couples to achieve a balance of power.

Having children can pose a threat to sexual intimacy for lesbians that also differs from the dynamics in most heterosexual relationships. The stereotype for lesbians, even after the lesbian sexual revolution of the 1980s and 1990s, is that long-term monogamy kills sex. There have been various theories on why lesbians are purportedly the least sexually active couples in society (gay male couples being the most sexually active). The most common theory is that, over time, lesbians become too merged and emotionally enmeshed to feel the tension of difference necessary for sexual excitement. Having a child, especially the process of pregnancy, childbirth, and breastfeeding, can seriously diminish sexual activity for any couple, and lesbians are no exception.

Nonetheless, having a child may well serve the purpose of making boundaries between lesbian partners more firm. The existence of a third person to respond and relate to can create healthy divisions, as well as difficult ones. The rearrangement of roles and interactions and the distance between partners that can occur when a child becomes the central focus can actually renew sexual interest between partners.

The one challenge that may be more insurmountable for lesbians than for heterosexual couples is financial. Women still make less money on average than men do. In the 1990s, almost half the female-headed families with children under eighteen fell below poverty level, according to the *New York Times.* Some of the female-headed families in poverty are undoubtedly lesbian families.

But the most intense stress that lesbians as a group face that heterosexuals do not is the absence of social affirmation and legal protection. The role of the nonbiological mother can be particularly challenging in this regard, and a woman can find herself going through, once again, the invisibility and difficulty in defining herself that she may have experienced when first coming out. Anyone who has pushed a stroller with a baby down the street knows how often strangers will stop to take surprisingly intimate liberties, often patting and touching the child and asking questions such as, "Is this your first?" or "Is she yours?" The briefest conversation can lead to the necessity of either lying or coming out for the nonbiological mother.

In fact, being forced to come out to strangers on an almost daily basis is one of the hallmark traits of lesbian and gay parenting. There are passersby, neighbors, preschool teachers, school administrators— the list goes on and on as we deal with our children growing up in the society at large.

CONTROVERSY IN THE LESBIAN COMMUNITY

The lesbian baby boom is not without controversy in the lesbian community. There is a lesbian-feminist analysis positing that, by virtue of their separation from men, lesbians are in a unique position to spend energy changing the patriarchy, unburdened by allegiances to men and responsibility for children. The stereotype of the nuclear family as consisting of the ruling father, submissive housewife-mother, and captive children is one of an unhealthy alliance, one that needs to be eliminated in order to form a more equitable society without hierarchies based on gender, age, or income-earning capacity. Many lesbians would (and do) argue that the move toward lesbians having children is regressive, a neurotic submission to women's early childhood socialization that reared them to see motherhood as an essential part of their identity. Even alternative family formations with multiple co-parents sharing responsibility for a child are suspect, because the energy that goes into raising children and forming family is energy that is lost to the collective effort to change society.

Separatism is no longer a major force in most lesbian communities, but the presence of boy children in lesbian families has often provoked controversy around public lesbian events. Can boy children come to women-only concerts or encampments? At what age do they become the "dreaded male" who would alter the safety of women-only space? Are lesbians automatically suspect when they have male children, no longer deserving of community support?

Some say that having children can also make it easier for a lesbian to pass, to be presumed to be straight in public situations because of the presence of children. This acceptance can be threatening to butch-appearing lesbians who can never pass, who are always at risk of being discriminated against or even harmed because they are obvious lesbians. When other lesbians join the mainstream by appearing to be simply "women with children," butch lesbians may feel dangerously isolated and betrayed.

These arguments continue, yet the positive side of the baby boom in the community is increasingly recognized. While it is true that in some settings lesbians with children can pass more easily, this is rarely true if the setting involves interaction and conversation with others. When lesbian mothers are asked about husbands, fathers, or other commonplace facts regarding their children's upbringing, it has to come out that there is a lesbian co-parent. And having children turns almost every public setting into an occasion for interaction because young children have no social limits compared to adults.

Having to come out to strangers on a daily basis has a great impact on the lesbian/gay rights movement. As Harvey Milk said in a speech in San Francisco shortly before his death, becoming visible, coming out, is the most important thing each of us can do to gain civil rights.

Parenting children is at the far end of the spectrum of permissible activities for gays and lesbians in the eyes of many heterosexuals (although lesbians, being women, are somewhat more acceptable to them as parents than are gay men). To demand the right to have and raise children, to do so through creative use of medical technology and in a way that is still outside the law, is an enormous challenge to the status quo. As Liz Hendrickson, of NCLR, stated, "The most revolutionary thing we do for lesbian and gay rights is to have children."

We need new language to express this revolutionary development in our family life. The words *mother* and *father* are not adequate to describe our parenting relationships, or those of society at large either. *Father* as parent and head of family has lost meaning in a country where one-third of fathers take no responsibility for their children. And medical technology, specifically alternative insemination, has created the biological father who is not a father.

We need new words to describe the roles of our family configurations. Some of the terms in use are *co-parents,* for those doing the parenting, *birthmother* for the biological mother and *other mother* for the nonbiological lesbian parent, *donor* or *biodad* for a minimally or uninvolved sperm donor. Some children call both lesbian parents Mama, Mommy, or Mom. Some parents choose to be called by their first names. Children may refer to biological relatives of their lesbian parents by the usual titles: grandmother, grandfather, cousin, aunt, and uncle, but the nonbiological mother's side of the family may or may not choose to accept those roles. Stories abound about what children end up calling their parents and relatives, often something unplanned but endearing. Perhaps the children will be the ones to create the new language for our families.

The existence of lesbian families is no longer secret nor uncommon, but it remains controversial. We challenge some of society's most deeply held beliefs about the nature of family and how children are created.

FURTHER READING

Alpert, Harriet, ed. *We Are Everywhere.* Freedom, Calif.: Crossing Press, 1988.

Burke, Phyllis. *Family Values.* New York: Random House, 1993.

Cowan, Carolyn, and Philip Cowan. *When Partners Become Parents.* New York: Basic Books, 1992.

Lester, Joan Steinau. *The Future of White Men.* Berkeley, Calif.: Conari Press, 1994.

Martin, April. *The Lesbian and Gay Parenting Handbook: Creating and Raising Our Families.* New York: HarperCollins, 1993.

Orta, Lisa, ed. *The Family Next Door, a newsletter for lesbian and gay parents and their friends.* POB 21580, Oakland, CA 94620.

Pies, Cheri. *Considering Parenthood.* San Francisco: Spinsters Book Co., 1988.

Rabenold, Diana. *Love, Politics and "Rescue" in Lesbian Relationships.* Santa Cruz, Calif.: HerBooks, 1987.

Rafkin, Louise, ed. *Different Mothers: Sons and Daughters of Lesbians Talk About Their Lives.* San Francisco: Cleis Press, 1990.

Silverstein, Olga, and Beth Rashbaum. *Preserving and Protecting the Families of Lesbians and Gay Men.* San Francisco: National Center for Lesbian Rights, 1990.

———. *The Courage to Raise Good Men.* New York: Viking, 1994.

TWELVE

OUR CHILDREN AND THEIR LAWS

Ruthann Robson

Legal rules presume an Adam and Eve model for legal parents:
Each child has one father and one mother, no more and no less.
If Adam and Eve dissolve their own relationship, they can become
involved in a custody battle for the children. In a dispute between
Adam and Eve, the law initially places both of them in the same
position, having to prove that the "best interests of the child" require
him or her to be the custodial parent. A judge, cloaked with the
usual authority and an unusual amount of discretion, makes such a
determination by considering numerous factors, economic, social,
and psychological. If Eve is a lesbian, this is certainly a factor that
the judge will consider.

The manner in which a judge can consider Eve's lesbianism varies
from state to state in America, and from country to country. In the
United States, three different approaches have developed. The most
traditional and conservative practice is simply to exclude lesbians
from custody on the grounds that living with a lesbian mother cannot be in the best interests of the child. The second approach says
that living with a lesbian mother can be in the best interests of a

child as long as the mother does not flaunt her lesbianism, live with a lesbian lover, or engage in lesbian politics. The most liberal stance requires a showing of some actual harm to the child caused by the mother's lesbianism in order for lesbianism to be a consideration. There has been a gradual—if uneven—trend toward this liberal stance, with a majority of states now following the middle, fact-specific method, which subjects lesbian mothers to a great deal of scrutiny. In such cases, the judge makes decisions about whether a lesbian mother's affection toward her lover or participation in a lesbian/gay pride march is an appropriate parental activity. In all cases, even if the state law is relatively progressive, lesbians seeking custody can suffer from judicial bias because of the tremendous amount of discretion afforded to individual judges. While the efforts of many brave lesbians and their attorneys are responsible for much progress in the law, for lesbians previously involved in heterosexual relationships, retaining custody or visitation against men continues to be major legal battle.

Lesbians also continue to be subject to custody challenges from other relatives and from the state. In these cases, lesbianism is often cited as a circumstance sufficient to overcome the legal presumption that favors child custody with parents rather than third parties. For example, in many Adam and Eve cases, Adam's fight for custody may be instigated and financed by Adam's parents; Adam serves as a kind of "front man" for the child's grandparents. When Adam cannot perform this function (he may be deceased, in prison, or drug-addicted), his parents may sue for custody and hope to win because of Eve's lesbianism. In other situations, as in the highly publicized case of Sharon Bottoms, Eve's own parents or other relatives may seek custody. The key issue in such situations is whether Eve's lesbianism is an extraordinary circumstance that will allow the judge even to entertain claims of custody by nonparents. Generally, lesbianism alone is not enough to support a finding of extraordinary circumstances, unless the jurisdiction adheres to the most conservative rule. However, judges are adept at finding other circumstances, such as the lesbian mother's marijuana use, which they accord great weight. As in all custody disputes, the judge's discretion is the most unpredictable and important factor.

The government can also seek to deprive a lesbian of custody. In the United States, every state has statutes allowing state agencies to intervene in situations in which a child is "dependent," "neglected," or "abused." While we tend to think of child abuse as physical, states can deprive a parent of custody based on the judge's opinions regarding proper schooling, home environment, medical care, and supervision. In one case, a court upheld the state's removal of a preschool child from his lesbian mother because she objected to his prescribed speech therapy, didn't cooperate with state authorities, and lived a "chaotic" home life with her lover and her lover's two children in a two-bedroom apartment. For many lesbians, especially those in lower economic classes that attract more social service agency attention, state interference with child custody is a constant threat.

The lesbian baby boom has brought its own host of legal problems. If Eve is a lesbian and decides to have a child with Lilith rather than Adam, there will be legal consequences to their decision of which one will give birth. If Eve gives birth, she will be the legal parent and Lilith will be a legal stranger. The repercussions of this legal construction are most pronounced should Eve and Lilith separate. In such cases, Lilith has no claim for custody or even visitation. Even the most progressive courts have decided that regardless of the circumstances—even if Lilith had been the primary caretaker and de facto parent—if Lilith is not a legal parent, she cannot seek custody or visitation unless there are extraordinary circumstances, such as Eve's unfitness to be a parent.

This problem can be avoided if Lilith becomes the legal parent through adoption. As the adoptive parent, Lilith would have virtually the same rights as Adam in the Adam and Eve model. These so-called second-parent adoptions are a relatively recent phenomenon, but they are becoming increasingly available for lesbian co-parents. Some courts resist their use by reasoning that a child cannot legally have two mothers. In states where the use of second-parent adoptions is unsettled, lesbian advocates continue to litigate to make this process available.

A lesbian couple's decision to have a child together creates legal concerns. First is the regulation of their access to the insemination procedure. Formal and informal bars may prevent unmarried women from being inseminated by physicians or tapping sperm banks. In the case of known donors, these men may make paternity claims. In recent years, the fact that such sperm donors are often gay men has caused rifts in lesbian and gay communities. In arguing for recognition of paternity, the sperm donors assume the position of Adam in the Adam and Eve model; Lilith's existence is irrelevant. The legal response to the claims of donors is still unsettled, as is the response of lesbians and our children.

THIRTEEN

LESBIAN PARENTING:
RADICAL OR RETROGRADE?

Sondra Segal-Sklar

There have always been lesbians who are parents. However, for the past decade lesbians in the United States have joined the national baby boom with one of our own. Lesbians from across the spectrum of class, race, region, politics, age, identity as feminists, cultural identity, and degree of outness have been creating families more than ever before.

We are doing it in diverse ways, seizing the opportunities created by technology (although certainly not created for us): alternative insemination with an unknown donor; alternative insemination with a known donor, who may be the brother of the member of the couple who is not going to become pregnant, making her the biological aunt of her child as well as its parent; in vitro fertilization, using the egg of one woman but implanting the embryo in the other woman, giving both parents a biological relationship to their child. We are adopting in record numbers both domestically and internationally, and becoming foster parents. More recently, lesbians have begun adopting the biological children of our partners. And, of course, some lesbians are becoming parents the old-fashioned way.

We are doing it everywhere—from New York City's Upper West Side, where there are at least thirty lesbian families within a forty-block radius, to rural Alabama, where a lesbian family may be the only one within hundreds of miles.

We are establishing a nationwide network of support. There are lesbian and gay parenting organizations in most major cities across the country, adoptive family organizations that now include a large contingent of homosexual parents, diverse support groups for us as parents and for our children. There are holiday parties and weekend getaways and an annual international conference for lesbian and gay families that includes a miniconference for our children.

We live in an exciting time. An activist lesbian/gay rights movement has pursued equal rights and equal protection in many areas, has secured a place for our issues on the national agenda, and is making the Gay Nineties more than just a successful marketing device. And, while the meaning of *family* is being debated across the country, a generation of children is being raised by out lesbians. Although there is lots of speculation by both the straight and homosexual worlds, it is too soon to determine what impact this will have on our children or what impact our children will have on the world.

Many people, in both the heterosexual and homosexual worlds, still think the terms *lesbian* and *parent* are mutually exclusive, or should be. While some lesbian parents feel there are no real differences between them and other parents, other lesbians feel their parenting provides a radical alternative to traditional socialization. In this chapter I focus on issues of sameness and difference, particularly as they relate to two-mother families in a setting where there is a critical mass of lesbian families.

AIN'T I A WOMAN?

The ways lesbian parents are the same as other women who are parents are many, both important and mundane. Like other women, we grew up as girls in a sexist and heterosexist culture. We were exposed to societal norms and expectations for us as girls and women that included the expectation that we would become mothers, in a culture that simultaneously exalts and denigrates motherhood and extols and dismisses children. And we all live in a world in which class, race, gender, and "sexual orientation" have not disappeared as political, and therefore meaningful, categories.

In the daily grind and pleasure of parenting, we are alike in myriad ways. We want what is best for our children. We are overwhelmed with tending to their needs (and keeping the jungle back) while trying to maintain the other parts of our lives—economic, intellectual, sexual, social, political. We worry about money and the safety of our neighborhoods. We take our children to doctors and dentists, playgrounds and playdates. We deal with teachers and homework, TV and bedtime, Barbie and toy guns. We experience unbridled joy as we witness the acquisition of language, the evolution of physical mastery, and the unfolding of intellect, personality, and character. We dream about and plan for the future.

Many lesbian parents experience parenting as the great equalizer that eases an outsider status, provides a real sense of belonging to the wider culture, and enables connections with other women, from our own mothers and sisters to co-workers and strangers at a playground. Some of us experience ourselves as having more in common with straight parents than with nonparenting lesbians, and sometimes feel we get more support from that source as well.

Many lesbians believe that other factors such as race, class, age, single parenthood, and ethnic identity are much more central to both self-definition and to how we operate in the world. An observant Jewish lesbian family may join a synagogue and find a feminist rabbi, services that include the full participation of the women congregants, a tot shabbat (a special service for young children), and a welcoming environment in which lesbian identity is not an issue. A single lesbian mother can share the services of a caregiver with a straight single mother, working out scheduling, financial arrangements, and different household rules with no particular difficulty

Janet Linder

My feelings of pride and responsibility in being a lesbian mother are equally intense. Technology has allowed me to have a child without depending on a husband or other involved male. I'm grateful. My partner of fifteen years, our four-year-old daughter, and I are right in the middle of a whole new world.

I am proud of how we parent. Two women adoring and supporting this emerging being. Two women in a demanding joint project to promote Sophie's self-esteem, enhance her creativity, and find the balance of tempering her high spirits without extinguishing her flame.

I live by the "shoulds" I have designated as important to our daughter's development. I take her to the preschool miles away with out gay teachers and the strongest antibias program in the Bay Area. I know I may never move from this region because there are so many kids like Sophie here. I maintain a strong connection to the community of lesbians with kids. I make sure Sophie socializes and bonds with other inseminated kids in lesbian families to help her see her own reality reflected back. My hope is that seeing other lesbian families will give her certain roots that will help anchor her identity in the rockier adolescent times ahead.

I consciously use the words *lesbian* and *insemination* to help her get used to them. I search for books that show diverse families, and use them as a starting point to discuss differences and definitions of family. I try to remain open to her questions about who her father is (they started early) and the fluctuations of interest and emotion that she expresses about this subject.

At times I fear that my choices in life may wind up giving Sophie outsider status, and possibly angst over being different. I feel a burden of guilt sometimes—though it's fleeting—and a deep responsibility to help Sophie make good sense of her world. But I don't feel apologetic and I don't feel ashamed. It seems to me that one of the gifts gay people bring to the rest of the world is the notion that we don't have to let the prejudice of others stop us from being who we are. I hope that Sophie can pursue her dreams, as I have.

caused by "lifestyle." An older lesbian mother may find the age of other parents to be the single most important connecting factor.

Many lesbian parents, in or out of the closet, want our lesbianism to fade into the background and not be the significant shaping factor in daily interactions with our children and the institutions parents have to deal with all the time. Today, in a major urban setting or an area of the country where many lesbians live, this may be possible.

Lesbian parents can find a preschool where we do not have to obscure the structure of our family or have it be seen as a problem, where we can talk with the teacher about the language we use to describe our family, where both mothers are treated as "real," where, as at our New York City preschool, the burning concern shared by many parents (working-class or middle-class, black or white, single or couple, straight or lesbian) is how to discuss adoption with our children.

We may be able to choose among pediatricians who are aware of our concerns, arrange playdates with children whose parents accept our family structure, and even find a sitter more easily than straight parents, since many college students today think babysitting for a lesbian family is great!

But in an era when the official guideline is "don't ask, don't tell," we don't know where or when the line will be drawn, when or if our children will be hurt or rejected because of who we are.

OUT . . . ON A LIMB?

A group of lesbian parents and our children had a beach picnic last summer on a beautiful August day. There were ten families, with children ranging in age from six weeks to eight years. There were two-mommy families and single-mom families, both adoptive and biological families. The parents spread out on blankets and beach chairs and talked while the children played nearby. We looked just like any group of mothers out for an afternoon in the sun with their children (albeit a bit older!). My partner of over twenty years said,

"God, I remember days like this with my sisters and their children." Another woman said, "We could almost be straight!" Oh, but we're not. Our experience as lesbians makes us different from nonlesbian parents. We call into question the very meaning of family, how children come into the world, how families are formed, what constitutes a family.

Our decision to have a child is rarely casual or accidental. From the outset, it requires special thinking, processing, and planning. We consider options and consequences very carefully. The way we make this foundation decision, conceiving of our child together even if we do not conceive our child together, often becomes a model for how we will operate as parents at home and in the world.

As lesbian parents, we challenge traditional assumptions about gender roles, about who can do what in a family. In our families all roles, responsibilities, and functions are fulfilled by women. In our homes, power is not based on gender.

Within the privacy of our homes, we lead our lives, doing the things we do in the ways we choose to do them. We don't walk around thinking of ourselves as lesbian parents when we are helping our children with homework or putting them to bed. When we cross the threshold to intersect with the wider world, however, we often experience a serious disjuncture that does require us to think of ourselves as lesbian parents. We are confronted with bias from the external world that is both blatant and subtle, from institutionalized discrimination to everyday, often unintended, slights.

In addition, as with every marginalized group, when we step beyond the boundaries of our homes and community, we may bring with us internal mechanisms and behavior we have developed to protect ourselves and our families from being hurt. We wear a protective shield, sometimes thick, sometimes thin, and we monitor our expectations, our expression of affection, our language. We don't really know what these subtle and largely nonverbal dynamics convey to our children, nor how they shape their sense of well-being and personhood over the long run.

WHICH ONE IS THE REAL MOM?

In heterosexual families both parents are sanctioned. They are legally the parents of their children, with the myriad rights and daily sense of entitlement that confers. They don't even have to think about it. They adopt or conceive their children together. Both their names are on the adoption documents or birth certificate. Each parent can travel with the child or take her or him to an emergency room for medical treatment. Both have titles that are recognized, carry meaning, and validate their relationship to the child a thousand times a day. They each think that she and he are the real parents. And everyone else thinks so too.

Our situations are different. We have to deal with legal, practical, and psychological issues that arise out of the fact that society does not automatically recognize and honor our families, and that in "double-mommy" families we are not both legally sanctioned parents.

In many states, the status of lesbian parents as sexual partners and/or as parents is illegal or highly vulnerable. In Georgia, a sodomy statute is still on the books. In New Hampshire, the "Live Free or Die" state, a known lesbian cannot adopt a child or become a foster parent. In New York, an "unmarried couple" (and lesbians are still not permitted to marry) cannot adopt jointly.

We may have to struggle for the right for both parents to be present when our child is born, and we rarely have the right to have both our names on the child's birth certificate. In most cases of domestic adoption, and always in international adoption, we cannot present ourselves both as parents.

Once we have our children, lesbians still face the very real threat of losing them. Although progress has been made, a lesbian in a custody dispute with a biological father is still likely to lose in most states, and in some cases may be permitted visitation only outside her lesbian household and not in the presence of her lesbian partner. A lesbian mother can lose custody of her children to the child's bio-

Louise G. Whitney

Poor child
Three months in utero
when I first made love
with a woman.
My world imploded
and passion was born
before you were.

A confused devotee
of the upper class,
I keened for Joan
in my labor.

Had I chosen Joan
they would have taken
you from me.
My mother at the head
of the pack.

I chose you over Joan
because I thought you were forever.
If there is no happiness
then at least a dynasty.

What happened
under that shadow.
They say
You have a thought disorder
Schizophrenia
Showed up when
you were sixteen.

You were delicate and fluttery
Did you get enough, Stephen?
Or had I already been devoured
by forbidden love?

logical grandparents or another biological relative who stakes a claim. The nonbiological or nonlegal mother of the child, who may have raised that child since birth, has no legal protection in a custody dispute with the "real" parent. If her lover becomes incapacitated or dies, she can be considered a "biological stranger" in a custody case—losing her child (and the child losing both parents) to the biological father, who may never have had a parenting relationship to the child, to an aunt or grandparent, or, believe it or not, to the state. On a practical and economic level, we cannot obtain insurance or file income tax as a family. Our child is not entitled to receive Social Security benefits from both of us, or necessarily to inherit our house or apartment when in later years we move or die.

The nonbiological/nonlegal parent cannot travel across international borders with her child without written permission from a biological/legal parent. She may need written permission to have the child treated in an emergency room, and her presence can be excluded during treatment because she is not the "real" parent.

If lesbian parents break up, the relationship between the nonlegal parent and the child is not protected by the courts. We draw up parenting agreements, hoping this document of intention that carries no formal legal weight will have meaning to a judge if we ever have to go to court. We write our wills, sign legal and medical powers of attorney, combine our bank accounts, formalize our domestic partnership, and pay thousands of dollars to lawyers to mitigate against the lack of legal protection. (See Ruthann Robson's "Our Children and Their Laws.")

Every form we ever fill out for our child, from the preschool application to the college application, calls our authenticity into question. We cross out Father and put in Other Mother. We white out Father and Mother and put in Parent/Parent. We attach a short, friendly note suggesting the institution consider changing its forms to embrace (or at least not oppress) families that don't fit that description, and sometimes we are successful.

At school, we say that our family requires two Mother's Day cards to be made, that the diagram of our child's family tree will look different, that on Father's Day children should be encouraged to make a card for "an important male" in their world, reminding the teacher that many of the children in the class, not just ours, do not have a father. We give them the language we want them to use when another child on the playground says, "But s/he can't have two mommies." We give our answer about family diversity saying, "Yes, s/he has two mommies. No, s/he doesn't have a daddy. Some families have two mommies, some families have two daddies, some have one mommy, some have a mommy and a daddy . . . "

At the same time, we hope that teachers and other parents won't see our child only through a single lens, assigning everything to the fact that s/he is the child of lesbian parents, misinterpreting her or his behavior and perhaps missing what's really going on.

We never see our families validated by the culture that inundates our children. Families like ours are not on *Sesame Street* or *Barney*, not in most children's books, not in movies. There are no songs about us on Raffi's albums. There are no marketing campaigns to celebrate or merchandise the wedding of Ariel to Snow White. There is no Lesbian Barbie.

For our child's well-being, and our own, we spend time thinking through scenarios in advance, planning how we will answer questions about our families so that our child's sense of confidence and security is not undermined. When a checkout clerk at the grocery store asks, "But which one is the real mom?," we have to have our answer ready or decide in that moment whether and how we wish to come out as a lesbian family to a line of strangers.

We are political activists and educators, whether we wish to be or not. We educate people—grandparents, extended family, other parents, the director of the preschool, playmates, doctors, neighbors, strangers—about our families. Sometimes this is oppressive and exhausting, and sometimes it is exhilarating and rewarding. We are in this position as a result of discrimination, but it does put us on a creative path that can have positive impact on how we parent.

Beth Rosen

My partner and I decided to become parents after living together for six years in New York City, where people provided a great deal of the support we felt we would need. When Emily, our daughter, went to public school, the other children started asking her questions about her two moms and her father. These were innocent kids, and she handled their questions well. For the most part, the other parents were warm and friendly to us.

Emily's new friends came to our home often. Then, in second grade, one boy invited her to his home but never came over to ours. When Emily realized that "Gary" was not allowed over, she asked me to call his mother. I did, and she made it very clear that her religious beliefs did not find our lifestyle acceptable. She wanted to take a stand against it, and so decided not to allow her son into our home. When we explained this to Emily, she cried and then became extremely angry.

Her sadness and anger lasted for weeks. One day, after discussing the situation, we encouraged her to write a letter to Gary's family. That seemed to help her put some of the painful feelings behind her, and soon Gary told her that he *could* come over. When she called him that night, though, he said that he couldn't. Emily asked why, and his mother got on the phone and told her the same religious dogma she had told me during our first conversation.

We watched Emily listening quietly on the phone. When the woman was finished, Emily asked, "But what does Gary think?" He got back on the phone and said he could not come over. She hung up and burst into tears. Now she was not only sad and angry but frightened by the family's religious beliefs.

Two months later, some of the kids at school talked about creating a club that would meet at different houses. Emily made it clear for the first time to her classmates that Gary wasn't allowed to come to her home. Within minutes, all the children rallied around her and reassured her that this made no sense. The children started ostracizing Gary, and the teacher gathered them together to discuss the problem. She tried to get them to see that all points of view are acceptable.

That night we got phone calls from lots of the kids and their parents, showing support. The teacher also called to say that she was going to speak to Gary's mother to see whether she would reconsider. The next day I found myself in the same position with the guidance counselor. While it felt great to receive their support, I had to remind both of them that Gary's mother had a right to her beliefs. She was still in charge of how she raised her son. I was surprised to find myself in the role of teaching tolerance for an opposing viewpoint to the school staff. Emily had gotten support from the kids and parents, and now Gary needed support.

Six months later, Emily let go of wanting Gary to come over. Fortunately, she has not encountered this kind of prejudice again, but if she does we feel she is prepared. She has pride in her family and herself because she knows most of the children and the community accept us the way we are.

THE POWER OF DIFFERENCE

Like all parents, lesbian parents are continually challenged by our children. We open up to the world in fresh ways as they think about something for the first time. They want to know how the moon stays up in the sky, what energy is, why everyone dies, how we, their parents, fell in love.

But these are children of lesbian parents in a new era. Some of the questions they ask seem to be brand new in the history of the world. And we must create the answers. When they ask, "How do babies with no mommies get born?" it takes a few beats to realize they are talking about children of gay male parents. If they don't have a dad, they ask, "How did I get made?" They wonder why a classmate has only one mother, asking, "What happened to her other mom?" They ask about sex in their two-mother household. They want to know what makes a family.

As lesbian parents, we have the opportunity to think about things that, historically, women have not had the chance to consider. We think through the consequences of how we name our child and how we name ourselves to our child. We try to understand the meaning of naming, the power of a name, the impact our choices will have. In some of the most commonly used approaches, one mother is called Mommy and the other is called by her first name; one mother is called Mommy and the other is called Mama; or both are called Mommy, sometimes with first names added, as in Mommy Sondra.

The child's last name also has to be decided. Some families give the child the last name of the legal/biological mother; others give her or him a hyphenated name combining both parents' names; some choose to create a brand-new name for their child. And in some families, both parents and children share the same family name.

We come out to our children, a complex and delicate task that has to be repeated and amplified as they move through different stages of development. We discuss their origins and talk about sensitive issues surrounding adoption and alternative insemination. We explain why they don't have a daddy. We tell them about conception, birth, and sex—both straight and gay.

Since "don't ask, don't tell" is an alien concept to most children—who like to ask and like to tell—they out us in situations where we are not seeking it or are not prepared. At a Passover seder, surrounded by grandparents and guests, they add to the discussion about good and bad laws, injustice and freedom, by asking, "Grandpa, did you know that two women are not allowed to marry each other?"—clearly a bad law. And we cope with (and sometimes delight in) the situation.

We also pose some new questions of our own. When a child has two mothers, is the impact of the mother/child bond diluted or doubled? Do our children receive more and better nurturing? Will they have more issues around merging and separation? What does the oedipal complex mean when both parents are women? What is the impact of growing up in a household where all the roles, responsibilities, and functions are performed by women and where power is not based on gender? Is the impact different on girls and boys? Are we raising sensitive boys and bold girls? Are we supposed to? Does lesbian parenting provide a radical alternative to traditional socialization? Are lesbian parents creating social change?

According to Nancy Polikoff, an attorney who writes about legal issues for lesbian mothers,

> The emergence of lesbian families provides a unique opportunity in history to raise children in a home with two parents of potentially equal power. The opportunity to grow up observing such equality in the home could have a lasting impact on children in lesbian families, and we need to embrace that possibility. If legal inequality diminishes or eliminates the experience of equal power within the home, we are missing the chance to make what might be our biggest contribution to future generations.

Audre Lorde has written powerfully about being a lesbian parent:

> There are those who say the urge to have children is a reaction to encroaching despair, a last desperate outcry before the leap into the void. I disagree. I believe that raising children is one way of participating in the future, in social change. On the other hand, it would be dangerous as well as sentimental to think that childrearing alone is enough to bring about a liveable future in the absence of any definition about that future. For unless we develop some cohesive vision of that world in which we hope these children will participate, and some sense of our own responsibilities in the shaping of that world, we will only raise new performers in the master's sorry drama.

Clearly, how we parent matters, but parenting is not enough. As lesbian parents, we have the greatest imperative to participate in social change—even if we don't always have the energy to do it—

because we *need* a world that embraces diversity and that is truly fit both for ourselves and our children to live in.

THE QUESTIONER: AN EPILOGUE

The Questioner is an oral history/research form I developed in the creation of theater works as an artistic director of the Women's Experimental Theatre. This Questioner was presented to a group of lesbians—parents, future parents, friends of parents, nonparents—to raise issues for discussion.

When you were growing up, did you always expect to have children?
At what point, if any, did you give up that expectation?
Was it related to being a lesbian?
What stands in your way of having children?
What supported your decision to have a child?

If you are a couple, do you both consider yourselves mothers?
Does your child relate to you both as mothers?
Is there competition between you?
When you are not the Mommy of the moment to your child, is your sense
of realness undermined?
Does the world relate to one of you as the real mother?
How does this affect your family?
Is the double mommy a double whammy?

How do you name yourselves to your child?
What does s/he call you at home? In public?
What is your child's family name? Is it different from yours?
Is your child's family name the same as your parents'?

How do you describe your family structure inside and outside the family?
Have you come out as a lesbian to your child?
How do you talk about the way you created your family?

How do you discuss adoption or alternative insemination with your child? With others?

How does your family relate to the theme of Daddy?

When you were growing up, were sex roles rigid in your family?

Who raised the children?

How does this impact on your desire to parent and on your parenting?

Are roles fluid in your family now?

What is the impact on your child of having all family roles and functions performed by women?

What are your investments in your child's sexual orientation?

Will you be disappointed or worried if your child is gay?

What if your child is straight?

Will your child be required to be gay?

How do your families of origin relate to you as a family?

Do both sets of your parents consider themselves grandparents to your child?

Does your partner's family relate to you as an in-law?

Does anyone in your family send you an anniversary card? A Mother's Day card?

Do you care whether they do?

Are your children allowed to tell others that their parents are lesbians?

Are they required to tell?

Do you modify your behavior in front of their friends?

Have they asked you to?

How have you prepared your children to cope with the homophobia (and other bigotry) they encounter in the wider world?

How old are you?

Has anyone mistaken you for your child's grandmother?

Now that you are a mother, do you find yourself passing as heterosexual?

Do you have more in common with straight parents than with the non-parenting lesbian community?

How do you maintain your outsider status as a lesbian when you are a parent? Do you seek to?

Does being a lesbian parent give you a sense of entering the mainstream, or does it increase your marginality?

How do you maintain your critique of the family while becoming one?

Was Radclyffe Hall a mother—or is this a contradiction in terms?

Do lesbian mothers have sex?

Do lesbian parents have more or less sex than other parents?

Once you become a parent, can you still be a lesbian?

What is better about growing up in a lesbian family?

What is unique about what we bring to parenting?

What is special about our children?

How will the lesbian baby boom impact on the lesbian community and on the wider world?

FURTHER READING

Benkov, Laura. *Reinventing the Family: The Emerging Story of Lesbian and Gay Parents.* New York: Crown, 1994.

Caspar, Virginia, Stephen Schultz, and Elaine Wickens. "Breaking the Silences: Lesbian and Gay Parents and the Schools." *Teachers College Record* (Fall 1992).

Coss, Clare, Sondra Segal, and Roberta Sklar. "Daughters, Part I of The Daughters Cycle Trilogy." *The Massachusetts Review* 24, no. 1 (1983).

Martin, April. *The Lesbian and Gay Parenting Handbook: Creating and Raising Our Families.* New York: HarperCollins, 1993.

Pollack, Sandra, and Jean Vaughn, eds. *Politics of the Heart: A Lesbian Parenting Anthology.* Ithaca, N.Y.: Firebrand Books, 1987.

Rafkin, Louise, ed. *Different Mothers: Sons and Daughters of Lesbians Talk About Their Lives.* San Francisco: Cleis Press, 1990.

Rich, Adrienne. *Of Woman Born.* New York: Norton, 1986.

OTHER RESOURCES

Alyson Wonderland Publications
    40 Plympton Street
    Boston, MA 02118
    617-542-5679

    Books for children of lesbian and gay parents.

Center Kids
    The Family Project of the Lesbian and Gay
        Community Services Center
    208 West 13th Street
    New York, NY 10011
    212-620-7310

Gay and Lesbian Parents Coalition International (GLPCI)
    P.O. Box 50360
    Washington, DC 20091
    202-583-8029

National Center for Lesbian Rights (NCLR)
    1663 Mission Street, 5th floor
    San Francisco, CA 94103
    415-621-0674

PART THREE

Sex and Gender Identity

FOURTEEN

CLIT NOTES

Marny Hall

Their eyes met across the crowded bar. In that magic moment, each imagined their future together. The languid blonde envisioned a one-night stand, the most torrid of her life. The buttoned-down butch saw the soulmate she had been waiting so long for, the life partner who would move to the country with her and have her baby. Overwhelmed, they blushed and looked away. Slyly, hesitantly, each raised her eyes again. This time, Dyke A imagined being lashed to the bed; Dyke B, a long romantic walk on the beach. Dyke A pictured nipple clamps and dildos; Dyke B, growing old together. Finally, without ever having said a word to each other, their respective fantasies fizzled and they left the bar . . . separately.

Hoots and whistles of appreciation greeted this skit, performed by a Bay Area lesbian and bisexual theater group. The caricatures of the initiative-impaired wannabe lovers were as reassuring as they were funny. For just a moment, the complexity of our love lives had been reduced to a misunderstanding between two contrary cartoon characters.

Offstage as well as on, such dichotomies (dyke-chotomies?) are a welcome time-out from the daunting confusion of genders and desires that characterizes lesbian life in the 1990s. In fact, in the last couple of years, even some formerly p.c. stalwarts have shamelessly invoked butch/femme scales, S/M/vanilla quotients, and true love/trash tendencies to explain their matches, mismatches, ecstasies, miseries—almost everything, in fact, except the care of their pets. I take that back. One friend recently told me that her new dog was disobedient because she hadn't yet realized who the butch was in their relationship. Such shorthand is funny, useful, soothing, but is it even remotely accurate? Do such stereotypes correspond to our lives? Do our love affairs sort neatly into brief encounters or serious relationships? I decided to ask my friends. Always eager to tell all, they positively blossomed under the glare of my "research." They all knew someone else I "had to talk to," and eventually the small, informal group expanded to a dozen.

At first I despaired over the uniform nature of the group. Though ethnically and racially diverse, the interviewees were all over forty and, though they would gnash their teeth at such a designation, middle class. They could hardly be considered a cross section of the lesbian community. But when the group turned out to be as sexually diverse as it was socially uniform, I decided the skewing had been felicitous. By inadvertently keeping certain aspects of the group constant, I had, in a sense, proved that a specific class or age wasn't necessarily predictive of a particular erotic blueprint. It was, however, predictive of a thoroughly annotated sexual history. Years of heartthrobs and heartbreaks, brief encounters and lasting relationships, had been distilled, by each woman, into her personal erotic canon. And the activities and arrangements that best suited each woman defied easy categorization. Some were in shifting and multiple relationships, some had chosen long-term partnerships, and one, though determinedly single and celibate, was passionate about her dog. Though they were all lesbians, their diverse erotic tastes belied one simple designation. Two identified as S/M bottoms; at the opposite extreme, two gentle souls dared not risk even a Swedish massage. Though most were turned on by some combination of hands, mouths, vibrators, and fantasies, one cerebrally endowed woman could think herself to multiple orgasms. And another, despite arduous efforts, remained intractably nonorgasmic. These women's sexual dalliances also ran the gamut, from the woman who could count a lifetime of lovers (all women) on one hand, to the one whose lifetime count, by her best estimate, approached a thousand partners of diverse (and sometimes surgically altered) genders.

This variation in experience, attitudes, and perhaps even biological wiring kept all my conclusions at bay. Each time I was tempted to generalize about differences between sex inside and outside committed partnerships, a fresh interview generated an exception to my formulation. As it turned out, such exceptions proved to be the only rule about lesbian sex.

THE GOOD/BAD OLD DAYS

"Casual sex" was a distant memory for about half of the women I interviewed, a dyke passage that had occurred before they had "settled down," joined Alcoholics Anonymous, or otherwise come to their senses. As impersonally torrid as some of their early encounters had been, they never reached the legendary anonymity commonly ascribed to gay men. But even though no one had been groped through a glory hole or butt-fucked in a steamroom by a dozen naked strangers, their tales were lively enough to merit considerable . . . uh . . . scientific interest.

For Torey, forty-three, drugs were the high point of her early debauches: "Once I had a five-way, but I only remember two of the principals . . . and of course the Quaalude." On another occasion, she recalls, "someone from the bar took me home and we did cocaine all night and made love like beasts. I never saw her again. She called but I never responded."

For Flynn, casual sex was linked with her first heady whiff of sexual freedom: "I wanted to be more than a lesbian in theory. A woman in my group made it clear she was interested in me. After a dance party, we came to my place and had sex. It was impulsive. I wasn't feeling romantic, but it was fine sexually . . . mutually orgasmic. . . . Afterward, I got nervous that she would expect to have sex again, and I didn't particularly want to."

Elaine recalls making a beeline for the bars in New York City the day after she finished college: "I fell in love instantly with this butch named Troy with a blond D.A. and a red blazer, but she wasn't interested in me. Another woman picked me up. I can't remember her name, but I remember feeling terribly grown up and illicit when we registered for a room. We had hot sex all night. I was surprised that I could have such a good time with someone I hadn't even noticed. I think I saw her a few more times."

Reba used casual encounters both as a heartache remedy and as a way of punishing a negligent lover: "When I was in college, I was emotionally involved with a woman who was involved with everyone but me. I decided I needed to have sex with someone else and climbed in bed with a dormmate and started having sex even though I wasn't attracted to her. We had sex a couple of more times, but after she showed me how to masturbate I stopped having sex with her." On another occasion, she remembers having a hard time with a lover: "I needed a distraction. This woman I was just getting to know turned me on in a restaurant by telling me in great detail how she would make love to me. I got into bed with her and she didn't do any of the things she said she was going to do. All she did was hump me. It was a big disappointment."

These women obviously cherish their misadventures. Such wild-oats credentials are perhaps as essential to our fledgling dyke identity as our first steps toward coming out. And now that these women view themselves as mature and stable, they can look back with humor, and perhaps even gratitude, that they survived what now seems like youthful indiscretions.

Their nostalgia also propped up the present in another way. For those who are part of a couple, a regularly invoked history of limited engagements seems to offer ongoing proof that current partnerships

Judith P. Stelboum

On my fifty-seventh birthday, I scrubbed the last lizard decal off my forearm to prepare myself spiritually for my first real tattoo. I never lied when anyone asked whether the lizards were real, but displaying fake tattoos felt more and more uncomfortable. I am simultaneously frightened of and attracted to lizards. Terrestrial or semi-aquatic, changing colors, lizards are hard to pin down. Dating from the Mesozoic period, the lizard embodies a prehistoric, prepatriarchal ur-world of kaleidoscopic change and unlimited possibilities. I, like the lizard, am constantly adapting or in transition. The lizard is a creative stimulant, individually representational and archetypically symbolic.

I drive to Seabrook, New Hampshire, for my appointment with Juli Moon. One of the few women in the field, she is internationally respected for her designs and color. Almost all of the lesbians Juli tattoos, regardless of age or class, want strong, individualistic images on visible body parts, referred to as "public skin." Most straight women regard tattoos as body decoration or as sexual enticements and prefer them on their butts, groins, or breasts. Juli sees tattoos as psychic armor repelling those who abhor them and attracting those who respond to them.

Because the needles of the tattoo machine move so fast, the sensation creates only a slight burning or pricking, and is not as painful as an injection or electrolysis. Two and a half hours after she starts, just as my arm begins to tense, Juli is finished. I gather my courage and look down at my arm.

My tattoo is powerful, sensuous, and beautiful. The lizard's nine-inch, S-shaped body curves from my wrist to my outer elbow. The vibrant colors mutate from green earth to blue water to blue-lavender sky. An orange-yellow crescent moon surrounded by stars symbolizes the goddess, a crab represents my astrological sign, and a subtle pink triangle marks her serpent head. Scales in variegated green swirl on the lizard's arms, tail, and legs, and stylized ocean waves represent rebirth and renewal. Her sharp claws, strong arms, and legs seem to move her sinuously around and up my arm. She is fast and dangerous. Her long, green, tapering tail with a yellow spiky ridge is capable of whiplike blows. The extended, red-forked tongue is both sexual and threatening. The lizard is the outward affirmation of my present passage, visible to me, and to the rest of the world, as an energy and life force rising up from within me.

Before leaving Juli's studio, I lift my arm up in front of me, emulating Wonder Woman raising her magic bracelets. With the new lizard goddess boldly facing the world, I make an instinctive, sharp, hissing sound. We all laugh, but it feels right to me.

are serious and enduring. But were the polished accounts I heard all that trustworthy? I suspected there was more to some of these stories. And, indeed, when I asked for more details about one-night stands, casual didn't seem so casual after all. Bedding someone was often followed by a flurry of phone calls, and perhaps even encores. Were these early encounters all that different from the first tentative passages into relationships that had a longer life? Once these embryonic relationships miscarried, were they then decreed casual?

CASUAL SEX, NINETIES STYLE

Just as my conventionally married friends need to distance themselves from their days of wine and roses (or cocaine and croissants), they distance themselves from women who have casual sex. They can't imagine climbing in the sack with someone they don't know. Nevertheless, they are intrigued by the sinful possibilities, perhaps proving, as Oscar Wilde said, that "wickedness is a myth invented by good people to account for the curious attractiveness of others." The women I spoke to who consciously seek out partners for casual sex, as it turns out, are less wicked—and less casual—than the noncasuals hope and fear. Even in most large cities, places where women who want a sexual partner for the evening can rendezvous are scarce. Consequently, play partners have probably rubbed shoulders at one of the few sex clubs or play parties before they ever get together sexually. They may in fact have been acquaintances for months who suddenly perceive some chemistry. In "Desperately Seeking Same," an article about lesbian life in the nineties, author Masha Gessen laments that she had to resort to the classifieds to "get laid by someone I didn't know rather than by an ex-lover or an ex-lover's lover or a lover's ex-lover or an ex-lover's ex-lover, which would be the extent of my options if I went to a lesbian sex club or back room bar in any major city."

Further reducing the casualness of brief encounters is the specter of AIDS. Practicing safer sex means sharing a generous dollop of one's history, health, and erotic appetites before having sex. Finding out if one is bisexual, prefers to top or bottom, or has a history of STDs can often jump-start a rudimentary relationship. And since sobriety is now de rigueur at most sex clubs and S/M parties, altered states are no longer a way to avoid knowing or remembering your partner.

Because of all these changed circumstances, casual sex, at least among the women I interviewed, wasn't the combustible mix of anonymous pleasure and danger I had expected. Nor was it, contrary to my expectations, always relationship-free. No matter how bracketed by limited expectations, well-defined roles, or other mutual agreements, brief encounters could (and frequently did) spill over into continuing affairs. In fact, one of the women remarked that she had to practice a Zen of Brief Encounters zealously in order to turn down a follow-up if the first round had been satisfying. Another commented, "Sometimes we just smile and walk away at the end . . . [but] sometimes I get a sense that I want to get to know the person in other contexts. . . . It's a 'more' feeling." In fact, when I interviewed her, Gita was in several long-term relationships with women she had met at play parties.

Of course, some casual encounters do sort neatly into episodes. Others, however, inaugurate longer affairs, partnerships, or friendships. This tendency of casual sex to hover somewhere between an encapsulated present and an open-ended future is particularly evident in Robin's account:

I noticed someone I was attracted to. We exchanged a few sentences and started touching. . . . We had a wonderful time . . . tender, caring, exciting. Afterward, we talked for a while and showered. I made sure to get her address and phone number. For the next couple of weeks, I played with the idea of calling or writing. Then I got a note from her. She had been wondering whether to call me. She wasn't sure if she would, but she told me she had a wonderful time and she gave me her address

Yemaya KauriAleeto

I first saw piercing at a festival in California where there was a piercing booth and many lesbians proudly displayed their nipple rings—including my long-distance lover, who had a new stainless steel barbell through her nipple. I left knowing I wanted one but wondering what my teenagers would think about "pierced Mom."

I returned to California the following year and discovered that my now ex-lover also had a barbell gently nudging her clit; her lover was similarly pierced. I knew it was time for me to get pierced.

I purchased a beautiful lavender ring and a needle. The excitement of having the ring secretly tucked in my pocket gave me a rush—I couldn't wait to have this cool metal through my nipple.

That evening the three of us lit candles and incense, drank wine, and listened to music as we prepared for the ritual. I would do the piercing while they provided support. My ex-lover sat behind me, holding me against her bare breasts, lightly stroking my bare skin. Her lover sat in front of me, fingers caressing me until my entire body was relaxed. I was ready to begin.

I gently pushed the needle against my skin, not yet piercing but testing the cold, sharp point against my tender nipple. And then I pushed harder. The point of the needle disappeared into my flesh and, instantaneously, a rush unlike anything I had experienced before flowed through my body. I felt light and transcendent.

After several minutes, I pushed until the tip of the needle pierced through, experiencing another rush of pleasure. I was fully pierced: The needle extended equally from both sides of my fully erect nipple.

I reclined and enjoyed the sensation while they gently threaded the ring through my nipple. It was as erotic as I had imagined. The lavender ring against the brown skin of my erect nipple looked fabulous—a beautiful complement to my plus-size figure. And I was more aroused than I could ever remember being.

The sensation stayed with me. My nipple was constantly erect, and I was constantly wet. I told only a few people about the piercing, wanting to savor the experience for myself. And I knew I would want to share this experience with a new partner, should she materialize.

My kids eventually found out and were amazed that the same Mom who attended PTA meetings and baked cookies had been pierced. Their response? "Go, Mom!"

And now, my partner and I plan to have a double-ring ceremony: my nipple and her clit hood. It promises to be a most erotic event. The kids are definitely *not* invited.

and phone number again. I sent a similar note back to her. Neither of us ever called. It's a delightful memory. . . . One of the most pure, definable relationships I've ever had.

If Robin had made a follow-up date before she left the club or simply walked decisively away, the interplay between casual and meaningful might have been concealed. And even in situations when there isn't a tidy resolution, our need to categorize all our encounters compels us to make one up. In a spasm of inventiveness, Robin collapses both ends of the whole casual-meaningful continuum into a new form: a brief, but nonetheless meaningful, relationship: "one of the most pure, definable . . . I've ever had."

Some of the women I interviewed insisted that they could only have sex in the context of meaningful relationships; others staunchly defended casual sex. Their actual behavior, however, didn't always fall into such polarized camps. Advocates of lasting relationships reported plenty of brief encounters. But the long-termers were likely to interpret these encounters as wild oats or mistakes. Conversely, identification with the casual-sex contingent was by no means a declaration of emancipation from traditional romance and marriage. In fact, the question—Is she a trick or an intimate partner?—seems to loom as large on trashy turf as it does on serious dates.

Rather than reflecting our identities accurately, our depictions of ourselves seem to be our attempts to make sense, after the fact, of complicated and often contradictory behaviors. Besides supplying some much-needed cohesion to our confusing love stories, claiming our own niches may be a psychological necessity—crucial self-protection in the increasingly balkanized sexual/social world in which we find ourselves. After all, even if the designations *meaningful* and *casual* don't begin to capture our sexual differences, they do place us within a particular clan in the lesbian tribe. And as my interviews proceeded, I continued to find that our lust for such location was just as compelling as any of our erotic desires.

A TALE OF TWO EROTIC ADEPTS: KELLY AND DIDIER

Kelly, an incorrigible romantic, calls to inform me that she has finally found her life partner. As soon as I hear her raves, I start raving myself: "Look at your track record. Stop moving them in. Can't you enjoy it and leave it at that? Stop marrying them. I can't live through another divorce." I reason. I coax. I beg. I protest. I threaten. All to no avail. Newly entranced, she dismisses my remonstrations with an airy, "This is really the one."

The more easily she has done it, the more easily she seems to do it again. At least there might have been a six-month entr'acte in the olden days. Now barely six weeks elapse between the time one ex is axed and her successor is installed. And even though she is falling in love more often, Kelly's faith in forever after has never faltered.

If we apply the true love/trash test, Kelly clearly falls on the traditional side of the dichotomy. But what if we look at another dimension: her ability to conjure up an imaginary world? If we consider the ease and frequency with which she falls in love, she has more in common with Didier, one of the women I interviewed. A rabid antiromantic, Didier seems, at first glance, like Kelly's polar opposite. Didier identifies herself as "an endorphin adept." She can be turned on instantly—by the merest suggestion of what is to come, or the contraction of a muscle unconnected with her erogenous zone. Her whole body is an erogenous zone. She is, she says, "hooked up." Rather than looking for one ideal lover, Didier seeks partners who will improvise erotic scenes with her. And when she plays the role of the proud maiden who is abducted, tied up, and ravished by a ruthless pirate, it is her own erotic "hook-ups" and the scene itself that arouse her. Her actual partner, when not convincingly piratical, is irrelevant, or perhaps even distracting.

Kelly identifies herself as a vanilla femme who wants to find that special someone to grow old with. Didier says she is an S/M switch hitter. When I interviewed her, her only complaint was a shortage of play partners. Kelly's gold standard of monogamy and Didier's identification as a polymorphous perverse sadomasochist may seem to place them in opposite erotic camps, but, in fact, they are quite similar. Both are skilled erotic conjurers—adepts who are able to imagine virtual worlds that have only the remotest correspondence with their daily lives. Because Kelly's destiny story fits so seamlessly with the larger culture's romance master narrative, it seems real compared to Didier's obviously contrived scripts. But Kelly's dream spouse is no less a confection than Didier's pirate. And their apparently opposite erotic philosophies hide a shared belief: Both are convinced that their psychological well-being and their sex lives are inseparable. For example, Kelly knows that, to be happy, she and her ideal spouse must have great sex. And Didier believes good sex will somehow undo a painful past.

Our stated preferences seem to hide more than they reveal. How, then, can we move beyond such distorting ideological frameworks? Are there ways of mapping our erotic lives that are more accurate than the formulaic polarities of meaningful versus casual or vanilla versus S/M? If I consider the interviews as a whole, the one feature that emerges clearly is the extent of the women's erotic inventiveness. Everyone, it seemed, had either molded her intimate relationship into a curious and unconventional form, or had reinvented her sexual partners in surprising ways. Perhaps this inventiveness is the alternative framework I need. In such a framework, even the usual polarities are simply another example of erotic invention. If we see them as collective crystallizations instead of forced choices, they are less tyrannical. And a framework of erotic inventiveness also provides me with a way of noticing and recording erotic practices that haven't yet been given labels.

BECOMING LESBIAN:
LEARNING THE ABCs OF EROTIC INVENTION

As lesbians, we have to imagine someone from a forbidden category into erotic being; that is, we come to believe that a member of our own devalued gender is attractive. And as soon as we accept such a radical proposition, we face another daunting hurdle. Lovers make love. And we have to imagine a way to "do it" in a culture that defines sex phallocentrically. Perhaps this explains the sexual inventiveness of lesbians.

If we're seasoned lesbians, sex with women seems perfectly normal. But in the beginning, it was so difficult to imagine that we were obliged to reinvent ourselves, to enter a special category. After we learned the ropes, we forgot, perhaps mercifully, having taken this quantum leap. But once kindled in this fashion, our erotic imaginations never quit. Not only do we not need a penis to be erotic; often, we do not even need a body. Most of the women I spoke to were able to experience ecstasy at a distance. Separated from the object of their desire by a dinner table or a continent, they could still be transported: "If I'm having dinner with an acquaintance, good food is just food," one interviewee commented, "but the whole meal is transformed if I have emotional or sexual feelings about my dinner partner. And I don't even need to touch her."

Another woman had fallen head over heels in love with an acquaintance she had talked to and danced with only once. After the encounter, she waited anxiously for letters, and fantasized furiously about the woman. Though never explicitly sexual, it was one of the most erotic and sexually charged experiences she had ever had.

A few of the women had woven entire relationships out of such gossamer. One said that she purposely didn't let her partner stimulate her to orgasms. She wanted to keep the ecstatic feeling as long as possible and was afraid sexual release would diffuse it. Another said she reached orgasmlike states regularly simply by hugging her partner.

Of course, such disembodied transports aren't the exclusive province of lesbians. Straights, too, have been known to fall in love and conduct entire affairs from a distance. But the lesbians I interviewed took such magic for granted. Could the coming-out process of imagining result in a new erotic skill—something we might call EESP (erotic extrasensory perception)? Accounts of such no-hands delights are commonplace in lesbian literature. One long-term part-

Amanda Kovattana

There aren't very many of us, and we're not talked about except academically in books on lesbian sexuality and queer theory. Yet how many lesbians and bisexual women were initiated by lesbian vampires? We are the public relations department of the lesbian community. We are undercover agents in mainstream culture, luring the curious, the latent, the travelers. In *The Lesbian Erotic Dance*, JoAnn Loulan named us lesbian vampires, women who are "practiced in the art of seducing heterosexual women."

I was born a lesbian vampire out of necessity. There was no one to give me an initiatory kiss. My girlfriends in high school all waited for me to make the first move. I advertised my interest in women by calling myself "bisexual" or simply "queer," always with sexual rather than political connotations. I separated myself from the lesbian community by keeping my hair long. For parties I indulged in costumes: hats with veils, vintage cocktail dresses, rhinestones, or sometimes a man's three-piece suit and makeup, à la Marlene Dietrich. And though I didn't smoke, I would traipse around with a cigarette holder and a lighted cigarette. I perfected a high level of intuition, knew just when to take her hand, how to flatter the insecure, make the plain girl feel attractive, how to take it so slowly that she didn't realize she was crossing the line until I kissed her.

As a lesbian vampire, I both betrayed and represented the lesbian community. By looking for partners outside the community, I was rejecting lesbian culture. I was shunning the monogamous, couple-intensive, insulated, merging nature of the lesbian community. By infiltrating straight culture, I could erode boundaries, challenge male precedent, recruit, and act as a bridge between the two communities. Few of my conquests crossed over to lesbianism, but most were expanded by the sexual option I presented to them.

But I paid for wanting straight women. They were closeted bedroom bisexuals. Some were waiting for Mr. Right. Others returned to their husbands, their curiosity abated. They made me feel illegitimate and sometimes inadequate because I was not a man and could offer no heterosexual privileges. I was still the other.

The lesbian vampire challenges the monogamous expectations of both straight and gay culture, while tapping into the fluidity of sexual identity. I look forward to a time when she earns her place as a priestess of initiation.

ner interviewed in *American Couples* remembers: "We first told each other we loved each other after we had been writing: I [asked her] 'is it possible to fall in love with someone through the mail?'"

In her autobiography *Lily Briscoe: A Self-Portrait,* the lesbian author and artist Mary Meigs describes a similar nongenital form of ecstasy: "While my soul fainted with joy and my body quivered . . . [we] would build an airy pleasure dome for weeks and months, without the intensity and obligation of sex; there were no let-downs, only a sustained state of bliss." (See also her "About Being an Old Lesbian in Love," in this volume.)

Such magic is not confined to vanilla romance. In *Sensuous Magic* Pat Califia, cutting-edge "sexpert" and writer, defines an S/M orgasm as "the reaching of an emotional, psychological, or spiritual state of catharsis, ecstasy or transcendence during an S/M scene without having a genital orgasm."

Among lesbians of every stripe, EESP seems to be a common form of erotic expression. Yet it goes unrecognized, typically lumped together with the idealizing of one's lover that, according to conventional wisdom, is true of everyone in love. Perhaps EESP is a universal phenomenon. If so, it is especially universal for lesbians.

COUPLE SEX: FRICTION AND FANTASY

Four of the women I spoke to were in long-term relationships. For them, the initial magic had evolved into a growing awareness of the mechanics of their own and their partners' orgasmic response. But even though this seasoned sex fell short of the earlier bliss, these women reported taking great pains to find time for it in their packed schedules. Somehow a niche—often, it seemed, a weekend morning—was chiseled from the demands of careers and social lives, chores, and the care of pets and children. Considering the struggle, why did they bother? It wasn't simply for orgasm. All four reported more reliable, if less pleasurable, orgasms when they masturbated·

alone. Nor was sex simply the best way for couples to wrest a few moments of intimacy from impossible schedules. Two of the women, in fact, preferred other ways to be close. After all their years together, one woman said she felt closer to her partner after particular conversations than after sex. Another claimed her most intimate moments with her lover occurred during long hikes.

It seemed that continuing couple sex was, like butch and femme, or S/M and vanilla, another badge of membership. Sex distinguished lover relationships from mere friendships. And "doing it" regularly certified that partners had avoided the lesbian-bed death epidemic.

Because partners couldn't predict that they would desire each other at, say, 10 A.M. every Saturday morning, they relied on certain techniques to awaken slumbering libidos. One woman observed that their vibrators had sustained them. Another said, "It's no big deal to have sex if one of us is in the mood and the other isn't." Their sex life depended on a certain irreverence about the importance of recip rocal orgasms.

As well as such sex-promoting techniques and attitudes, all four depended on erotic invention. Three reported tuning in to unspoken, unshared fantasies when their partners were stimulating them orally, manually, or with vibrators. Another said she and her lover cooked up scenarios together. They had developed one that they had varied slightly over the years. One or the other would start by describing other people as backdrops, voyeurs who had come to watch them. Initiating the fantasy, she said, had become "a way to synch into sex . . . like turning the lights down low."

Just as a wild-oats stage often authenticates lesbian identity, continuing to "do it" postpassionately gives lesbian long-term relationships a certain consequence not conferred on them by the outside world. And, ironically, in order to be perceived as "real" intimates, they became unreal to each other during sex. For a brief interlude every week or two, these long-term partners agreed explicitly or tacitly to uncouple—to reinvent each other as exotic strangers.

FLEXISEX: DISSOLVING THE LOVER/FRIEND BOUNDARY

As well as converting spouses into strangers, these women also melted down the boundary between friends and lovers. Marlene took special pains to celebrate this collapse of old polarities.

Marlene, a wilderness guide, met her friend and sometimes lover, Kip, when they were both rookie lesbians. For the next two decades, they lived hundreds of miles apart. When they found themselves in the same locale, they would backpack, gossip, commiserate about breakups, and sometimes have sex. Chafing at the way their multi-faceted relationship seemed less visible to their lesbian friends than more conventional commitments, they decided to have a ceremony to honor their bond. They sent out announcements inviting women to help them celebrate "21 years of open love, uncommitted sex, firm friendship and wild adventures." In keeping with the spirit of their free-form relationship, each brought another date to the ceremony. Marlene started out in a tux and Kip in a dress; halfway through the ceremony, they switched costumes and roles. The final touch was the ring ceremony: They brought 100 gay freedom rings, which they handed out to all the guests.

For Marlene and Kip, sex, like backpacking, is one of a number of pleasurable activities that have deepened their friendship over the years. In contrast, their official long-term lover relationships have not endured.

Another of the interviewees, Leah, also cherished friendly sex. She divided her sexual relationships into three categories: strictly recreational, in-love partnerships, and encounters with loving friends. Recreational sex had been sporadic, and the in-love type had landed her in a long-term relationship that had been destructive. Of the three types, it was the friendly sex that, over the years, had been most sustaining and unproblematic.

For Hettie, friendly sex consisted of encounters with ex-lovers who lived in other parts of the country, but whose paths crossed hers from time to time. When these serendipitous meetings occurred, they would get together for dinner. If both happened to be out of monogamous relationships, they would spend the night together. The sex wasn't electrifying. It was another way, like their dinner conversation, to certify their rapport and, as Hettie said, to "take a stand against the passage of time that was changing everything else."

Since their bonds didn't depend on sex, these sometimes sexual friends were never estranged during nonsexual interludes. Their erotic relationship on hold, they could still be dinner companions or backpacking partners.

Lesbian erotic inventiveness is a great source of fun and pleasure, but it is practical as well. These women's ability to be part-time lovers increased the feelings of loyalty and closeness already associated with their friendship. The deepened bond seemed particularly sturdy. It held firm during changes and separations. And it was a form of social security that could be tapped during lonely stretches, breakups, or other trying times.

COLLECTIVE EROTIC INVENTION

Just as we are constantly reinventing ourselves and our intimacies, our communities are constantly reinventing us. S/M or vanilla, merger queen or endorphin adept, butch or femme, our individual inventions can never be entirely separated from a collective and shifting zeitgeist. The most recent shift, however, has not been to everyone's liking. One interviewee told me that she noticed that twenty- and thirty-year-olds she met seemed to practice much rougher sex than her older partners. She simply had to get used to it, she said a bit peevishly, if she wanted a range of lovers. Another interviewee, who had always had multiple partners, told me that all the available women she had encountered recently had turned out to be into S/M. She had decided to get proficient at whips and cuffs simply to get laid.

I've noticed a similar sea change among some of my friends. A new sporting spirit prevails at most birthday gatherings I attend.

Slick Harris

A short story about a femme woman's passion for her butch lover's dildo gave me the courage to buy my own equipment. I certainly wasn't brave enough to go into a sex shop. Although ordering from a catalog is convenient and anonymous, it has its drawbacks. As a novice, I made a few mistakes because I didn't fully understand the difference between "representational" (*very* realistic) and "fanciful" (whimsically shaped) dildos.

It was easy to fasten the harness and dildo securely in place. I practiced fucking my pillow, a stuffed pig—anything that didn't move. I jerked myself off via this silicone cock, and actually came while imagining I was spurting all over my belly. I watched myself in the mirror, incredibly turned on by the sight of a realistic cock hanging between my legs. Why shouldn't I be? I was simply giving life to the fantasy fucking I had been practicing for years. Long ago, I had figured out what I wanted to do in bed, and my sexual encounters reflected my desire. I always starred as the butch top, using my hand, my body, or my imagination to fuck.

When I had experimented with my new toys to my satisfaction, I was ready for action. On our first date, I announced to my new lover, "I just want to fuck you," and was astonished to hear the delighted reply, "You're in luck!" Indeed I was, and although we were dildo-fucking virgins, the sex was so hot and we fit so well that it seemed as if we had been together forever.

There is something so sexy about the preliminaries: selecting a dildo, inserting it into the harness, tightening the straps, feeling the weight on my pelvis, putting on a condom, applying generous amounts of lube, gazing at my cock or the anticipation burning in my lover's eyes. As for actually getting into it . . . well, I leave that to your inventive imagination.

Since that first exhilarating experience, I gained confidence and a dildo collection. My "toy chest" is overflowing. I just had to have a cock to suit every mood, including a soft, compact model for packin' (wearing the dildo inside my jeans). The irony is that a cock suitable for street or bar wear is too small and pliable for real fucking. One must be resigned to looking tough with a limp dick, or interrupting hot foreplay and changing gear in order to become a functional top. There are dildos that vibrate, inflate, pump, and ejaculate, but, as in other areas of mechanical engineering, the right tool for the right job is the way to go.

Some celebrants are still getting the usual haul of labyris earrings and Amazon posters. But today's lesbian birthday girl is just as likely to receive handcuffs, a double dildo, or a lifetime supply of rubber gloves. In another sign of the changing times, the local vibrator store has added a display rack devoted strictly to leather items. A psychologist colleague recently confided that she used to refuse to do therapy with S/M couples, but she has decided to amend her policy. Still trying to salvage some of her politics, she now draws the line at partners into blood sports. And, scanning the 1994 annual Gay and Lesbian National Health Conference program, I noticed a workshop designed to explore S/M as a "normal healthy sexual identity, despite the Diagnostic and Statistical Manual's assessment of it as a psychosexual disorder." Lesbians are forging a new consensus about the activities that constitute sex.

The infusion of S/M into vanilla isn't the only contemporary sign of a changing dyktegeist. Public participation in private acts, for example, was much in evidence at a recent performance by Annie Sprinkle. Self-proclaimed porn star turned sacred temple prostitute, she converted the most traditionally solitary activity—masturbation—into performance art by vibrating to orgasm onstage in concert with a handful of her Sapphic sisters. Noisemakers were distributed to the audience, and we were encouraged to participate percussively in the mounting rhythm. Never a fan of any organized religion before, I found myself an instant convert to this brand of evangelesbianism.

Along with the fusion of S/M and vanilla, casual and long-term, friends and lovers, that hoariest of dualisms—the spirit and flesh—collapsed as Annie vibrated to holiness. I suspect if I continue to interview women, even the recombinant categories formed by the collapse of old polarities will make way for as yet unimaginable erotic inventions. A truly representative map would have to include every protean shift of every lesbian over time. But even that wouldn't capture the larger waves that are constantly refashioning and refurbishing our individual preferences and experiences.

Ultimately, it comes as no surprise that talking to a small group of lesbians about their erotic experiences only illustrates the slipperiness of sex. And perhaps the fuzzy provisionality of sex gives me an excuse to stay at my post, spotting new inventions that are already in the process of becoming passé. And, of course, there are the pleasures of listening, and watching.

I have a new interview scheduled. My last interviewee told me that I shouldn't miss Dion, "someone with some incredible experiences . . . very articulate." A woman matching her description saunters into the coffeehouse where we have arranged to talk. Our eyes meet. Self-consciously, we busy ourselves with introductions and the search for a private table. Finally settled, lattes ordered, I bring out my recorder. "Is it okay?" I ask. I imagine that her smile of assent dips ever so slightly beneath the shiny formal surface of the interview. She begins her story. Every now and then I probe for the telling detail. Her response is a beguiling tangent and, if I'm lucky, a Mona Lisa smile. Buzzed on the caffeine and the merry chase she is leading me on, I am surprised how quickly the hour passes.

After she leaves, I order another latte and replay the interview in my head. Dion had dallied with a number of imaginary partners while in conventional relationships. Among her favorite roles: a sultan's captive princess, an ingenue's headmistress, and a frat house mascot. She was, in short, expert at combining real coupling and imaginary scenarios. And I realize I'm no slouch at invention myself. What were pirates and maidens, after all, compared to my own favorite scene: the sensitive sex researcher forever in pursuit of her elusive subject?

FURTHER READING

Barrington, Judith, ed. *An Intimate Wilderness: Lesbian Writers on Sexuality.* Portland, Oreg.: Eighth Mountain Press, 1991.

Blumstein, Philip, and Pepper Schwartz. *American Couples.* New York: Morrow, 1983.

Burana, Lily, Roxxie, and Linnea Due. *Dagger: On Butch Women.* San Francisco: Cleis, 1994.

Califia, Pat. *Sensuous Magic.* New York: Masquerade, 1993.

Loulan, JoAnn. *Lesbian Sex.* San Francisco: Spinsters Ink, 1984.

Nestle, Joan, ed. *The Persistent Desire: A Femme-Butch Reader.* Boston: Alyson, 1992.

Rothblum, Esther, and Kathleen A. Brehony, eds. *Boston Marriages: Romantic But Asexual Relationships Among Contemporary Lesbians.* Amherst: University of Massachusetts Press, 1993.

Stein, Arlene. *Sisters, Sexperts, Queers: Beyond the Lesbian Nation.* New York: Penguin, 1993.

Stevens, Robin, ed. *Girlfriend Number One: Lesbian Life in the 90s.* San Francisco: Cleis, 1994.

Tomaso, Carla. *The House of Real Love.* New York: Penguin, 1992.

FIFTEEN

SAFER SEX

Marcia Munson

Is lesbian sex safe, safer, or safest? After over a decade of caring for our brothers and friends with AIDS, many lesbians are now frightened for our own safety. Our fear may be larger than the danger. Woman-to-woman sex is an unlikely way of spreading the AIDS virus. Transmitting HIV requires getting live virus from an infected person inside the body of an uninfected person.

Semen and blood from an HIV-positive person contain plenty of the virus. Vaginal fluid contains less. In anal or vaginal intercourse, about two teaspoons of semen are deposited into a vulnerable body cavity. If the semen contains the AIDS virus, it can easily enter a partner's bloodstream through tiny tears in the vaginal or rectal lining, through the cervix and into the thin-walled uterus, or even through intact vaginal and rectal mucous membranes. That's why anal intercourse with a man and vaginal intercourse between a woman and a man are so risky. Examples of woman-to-woman activity that would be similarly high risk would be artificially inseminating a partner using fresh (possibly infected) sperm, or sharing injection drug needles.

Intact skin is an excellent barrier against HIV transmission, but whenever abrasion, burning, cutting, tattooing, biting, piercing, or whipping has created a break in the skin, another person's body fluid can enter the bloodstream through this opening. When the vaginal lining or the delicate rectal lining has been traumatized by fisting or intense penetration, it is especially important to avoid introducing a partner's blood or vaginal fluid into the vagina or rectum. S/M women have been leaders in teaching about the importance of using latex barriers and of sterilizing all knives and needles.

Immunoglobulin A, which neutralizes the AIDS virus, is found in the saliva of 449 out of 450 people. So how could the handful of anecdotal vagina-to-mouth cases of HIV transmission have occurred? Possibly by getting menstrual blood or vaginal fluid into the bloodstream through cracked lips, fresh piercings, open sores in the mouth, or the thin mucous membranes of the nose or eyes.

In the 1993 San Francisco/Berkeley study of seroprevalence among 498 lesbian and bisexual women, the 6 who tested positive for HIV had all used intravenous drugs or had sex with men since 1978. In a study of 18 lesbian couples released by the University of Turin, Italy, in 1994, one woman in each couple was HIV-positive and one woman was HIV-negative at the beginning of the research. After six months of recorded activity, including shared sex toys, anal manipulation, sex during menstruation, and oral sex, all previously HIV-negative partners were still negative. No scientific evidence of woman-to-woman sexual transmission of HIV was found in either of the studies, or in the four Centers for Disease Control studies done in the early 1990s. The CDC studies included nearly one million female blood donors, STD clinic clients, and women's health clinic clients. Each CDC study ended with a recommendation that HIV-prevention education for lesbians and bisexual women focus on the dangers of injection drug use and heterosexual sex. But in reaction to the limited research on lesbians and HIV and in memory of the five suspected woman-to-woman cases of HIV transmission reported from 1984 to 1994, some American dykes continue vigorously to promote latex gloves and oral sex barriers.

In the absence of proof of HIV transmission during woman-to-woman sexual activity, some European activists see the marketing of latex safer-sex products to lesbians as just another capitalist plot to take women's money. When oral-sex protection is pushed to lesbians but not to men, some feminists note the sexism in the safer-sex message. Some women's health activists wish dykes would focus on issues that more seriously threaten the lives of women, such as breast cancer, which killed 46,000 American women in 1993, compared to AIDS, which killed 5,000 American women. Homophobia and sexism combine to silence the most ignored public health message of all: that one of the most effective safer-sex choices women can make is to have sex only with other women.

Yes, lesbians do get AIDS—mostly from sharing IV drug works and from having sex with men. Yes, it's theoretically possible to transmit HIV from woman to woman, so it's wise to avoid getting another person's vaginal fluid into your bloodstream. Of course, never exchange blood. Sometimes this means using latex gloves, condoms, Saran Wrap, bleach, or soap and water. (The AIDS virus is killed easily with bleach or soap and water; it cannot travel through intact skin, latex condoms, or gloves.)

As debate intensifies across the Atlantic about whether and when lesbians need to use latex barriers for sex, many long-time dykes regret that discussion of safer sex over the last ten years has focused only on AIDS. Though lesbians have long been known to have a low incidence of all sexually transmitted diseases, some commonsense wisdom from the past about avoiding STDs needs to be reiterated among lesbians:

1. Herpes can be spread from mouth to genitals. If you have a cold sore on your lips, don't go down on your girlfriend or even kiss her.

2. Getting a partner's vaginal fluid inside your pussy could spread syphilis, gonorrhea, chlamydia, bacterial vaginosis,

Betty Rose Dudley

The first woman I ever made love to was myself. I mean more than masturbation. In my mid-twenties, I'd had quite a bit of sexual experience with men, yet knew that I only wanted love with women. I fantasized making love to women; I even practiced sex with my dolls. But in real life, men were easier. They did all the work, and I didn't get emotionally entangled. Then one day I decided I'd had enough.

Before I had been a man in most of my sexual fantasies. This was real life now. I stood looking at myself naked in my bedroom mirror and realized that I was a woman, a lesbian.

I was scared. It hadn't occurred to me that a woman might want me as a woman. Would *I* want to make love to me? I was fat. With men, all I ever had to do was act available. I knew that women weren't going to be so easy, especially for a fat girl. I also knew that I wasn't the woman of my dreams. I had never heard of anyone dreaming of a fat girl. Would I want a fat lover?

I decided to find out. I stood and looked at myself in the mirror and memorized my body. When I held an image in my mind of what I really looked like, I became both lover and other. I closed my eyes, walked up to myself, nuzzled my ear, and took myself to bed.

I explored my body through both visual fantasy and actual touch. I played with my ears and caressed my throat as I licked my lips. I paid attention to how I liked my nipples touched. I watched myself from every angle, going as slowly as possible, trying to take in as much detail as I could. I gently caressed and kissed my fat belly and slowly, very slowly, spread open my fat thighs and felt my own wetness. I put my fingers into my fat, wet cunt and imagined what it would be like to open myself up and lick my clit. For the very first time, I tasted myself. Oh, how sweet that taste was.

When I looked at myself in the mirror again, I knew that, fat and all, I wanted me. I was still not the woman of my dreams, but I knew who I was. I was the first woman I had ever made love to. For the first time in my life, I felt deeply, profoundly, and positively female.

trichomoniasis, or hepatitis. Always wash hands and sex toys well before sharing.

3. Getting bacteria from the anus into the vagina could spread chlamydia or cause a vaginal infection. Don't move sex toys or fingers from the ass to the vagina without washing them first.

4. Eating the blood or feces of a person infected with hepatitis can spread this potentially fatal disease.

5. Urinate after having sex to prevent stray anal bacteria from traveling up the urethra and causing a bladder infection.

6. Always fasten your seat belt while driving to or from a sexual encounter. You're far more likely to die in a car crash than from an STD you might get from a woman.

FURTHER READING

McIlvenna, T. *The Complete Guide to Safer Sex.* Fort Lee, N.J.: Barricade Books, 1992.

O'Sullivan, S., and P. Parmar. *Lesbians Talk Safer Sex.* London: Scarlet Press, 1992.

Raiteri, R., R. Fora, and A. Sinicco. "No HIV-1 Transmission Through Lesbian Sex." *Lancet* (1992): 344–70.

SIXTEEN

GUESSING GAMES

Kath Weston

Can you always tell one when you see one? Of course not, but that doesn't keep people from trying. In the United States, the shifting sands of gender are sculpted, in part, by the widespread belief that lesbians can be identified at a glance. "Is she or isn't she?" people wonder. To back up their speculations, they look for clues, confident in their ability to infer sexual identity directly from bodies. And these guessing games are far from a heterosexual pastime. Gay women and men play, too.

In most cases, the clues people seek are not about sexuality per se, but about gender. Rather than ask whether anyone has ever spotted So-and-so kissing another woman, people are more likely to assess her gay potential based upon the timbre of her voice, the way she occupies space in a room, the boyish cut of her clothing, or her "nontraditional" job. Using gender to infer sexual identity is not a new gambit in the high-stakes game of representation. During the first half of the twentieth century, psychiatry gave credibility to the notion that homosexuality is accompanied by gender inversion (exhibiting "traits" of the "opposite" gender). Lipstick lesbians aside, most popular representations still depict "real" lesbians as masculin-ized women, assuming all the while that everyone agrees upon the meaning of *masculine.*

Even after So-and-so's gay identity becomes known, or at least assigned, the speculation doesn't end. Players regroup for Round Two. Now the questions revolve around how she genders herself les-bian: Is she butch, femme, neither, both, androgynous, or (in hushed tones) one of those halfway middlers? Less discussed, but no less important, are the ways that race, class, age, and ethnicity thread through these ostensibly gendered categories.

Guessing games are a constant reminder that gendering involves much more than claiming an identity. They point to deep-seated cultural assumptions, including the notion that the world is made up of two fixed genders and that individuals display a consistent set of gender traits. Via the categorizing moves required to play the game, people become engaged in the process of creating gender. They also learn to twist and bend received notions of what makes someone "that kind" or "that way."

The following narratives zero in on attempts to judge who's who and what's what at the place where gender meets sexuality. I have excerpted them from interviews conducted in the San Francisco Bay Area from 1985 to 1990 as part of an anthropological research project on the gendering of "same-sex" relationships. Only one of the four women interviewed here considered herself butch or femme. Yet all four women used these categories to explain past events, present relationships, and everyday encounters. So don't be too quick to dismiss femme and butch as outmoded stereotypes or identities only a few lesbians claim. Who knows? They might just provide a starting point for rethinking gender.

MARTA ROSALES: "GOD, IF I EVER MEET ONE OF THEM!"

"I remember growing up, and my father would say someone was *marimacha.* '*Marimacha,*' he said; you know, 'You *dyke.*' And I always used to be so afraid. *Marimachas* were just like awful abominations. I thought, 'God, if I ever meet one of them!' *My* idea of a lesbian was someone who was in leathers, and they were really tough. I just was so frightened by that."

Before she moved to the Bay Area from Southern California, Marta Rosales* said she "didn't think there were [*marimachas*], really. I know they talked about them. There was one—but she wasn't Hispanic—at my dad's work. *She* was over *him*. Ha-ha! It was great, now that I think. Damn! All the men were scared of her. This was the stereotype I had: She wore steel-toed boots. She wore men's straight-legged jeans. Wallet in her pocket. These little Hawaiian shirts that she'd roll up. She had these nice arms—nice arms, oh! I still remember that! She had this real curly hair, that she kept with gel. I mean, *this* was a dyke to me. My dad would say, '*La marimacha* Pat.' I was so afraid of her.

"When I was fourteen and a half, I started working with my dad. And here was Pat, who didn't like anyone. She liked my father, for some strange reason. She respected him as a worker, but he looked down at her for being a dyke. He'd say, 'Good morning, Pat,' and she'd say, 'How ya doing?' and then I would just run away. I was so scared of her! But that was the only dyke I ever really knew. And she was in such a position of authority. She was in charge of everybody else."

Marta described her younger self as "very untraditional. I wasn't like my sister. I wasn't like my brother. I was fascinated with bicycles, and I used to take them apart and put them together. *I* showed my brothers how to ride their bicycles. *I* showed my brothers how to *fix* their bicycles. Then I decided I wanted a scooter, and that wasn't enough, and I got a motorcycle. Here's this Hispanic family, the *girl* buying a motorcycle. 'Oh, what people are gonna think!' And I said, 'I don't care what people are gonna think about me, Dad. I decided to get a motorcycle.'

*Pseudonyms are used in this chapter to maintain confidentiality for the women who generously committed their time and thought to this project.

"Then I used to wear my little 501s and tool around on my bike. I was really happy. But people then started asking me. I didn't have a boyfriend [after] high school. They would come up and say, 'Are you a lesbian?' I said, 'No, I'm not. I am not. I don't know what you're talking about.' I was real heavy into denial. What I used to resent [was] not so much that they would think I was gay, but because they were stereotyping. Because here was this woman who had a motor-cycle, who wore jeans, and was so nontraditional."

When Marta moved to the Bay Area to continue her education on a scholarship, a friend introduced her to an out lesbian who "broke down a lot of stereotypes. Even when I first started coming to the bars here, if someone was very butchy, it was like, 'Oh, my god!' But she broke down all that. She had her master's in criminal justice, and she was intelligent. Oh, my god, this woman had an IQ!"

Shortly afterward Marta met her lover, Toni Williams. "I remem-ber Toni gave me a ring. I had my ring on [my right hand] and somebody [at work] said, 'Marta, you're married?' And I said, 'No. Isn't it one of your fingers on *this* hand?' And they said, 'Well, why didn't you answer [right away]? You're not *gay* or anything, are you? You're not one of those?' I would just like for them to get to know me, for who I am, not for what I am. Here's Marta, who everybody just looks up to, and is so good. This whole Madonna complex, really!"

Marta believed her upbringing as a Mexican-American woman had raised obstacles to coming out. "There are more now that aren't Catholic, but the majority [are] very religious. You're going to grow up to marry a man and cater to a man. [Although] that may not be so much the thinking *now* ... the [Mexican] culture, with the American [culture], it's mixing. You're engraved with that. You're going to grow up, and you're going to learn how to cook, you're going to learn how to be a good mother, and you're going to learn how to do everything for someone else except yourself."

When it came to the categories femme and butch, Marta felt she had "a little of both. I can't say one or the other, because I really go in spurts. I think I'm more butch and very much in control, but I have very feminine qualities, in another way.

"But on that butch/femme distinction, is it do you just have oral sex? Some people don't like dildos. Some people don't like anything about that kind of role playing. When I was in senior year [of college], about two years ago, they said, 'God, you know, you're really butch.' And I thought, well, what is being butch? 'Oh, that means when you're more controlling, or you're more aggressive.' And I'm aggressive in some things, but oh, gosh, I'm just not in other things. So I would say I'm both."

In earlier years, Marta thought of herself as more femme than butch. "I used to think it was dress. I usually wear pants because they're comfortable, but if it's anything dressy, I like to wear dresses. Because to me, they're dressier. I don't own very many dresses, only because I usually don't wear them, not because I hate dresses. If I had an occasion that I had to wear them more often, I would."

By the time of the interview, Marta associated the term *femme* less with sex or dress and more with "the emotions, and the dependency. I've always had a vision that femmes are so much more dependent. A lot of people will tease. They'll say, 'Oh, you're such a femme.' And I'll say, 'Oh, you're right. I guess.' I never get upset if people call me a femme. Because I'm very nurturing. I'm very dramatic. I'm emotional; Toni's not. But people who *really* know us will say, 'Toni's the femme and you're the butch. Because you're the one that really runs the show underneath.'

"Let's say I was with someone who was just as emotional, or even more dependent, and very into helplessness. Then I think they would see me more as butch. But I do get helpless. There's some things I cannot do, and I rely on Toni. And there's some things that she just can't do, and she relies on me. I think we're a pretty good balance. She sometimes tends to be a little bit on the butch, but I think I'm attracted to qualities like that, also. Which makes me think I'm more of a femme. Even though I have *both* characteristics, if you wanted an answer to categorize myself am I butch or am I femme, I would say femme.

"Even if I were to be in a bar, and say I saw someone come in. Someone had jeans on, with a little sweatshirt like this. I would say I would be more attracted to that person than someone who came in with wool slacks and a nice silk shirt. Because that's more down to earth, also.

"Two years ago, three years ago, someone would have said I was a butch because I was sitting on a motorcycle. Here I am, this little thing on a motorcycle, with the jacket and the helmet. You look at me and think, 'Oh, my god, what a *dyke!* That butch!' It was hilarious. Or people would just be flabbergasted. 'You drive a motorcycle? *You*, Marta? You're so quiet!' I said, 'I like motorcycles. It has *nothing* to do with that.' And I used to laugh! I said, 'Toni, people think I'm such a butch because I drive a motorcycle! And you know better!' So I said, 'I know what I'm going to do. I'm going to buy a pink helmet and tool along.' She says, 'Don't you dare!'"

SID STEIN: "I'VE SEEN SOME PRETTY CURVACEOUS BUTCHES"

"I don't think I've ever been taken for a femme. Except once, when I went [with] a friend of mine who's butch to a wedding for somebody who she worked with. They took me as a femme there because she seemed butcher than me, and they just figured one of us had to be a femme. So I won the femme award.

"When I first came out in the 1970s, it was sort of uncool to be butch or femme. But I was clearly butch in the relationship that I was in. And we used to play with it sometimes. You know, we'd get dressed up to go out. She would wear little lacy things and I would dress in a tie. In relationships I was mostly attracted to femmes. But it was like you weren't supposed to have roles. You were supposed to be evolved from that sort of thing. I thought of myself as 'butch etcetera.' Later on, when things relaxed a bit, I was more clearly defined.

"Some of it is obviously dress, the way we dressed. But that's just really superficial. And some of it's body language. She was very feminine in body language and I was much less so. And then some of it is the way that emotional issues were dealt with. She tended to be much more open emotionally, much more wanting to talk about stuff. And I tended to be much less that way.

"I think with lesbians it's easier to fool around with being butch if you're femme than it is for women who identify as butch to fool around with being femme. I mean, it's frightening for me to think about wearing a dress. It really is. [Or] putting on makeup. And I know that she didn't particularly have a hard time putting on my clothes or not wearing makeup. Having long hair, all those things were an issue for me. I couldn't do that.

"For me, to be feminine is to feel real vulnerable. It's frightening. It feels degrading. It feels like it's not me. It's confusing. So, I wouldn't do it. I guess it's not the same for women who are femme. I can certainly picture femme women picking up butch body language rather than vice versa." Looking at her past femme lovers, Sid saw "some of the vulnerability. I don't think it's degrading at all. It seems like it's natural. It's just that for me it would be. I'd be forced into something that's not me.

"I think, you know, some of it has to do with [being] molested when I was growing up. And I think that, in a lot of ways, I was treated as the boy in the house. My dad talked about me as if I was a boy, his son, and we did boy stuff together. I really attached to that: That was a safe time, to be around my father, but when I was a girl it wasn't safe. Being treated like a girl, female, anything like that is very uncomfortable for me, because it makes me feel unsafe.

"Sometimes I still have a hard time with having a body that's pretty feminine. Breasts . . . I have hips, thighs . . . I have a feminine

(What you see isn't what you get—a variation of a phrase in computerspeak.)

Rini Das

I grew up in a culture in which eating chicken was a luxury for women. By existing social logic, women in India left the robust, wholesome drumsticks for the men, while my grandmothers, mothers, blood aunts, nonblood aunts, sisters-in-law, girlfriends, and women acquaintances learned to savor and pepper the gizzards, brain, kidneys, liver, breasts, and wings. They lived through the enforced motions of the centuries, chewing the bones of chickens until their content laughter was without teeth.

This incongruous whisper of women osmosis-ed with me. I yearned for the drumsticks because I wanted to be free from the directives of the sexist landscape. Yet I knew how to use the drumsticks to lure my lovers and be lured by them.

Then I came to the United States, where one can fill a platter with combinations of any parts of the chicken that one wants. First I was awestruck by such choice, but I soon got used to it.

Then one tepid fall afternoon, I went to the motor vehicle office in Columbus, Ohio. The American person at the desk with the usual air of busyness attended to my needs; gruff! gruff! I got my license. The person decided to conclude that my non-sari-clad body, baseball cap, bass voice, and short name befitted a member of the penis owners' association.

The person put an "M" in the sex column on the license. Not checking the entry, I signed. On that day, I legitimized my malehood and got as a privilege all the drumsticks I desired. On that day, I could have stopped negotiating the world with my role play as a woman, a woman of color, a lesbian of color.

I have to get the proverbial Green Card to keep living in the United States—the land of choices—and it is easier to get it by marrying somebody. On that day, I got the dubious opportunity to marry someone of my own sex without having medical wonders implanted in me. All I have to do is walk into the homophobic perceptions of the two-hundred-plus-year-old institutions of this country, hold up my volatile crotch, uncrease my drooping breasts, shave my firm chin, and know my lover's favorite color when I am interrogated by my nemesis: the Immigration and Naturalization Services official. Then I am free.

Meanwhile, my hair is growing longer, and my auto insurance agent tells me that I will be statistically discriminated for and get a lower premium if I identify as a woman. My lover convinces me that she'll leave me if I keep putting the distended, burly, tasteless, industrialized drumsticks on her dinner plate. From India, my grandmother calls me. She yammers on and on about her dog, her gout, Romona—her distant cousin. When I interrupt and express my dilemma, she tells me, "Oh! My! You should have understood." She says that for generations all women were doing was duping the men. She says that they gave their men the big and the lumpy, whereas they shared among themselves the digs, the puzzle, the commas, the romance, the exclamations, the jazz, the color, the spice, the rap, the juice of the chicken minus drumsticks. She says, "We are blessed with this tradition. Cherish it." She is a lesbian. As for the driver's license, I have to get it changed. As for the rest of you, "Thanks for nothing!"

---

body. I think sometimes if women can't tell I'm a butch it's partially because my body type is fairly feminine. But I've seen some pretty curvaceous butches. Who made me think they weren't butches!

"I've talked to a lot of women who are butch dykes. They'll talk about not wanting to wear shorts. But I don't see shorts as feminine, particularly. Men wear shorts. I've certainly seen a lot of butches wear shorts, and they didn't particularly look like femmes simply because they were wearing shorts. But [for] the women I've talked to, it's [about] revealing parts of the body. They're more likely to be more feminine parts, you know.

"I didn't wear women's clothes until the last couple of years. The fact that I can do that now says that something's changed. My job makes it more changed. [Before working at the counseling center] I never shopped in a women's store. I buy fairly androgynous clothes, but to me, if it has buttons, it's a woman's jacket! When I first did it I felt, really, like people were going to laugh at me: a butch trying to dress up in women's clothes. I looked real strange. I felt strange. But now I don't feel strange, and I don't have to come home and change out of it, either.

"I didn't want to be a girl when I was a kid. I thought it was some kind of cruel mistake. I didn't want to have a penis, but I wanted to be a boy. I mean, I wanted to be a boy because I thought they had more exciting lives. I never really liked boys. I just didn't want to have breasts and get my period and all that stuff.

"Your role is created when you're a kid, and that's what you are. I think everyone is a little to one or the other [butch or femme]. To me, it doesn't matter what you dress like: You are a role. I have a friend here, an older woman in the city, and everyone thinks that she's butch because she dresses real butch and she's aggressive. And to me there's no way this woman is butch, because [of] her body language. It's just the way she puts her hands on her head, you know? It's just little gestures like that, that say, ah, that's a real femme gesture. She came up in the bars in the era when roles were pretty well defined. Then, she was a femme. [Now] she's slicked back her hair, wears a tie and big boots. But she's a femme.

"I think that butch/femme is beyond what we see ourselves as. Beyond what we want to be, really. I have a friend who goes back and forth. She's a butch. She can say she's a femme; she's a butch. She'll go through a period where she'll say, 'I'm really a femme at heart.' 'Okay, you're a femme at heart. Great. But you're a butch.' But we're not going to fight about it. Now she's a butch again, and she'll probably want to be a femme again for a while.

"Sometimes people don't know what I am, because they picture butches being a lot harder than me or a lot different than me. [They take me as] one of those 'in the middle.' They have a whole different picture of what a butch is. I'm not that, so what am I? They don't know."

How did Sid think she differed from this standard representation of a butch? "Well, I'm not particularly handy. I don't fix shit. I think people don't see that image of butch as liking to read, being kind of intellectual. [You're supposed to be] into that kind of heavy stuff, which I think is a misrepresentation of butches, but nonetheless, people have this image of butches that they are construction workers and hang out in bars and ride motorcycles. I don't ride a motorcycle. I tried to. I got scared, so I didn't do it.

"Middle-class privilege gives one the privilege to pass a little bit more in this culture. I don't pass for straight, but I pass in other ways. I'm acceptable in certain ways that I know women who were raised working-class who are butch are not acceptable.

"I have these friends from Los Angeles. We used to talk about cultural differences: that maybe Jewish butches were a little different, because Jews' education is so emphasized that a lot of times people were not particularly good athletes. I mean, that's a generalization, but. . . . Do good in schoolwork, read a lot, have good conversation, be able to argue. That kind of stuff was what was important in my family and [to] a lot of other Jewish dykes that I know. So consequently we didn't learn to fix things, and I didn't ever play a sport. I hated sports. I don't want to play softball. So I think those kinds of things make different kinds of butches."

LOUISE ROMERO: "THEY ALL SAY I'M FEMME, SO I GO AS FEMME"

"I didn't think I was ever going to work. I was just going to have babies. In fact, I didn't worry about anything, because I always thought, 'Oh, I'll get married, have kids, and the guy will always bring home the money.' Cook, clean the house, maybe a little part-time job doing something. Now it's like I really got to keep a flow of steady money in my pocket, money in the bank above that, where I didn't think I really was going to have to take care of all that stuff on my own. [After coming out] I knew definitely, no one's going to support me.

"I had a boyfriend [in high school]. We had planned to get married and everything. But he was real pushy. Actually, he was real abusive. He didn't like me smoking cigarettes, or he didn't like me working on the cars. He went, 'It's not ladylike! It's not ladylike!' I go, 'But I want to!' All he wanted to do was fuck all the time, and I'd tell him to go stick it in the light socket.

"I was trying to get rid of him. Meanwhile, I was having an affair with this woman, thinking, 'Oh, my god, what is this?' I didn't know I was a lesbian at the time. I just couldn't believe how attracted to her I was! When we first met, we didn't like each other. We almost got in a big fight. She hung around with the little hoods. I had this hat on because it was raining, and she took the hat and threw it on top of a pole. I called her a bitch and I said, 'Get my hat down. Who do you think you are?'

"I was real new. I'd just started high school, just got out of Catholic school, didn't know anybody because I didn't go to public school. So this woman did this, and I was real stubborn. I wasn't about to back down. Finally she shook the pole; the hat came down. But people were standing around: 'Hit her! Hit her! Hit her!' And it was like, 'Go ahead and hit me, bitch!' She never hit me. She just turned around and walked away, and then the next day she came up to me and started talking. We decided it was pretty stupid."

In her late teens, Louise's friend married. "She's always been into sports, so she knows a little bit of self-defense and she was showing me some moves. We were wrestling around. She said, 'Oh, you're not so tough!' All of a sudden I had her pinned down and I just kind of made a pass at her. She responded, and we started making out. Actually, we made out for a *long* time. It was kind of intense, because I was lying on top of her. Then we were staring at each other. And then when I realized she was looking at me, I eased up, and she didn't push me off. I mean, she could have, because I let go. So it was more like I let go and at the same time she was pulling me towards her.

"And then her husband drove up and we just sat there. We weren't doing nothing; we were really scared. The next day we talked about it, and we decided we liked it. We did it again. Then finally I broke up with my boyfriend. I wasn't happy with guys. There was always things you couldn't do because you were a woman. And plus, I didn't like doing it. I didn't like that penis in me. It gave me an upset stomach! I found women's bodies are so much softer. Males seem to be so hard. They tend to be more rough or something. Even with my first boyfriend, I wasn't really attracted to him sexually. It was no *desire*. I wanted to feel orgasms, but I didn't want all this other stuff that came with it!"

At beauty school, Louise met two gay men. "They were the only ones that I knew. I came out to them eventually. I go, 'I can't go out to the bars because I'm not twenty-one. But I want to meet some women!' 'Oh, honey, come with us. They'll never know.' So we did.

"Philip was dressed in drag. He dressed me pretty butch. I mean he stuck this leather jacket on me, stuff like that. I looked young then. I don't know how I got away with it. There were hardly any women [at the bar]. There was something like five women that were heavy-duty into more of the butch-type role. It was all right, but they didn't *speak!* They just sat there and drank. It was kind of intense. How do you approach all this? But at least I knew there was women out there.

"I was really happy, because I didn't have to worry. When I'd go to the women's bars when I first came out, I'd wear all this low-cut, sleazy stuff in style. You know: disco. See, I always worried about being around males and my tits and stuff. A lot of times I go out, I like to wear low-cut blouses, or I love not wearing my bra. I'd wear my T-shirts with my tits hanging out. I could dance and move around and I didn't have to worry about anybody grabbing me or trying to rape me or shit like that.

"Among lesbian women in the community, even if they're racist, they're not trying to be! That's what's funny. You know, they might say something, but I know it's no bad intention, or [that] they hate people of color. Because they just weren't taught, they just don't know.

"But sometimes they just think they know everything. I seen this one [white] woman with this [other] white woman talking about something that has to do with a *black* woman, and I think, 'I'm not black. You're not black. Why do you think you know everything?' This woman is such an asshole! She'd best learn to keep her mouth shut, that's what I tell her. Those kind, I just won't bother with. Unless I want to. If it feels safe, I'm willing, but if it doesn't feel safe to me, I won't do it.

"Most of my friends, they all say I'm femme, so I go as femme. Look, see, I've always been the same. I haven't changed my dress. I do like real pretty dresses: evening gowns, low-cut things. I do. But I hate high heels, so I can never wear those. I think male clothing is made better. Male clothes are more practical to wear, more convenient, more comfortable. If you think wearing T-shirts and Levis are butch, . . . I like dressing up and putting on makeup, too, when I go out. So I don't know if you consider that femme.

"In bed I've never had any butch/femme roles. I've heard about a few stories of women doing that, but I don't like doing that. Sometimes I'm a little aggressive, sometimes I'm not. Sometimes I like the opposite, sometimes I don't.

"I did date a woman that dressed rough and always marched around with the muscles. As a matter of fact, she was a boxer. She had muscles like this! Of course, rode her motorcycle; always in the [gay pride] parade on her motorcycle. When she was at home, she swishes in the kitchen. She'd always cook and she'd swish. I said, 'You're so butch, you swish!' The butcher they are, [the more] they have this little act. It's like they're such little, little, wimpy little things! That's what I've found. They're afraid of flies or something."

Carolyn Fisher: "In Five Minutes, I May Want to Wear a Dress"

"My parents will say they're German before they say they're Cherokee Indian. So as I grew up, it was more being German than being Indian, from whatever reason they had. I think because society looks down on Indians as being drunks, as being lazy, no good. Then when I was in junior high school, I had gotten beaten up because I was German, because we had watched a Holocaust movie. I got teased a lot. That's when I started becoming more proud of being Indian. Just because of the way society said, 'Germans are mean. Germans are no-good people. Look what they did.' And listening to my great-grandmother talk about Indians. It really excited me. It made me proud of it. It was like Indians basically did good, to where the Germans basically were mean and rotten people with bad tempers [laughs]. But now I'm proud of being both.

"You do applications, then if you put Indian they think you're full-blooded Indian, and if you put white . . . I don't like to put myself in the white category. Lots of times I don't feel white and I don't *look* white. If people ask me, I'll tell them. A lot of people tend to think that I'm Latin because of my dark hair, my eyes, my complexion. So that's usually how people know who I am, is because they think, 'Are you Latin or Italian?' 'No. I'm German and I'm Indian.' It's not as important as people knowing that I'm gay. It is a big part of me, though.

"The people that I went to school with didn't dress up, so it made it easy for me to fit in. I think it had a lot to do with being in the country. You walk out and you get all dirty. Everybody basically wore jeans and casual things. The country's not really into fashion. There's nobody to be fashionable for! A lot of women [there], they *look* like dykes. It's very obvious. But there, they just think you're an athlete. They think you're a tomboy. You're country!

"I think I learned a lot of things about myself [from coming out]. More things started coming to me. Like when I was younger, instead of playing with dolls, I was out playing cowboys and Indians. I felt a relief. I felt like now this is who I'm really supposed to be. And now I don't have to go around and put makeup on if I don't want to.

"For me, it's like with a lot of gay women. You could just *look* at them and you go, 'They're gay.' Because it seems like a lot of gay women wear a lot of the same things. The jeans and flannel shirts and T-shirts. They just have that air to them. And that's how I feel like I am. I feel like a lot of people look at me and just say, 'She's a dyke.' And that's okay. I feel good with that. But I was a different person when I came out. Because when people used to say, 'Well, you're just a little dyke,' it's like, 'No! I'm a tomboy! I'm a tomboy, I'm *not* a dyke!' I think I got mad because I knew it was true.

"It was my attitude. The way I dressed. It was far from feminine!

An 'I-don't-give-a-shit' attitude. This is who I am, and fuck you! Now that I look at it, it was more of a carefree attitude. More of a rough, tomboyish attitude. I wasn't out to impress people, *especially* men.

"My mind talks all the time. I have shit going through my mind all the time. I could *imagine* being with a woman, but then it was like, what am I going to do after that? How am I going to get married and have kids? I'm going to get hassled my whole life. Once again I'm going to be in rebellion. And once again I'm going against the grain of society. It was a hard decision for me. And when it really happened—when it came down to me knowing for sure, after being kissed—it was like, yeah, this is what I like. I don't like men touching me, but I like for a woman to touch me. It was *reality*. And if people don't accept you, screw them!

"I came out when I was around eighteen years old. I didn't know *no*body! In the straight community, it doesn't seem like they [mind going] across age that much. But when you get to the gay community, what I've run across is, once I tell someone I'm nineteen years old, then it's like, 'Nineteen years old! You're too young. I don't want to mess with it.' That's probably the hardest and most frustrating thing that I've come across. It's made me think twice of my sexuality.

"I like dark-complected people, Latin people. And just casual. Not real feminine, not real butch. Somewhat like me. Athletic, intelligent. Just recently, I used to be dating a couple of white girls. Which is really unusual, because of their backgrounds. 'Wow, I never went through this before! Going with a white girl.' And I had this thing in my mind to where lesbians aren't rich. Rich people aren't gay. Because I grew up having money. At first it was like, 'Oh, now you can't be gay!' But then after a while, the more it started sinking in that, yeah, I am gay, that meant that I had to break loose and do it on my own. That would mean that I'm not rich. And as I started meeting more [gay] women, there was women who were financially well off."

After moving to San Francisco, Carolyn had to support herself for the first time in her life, so she enrolled in a job-training program that placed women in blue-collar trades. "I could never picture myself working in the financial district wearing a little dress, or sitting behind a desk doing paperwork all day. It'd drive me buggy! I want to be out moving around, being physical and building things and taking things apart.

"I don't like to go out with people who are really femme, because they want you to dominate them the whole time. It's like someone giving you all that power, and I'm not into that. And then I don't like someone real butch, because they intimidate me. I've met some really butch women, and it's like almost looking at a man. I don't like that.

"I think another part of why I'm gay is that I hate for someone to dominate me. Sometimes it's okay, but not all the time. I mean, I tried going with men when I was gay, and it was opening doors for me, walking me home. Ugh! Don't do this to me all the time! I don't like the old-fashioned way of dating. I feel like things should be equal. And that's the way most of my relationships have been.

"Most of the women I go out with could go either way. They like that equalness. And I enjoy that. Some people tease me: 'You are butch, but then you're not. You just can't make up your mind.' I don't feel like I should *have* to make up my mind with something like that. In five minutes, I may want to wear a dress! Who knows? And in the next five minutes, I might want to just get totally butched out. I want that freedom to be able to do what I want. I find in the lesbian community there's a lot of labeling. You're a preppy, or you're butch, or you're femme. Why should I have to go to that? If I want to be casual, that's who I am.

"I've always been a little bit different than what people wanted me to do, and what people were supposed to do. If people were supposed to wear their hair long, I'd wear mine short. Coloring my hair, chopping it all off. I think it *would* be hard for me [to wear makeup and jewelry], because of the way a lot of the community sees lesbians as dykes: as rough and tough and motorcycles and leather and leaning to the butch side. But knowing my personality, I'd probably be like, 'Fuck it if you can't take a joke!'"

GUESSING GAMES: DOUBLE TAKES

Mari (Mary) + macha (the feminine of macho): a specifically Latina, and implicitly working-class, rendition of "dyke." Gossiped about but rarely glimpsed, *la marimacha* embodies an entire range of assumptions about what it takes to make a lesbian. To Marta Rosales's youthful eyes, *la marimacha* Pat was the only gay woman around, visible because she violated gendered expectations. More uniform than wardrobe, Pat's clothing conformed to classic represen- tations of the 1950s street dyke. From her steel-toed boots to her slicked-back hair, her appearance flew in the face of prescriptions for middle-class white womanhood. Marta's reaction to Pat—fear strong enough to make her run away and hide—is a common one in stories that set up a confrontation between childlike innocence and repre- sentations of the Other. That first "real live lesbian" trots on stage as big bad butch, an intimidating creature of another order. But in Marta's case, childhood terror mixed with a retrospective dose of desire: "Nice arms, oh! I still remember that!"

Such is the power of representations that when Marta attempts to measure herself against the standard set by Pat, she can't find a place for herself in the picture. Do I have to wear chinos and roll up a cigarette pack in the sleeve of my T-shirt to be a lesbian? Do I have to be Anglo? Do I have to be tough? Do I have to be like her? If I'm attracted to women but a far cry from all of that, what am I? Marta was not sure whether *marimachas* really existed or whether Pat quali- fied as *marimacha* ("there was one—but she wasn't Hispanic"). *Marimacha* is culturally coded Latina, not just a Spanish translation of "dyke." How could Marta visualize herself as *marimacha,* if the one individual who seemed to bring the category to life was Anglo?

Rather than attempt to regender herself to conform to these rep- resentations, Marta slowly began to modify her idea of what it meant to be gay. Encounters with different kinds of lesbians contradicted some of her original impressions. Imagine: a lesbian with a college degree (that is, not working-class) and "an IQ"! An entire range of gendered possibilities came into view.

Once it becomes obvious that not every lesbian is best described as *marimacha,* gendering recasts itself as a matter of intrigue and an open question. People avail themselves of new categories that elaborate gendered differences. As Marta tried to sort things out, she wondered what made someone femme or butch. Dress? Behavior (timidity, speech patterns, aggression)? Sexuality (oral sex, penetration, assertion, seduction, who's on top)? Emotions (passivity, expressiveness, independence)? Anatomy (the shape and size of breasts, hips, thighs)? Gesture? Occupation? Gender-coded activities? The "evidence" for classifying someone as one or the other tends to take the form of a set of standardized examples: tree climbing; motorcycle riding; wearing makeup or high heels; taking out the garbage; initiating sex. In the course of wondering whether particular individuals met these criteria, Marta also puzzled over how to interpret the criteria and even which ones to apply.

One of the first things people figure out when they begin to hazard a guess is that most "real live lesbians" (or heterosexuals, for that matter) do not fit neatly into gendered categories. Guessing games depend on a problematic tendency to treat people as though they possess a consistent set of gendered "traits." But the world is not so easily divided into masculine and feminine, butch and femme. Louise Romero said she knew gay women who claimed they had never met a femme who worked on cars. In other words, they would define someone who engaged in that (butch-coded) activity right out of the femme category. How was Louise to reconcile the apparent contradiction in her love of mechanics *and* low-cut dresses? Louise's friends called her femme. Was she caught in a framework that forced a choice between two gendered categories?

Marta certainly felt trapped between representations. People found it hard to believe that she rode a motorcycle because they viewed her as quiet and responsible, a "good girl." For Marta, it was "this whole Madonna complex" that rendered her an enigma. The admittedly oversimplified notion of a Madonna complex—which posits "the Madonna" and "the whore" as the two basic positions open to Latinas—runs gendering through Mexican-American identity. Madonna and *marimacha* just don't jibe. But where did that leave Marta?

To complicate matters, many things are not gender-coded in any straightforward fashion. Sid Stein's comments on some butches' reluctance to wear shorts offers a case in point. In and of themselves, shorts are neither masculine nor feminine attire. Both men and women wear them. Only the feminization of bodies brought about when a particularly revealing article of clothing highlights hips and thighs brings this item into the realm of guessing games.

Then, too, there are aspects of the gendering of heterosexual relations that do not find a counterpart in butch and femme. Although it is not uncommon for older men to go out with younger women, Carolyn Fisher found the pain of rejection from older lesbians who considered her too young to date so intense that it "made me think twice of my sexuality." Louise, who had always expected a man to support her, did not transfer that expectation onto her female partners after she came out as a lesbian. And at the same clubs where Louise was taken aback by the silence of women she later identified as butches, she remembered the freedom of dressing as she pleased without worrying about someone refusing to take no for an answer. Their remarks provide another indication that the gendering of lesbian relationships stands in a complex relationship to gendering in the larger society.

People do not carry around gendered traits like a portable CD player or display them like the message on a favorite T-shirt. Gendered traits are called attributes for a reason: People *attribute* traits to others. No one possesses them. Traits are the products of evaluation.

Take the butch who's fond of bubble baths. If her secret passion becomes known, her friends *could* use this potentially discrediting piece of information to reclassify her as androgynous or femme. But they are much more likely to use it to tease her. Why?

People tend to assimilate new material to the story already in place about an individual. Friends end up portraying the bubble bath as the humorous exception to the rule, rather than deciding that someone was a pseudo-butch or closet femme all along. But instances of recategorization do occur. When Sid toyed with the idea that anatomy should override dress or behavior for the purposes of assigning gender, reclassification became the name of the game: "I've seen some pretty curvaceous butches. Who made me think they weren't butches!" But she spoke with wry self-consciousness, since she had just finished describing the coexistence of her own butch identity with a "feminine" body.

People can subject attributes to endless interpretation and reinterpretation. Although women often cited initiating sex as a butch trait, seduction (surely a mode of initiating sex) qualified as femme. Disliking or declining sex was up for grabs in the gender sweepstakes. Players debating the finer points of butch/femme could have it both ways, calling upon one-dimensional representations of untouchable ("stone") butches who live for their femmes' pleasure, or old-fashioned femmes who lie there and take it.

Even Sid, who believed that butches "just are," also believed that butches are made. Growing up Jewish, she maintained, creates "different kinds of butches": "Sometimes people don't know what I am, because they picture butches as being a lot harder than me or a lot different than me." Although Sid contended that a lesbian did not have to be a jock to be butch, she realized that some people questioned her butch identity because she failed to conform to their preconceptions about what a stud should be. Her strategy? To call for more varied, culturally sensitive accounts of what it means to be butch.

Trafficking in the abstractions of gender traits artificially isolates gender from class, race, sexuality, ethnicity, and context. But none of these is discrete. When Carolyn first arrived in San Francisco, she had the impression that "rich people aren't gay." It took her a while to realize that she had fallen for a stereotype that links sexuality to class. Come to find out, queers are not all either unusually wealthy or down-and-out habitués of back-alley bars. In attempting to apply these images to her own situation, Carolyn remembered thinking that she couldn't be gay because her parents owned their own business. Likewise, when Marta predicted her attraction to a woman in sweatshirt and jeans over another in wool slacks and silk shirt, she was talking about a desire that combined class with gender and sexuality. Either outfit could come across as butch.

To grasp what's going on here, you need something more than gendered terminology, because forced dichotomies like butch versus femme do not accommodate multiple lines of identification. With the single word *untraditional,* Marta drew together race, ethnicity, gender, and sexuality in a way that underscored the shock value of her punchline: a Mexican-American family in which the *girl* buys the motorcycle. For Carolyn, childhood memories of playing cowboys and Indians became double-edged tools for figuring out "who I'm really supposed to be." How—or whether—she read herself into the category "Indian" raises a host of questions about power and identification, even in play. In Louise's account, there is an important slippage between her initial claim that she had never encountered racism among gay women and later allusions to racist incidents. A recurrent theme of safety and threat links Louise's discussion of her relations with men in general to the passages about how to relate to Anglo lesbians.

Informing all these discussions are elements of race, class, and ethnicity already built into the gendered representations with the widest circulation. Louise's rendition of femme departs radically from the middle-class assumptions built into Marta's first impressions of femme ("dependent, and very into helplessness"). For Louise, defending herself in a schoolyard scrap was perfectly compatible with femme because, in her working-class neighborhood, the ability to fight didn't necessarily mark you as a tomboy or dyke. Many people said that butches were supposed to be physically active, construction-worker types—all the things that Sid, with her fear of motorcycles, was not. By reworking butch to encompass the intellectual as well as the athlete, Sid interpretively linked education to Jewish culture in a way that countered images of butch as white, Christian, working-class. Street theorist that she was, Sid could not help but note the irony of using oversimplified representations of what's Jewish to counter generalizations about what's butch.

Coining the phrase "butch etcetera" was Sid's way of expanding the term beyond the fuzzy edges supposed to mark the boundaries of butch. There are other strategies to close the gap between self-perception and gendered representations. A person can edit inconsistencies out of her narratives, like the woman who goes into great detail about her softball team and her welding trade, but who "forgets" to tell new friends that she was once a high school cheerleader. A person can locate herself along a continuum from more butch to more femme. Like Louise, she can accept other people's evaluations at face value. Or she can launch herself into perpetual motion like Marta, tacking back and forth between femme and butch. In that case, she may define herself relative to a lover. The old adage that opposites attract, combined with the assumption that butch and femme are always defined as opposites, explains how people could take Sid for femme when she appeared at a wedding alongside an even "butchier" friend.

Women also argued for paying attention to context. Just because driving a motorcycle is a butch signifier, Marta protested, does not mean that everyone's interest in motorcycles relates to gender. According to Carolyn, rough-and-tumble mannerisms might indicate a country girl rather than another dyke-in-the-making. (Note, though, that the urban/rural contrast, like all dichotomies, oversimplifies by representing every city dweller as a white-collar worker with a desk job who never has to worry about getting her clothes dirty.) Their comments draw attention to the importance of what so-called gender traits mean to people.

If you're going to play guessing games, you might as well enjoy yourself. Marta's story about a pink motorcycle helmet drew a lot of laughs because she juxtaposed the color that symbolizes femininity with the machine that signifies toughness. After all, the woman saw herself moving between femme and butch. Why should she pretend otherwise? A "masculine" symbol here, a "feminine" symbol there. . . . Let that pink helmet be a lesson to anyone who tried to stick her with a matching set of gender traits.

Louise derived her pleasure from counterexamples. "You're so butch, you swish," she admonished her lover, a woman who enjoyed cooking in the privacy of her own kitchen after flexing her muscles in public. Marta took delight in the turnabout that placed *la mari-macha* Pat in a position of authority over Marta's father. A complicated negotiation of gender, race, class, and sexuality characterized this relationship: "She respected him as a worker, but he looked down at her for being a dyke." A Chicano worker answering to an Anglo boss challenges little about the power relations that structure labor markets in the United States, but a lesbian (and a butch one at that) supervising a man in a blue-collar job is turnabout indeed. Carolyn thought she would have a hard time wearing makeup and jewelry precisely *because* the most common representations of gay women are masculinized. Yet she responded with a power play: It's my prerogative to challenge your expectations of me and throw them back in your face.

In contrast to these anecdotes of playfulness and transgression, much of the repartee about gendered differences is organized by the erroneous presumption that people can be determined to be absolutely, unequivocally, essentially, irrevocably butch, femme, androgynous, or what have you. There's lots of cultural reinforcement for tracking down one's "true" self (whatever that means). But even four narratives give ample indication that people are not that consistent, and their identifications aren't limited to gender. Why, then, continue to play the game?

A hidden stake in guessing games is the power to claim the insight or expertise to determine who's who. Take Sid's friend—the one who calls herself femme, but whom Sid insisted upon characterizing as a butch dressed up in women's clothes. Did Sid see something her friend missed when it came to gender? Or was Sid's friend whatever she considered herself to be? What about the woman who says she doesn't like the way the terms *femme* and *butch* flatten out her experience, but whose friends argue that "anyone can tell" she plays fluff (femme) to her partner's stud (butch)? These are questions of voice and authority endemic to identity politics. Are people the best judges of their own minds and experiences? Who can speak for whom? Just how transparent is experience, anyway? Rather than being self-evident, isn't "experience" open to conflicting interpretations?

When all is said and done, no one has the inside track on the gendering of lesbian relationships. There is no consensus about what makes someone butch or femme, because there can't be. The search for gender traits is never-ending, because traits are not lying in wait to be discovered. But that doesn't make gendered categories like femme and butch meaningless. Gendering is produced in social interactions and structured by representations. Louise rejects a boyfriend who pressures her to stop working on cars. Carolyn searches for words to describe her first date with a white woman. Marta imagines gendering herself differently in relation to different lovers. Sid ranks body language over dress as an index of gendered differences.

Guessing games may be part of the process of creating and recreating gender, but that does not account for their popularity. What seduces people into looking for an authentic answer to the questions, "What are you?" and "Who is she, *really?*" Some of the pleasure lies in the playing of the game. Like Carolyn Fisher, many people have minds that talk all the time when they try to place one another with respect to gender. Where they find their answers and what they use as evidence have as much to do with history as idle talk.

FURTHER READING

Burana, Lily, Roxxie, and Linnea Due, eds. *Dagger: On Butch Women.* San Francisco: Cleis Press, 1994.

Faderman, Lillian. "The Return of Butch and Femme." *Journal of the History of Sexuality* 2, no. 4 (1992): 578–96.

Feinberg, Leslie. *Stone Butch Blues.* Ithaca, N.Y.: Firebrand Books, 1993.

Kennedy, Elizabeth Lapovsky, and Madeline D. Davis. *Boots of Leather, Slippers of Gold: The History of a Lesbian Community.* New York: Routledge, 1993.

Nestle, Joan. *A Restricted Country.* Ithaca, N.Y.: Firebrand Books, 1987.

Nestle, Joan, ed. *The Persistent Desire: A Femme-Butch Reader.* Boston: Alyson Publications, 1992.

Newton, Esther. "The Mythic Mannish Lesbian." In *The Lesbian Issue: Essays from SIGNS.* Ed. Estelle B. Freedman, Barbara C. Gelpi, Susan L. Johnson, and Kathleen M. Weston, pp. 7–25. Chicago: University of Chicago Press, 1985.

Stevens, Robin, ed. *Girlfriend Number One: Lesbian Life in the 90s.* Pittsburgh: Cleis Press, 1994.

Trujillo, Carla, ed. *Chicana Lesbians: The Girls Our Mothers Warned Us About.* Berkeley: Third Woman Press, 1991.

Weston, Kath. "Do Clothes Make the Woman?" *Genders* 17 (1993): 1–21.

SEVENTEEN

BUTCH MOTHERS, FEMME BULL DYKES:
DISMANTLING OUR OWN STEREOTYPES

JoAnn Loulan

In 1994, a memorial service was held for Rikki Streicher, one of San Francisco's most important and well-loved lesbian activists. She was sixty-nine years old when she died, and in her lifetime had started many of the bars, social clubs, and baseball teams that had been an essential part of the lesbian landscape of that city for thirty years. Speakers reminisced about the important part Rikki had played in their lives and the life of the community. Many people nodded as some characteristic behavior or attitude of hers was mentioned. She was blunt. She told people how they should conduct their lives. She mentored young lesbian politicians and organizers. She encouraged people to give their money and time to lesbian causes and political candidates. She was always open to opinions that might change hers. She was generous to all who crossed her path.

Judging from the people stuffed into the church, the anterooms, and the gardens, her reach extended to lesbians of all ages, to gay men, to straights, to city and county officials, as well as to state senators. The American flag flew at half mast over City Hall the day she died.

In the midst of the service, one young woman who got up to speak said she had been asked many times whether our fallen sister had been a "mother figure" to her. She and the rest of the assembled then laughed heartily. "No," the speaker said, "I wouldn't say she was a mother figure." No one offered a reason why this nurturing and loving presence in the lesbian community was not a mother figure, except that we all agreed she didn't look like one. She looked like a butch lesbian.

In all the time I had spent with Rikki, I never thought to ask her how she defined herself. Did she call herself butch? She was from that generation who had come out in the time of butch/femme relationships in the 1940s and 1950s and then were confronted with a whole new breed of sisters. Women coming out in the 1970s earnestly questioned all the values and standards of lesbian culture from a newly understood and incorporated feminist perspective. There was little understanding among this new generation of the butch/femme lifestyle. Many young feminist lesbians bought the line that straight culture had been repeating relentlessly: Delineations of butch and femme in relationships between women were a sorry attempt to copy heterosexual sex roles.

Butches and femmes were vilified. Many either retreated from this new judgmental community, welcomed a change and jumped on the androgyny bandwagon, or simply denied their identification while everyone around them categorized them anyway.

The feminist lesbian cultural revolution in the 1970s left many in the community out in the cold and left a gap in our heritage for women who came out at this time. In the most profound sense, this rejection of our past, our social and cultural history, has taken its toll on our sense of our sexual and emotional selves. How could we imagine it would be possible to make sense of our newfound lesbian identities while dismissing and denying our history and the women who had come before?

When we think of a mother, we think of someone who nurtures, forgives, teaches, protects, and keeps family and its traditions together. Rikki Streicher kept her bar, Maud's, open 365 days a year so lesbians would always have a place to go. She provided holiday dinners at the bar because she knew that many out lesbians could not go back to their family of origin for gatherings. She offered activities like baseball teams, pool playing, dancing, and, most of all, safety from a world of hatred. She created a family in the Bay Area that endured for decades. She certainly made and kept our family traditions. What does it mean that we don't think of such a woman as a mother figure? She was one of the great mothers of the San Francisco lesbian community from the 1950s until her death.

I mentioned Rikki's memorial because it underscores the point that in regard to our lesbian sexualities we still have our gender identification tied to the archetypes of the majority culture. We have a lesbian cultural stereotype that butches are dominant, assertive, aggressive, and self-reliant. We carry in our subconscious the cultural message that mothers are passive. This is a basis not only for society's misogyny but also for our own internalized misogyny. For even as the notion that women are passive objects is abhorrent to feminist lesbians whose consciousness has been forever changed by the women's liberation movement, we are nonetheless affected by it.

This is especially true when it comes to sex. We do not expect mothers to be active sex partners; we expect them to acquiesce to fathers. We are ashamed that our mothers have learned this behavior, and we want them to be different. We admire the stereotype that says butches are sexually active, and at the same time we are ashamed that we are valuing the perceived role of fathers in the sexual world. When we value that notion, we devalue our mothers. It also confuses us about what is active and passive when it comes to lesbian sex.

We think mothers should look like the mothers we grew up with, yet in the lesbian family, they don't always come in that package. And if there is an archetypal father figure in the lesbian community, we are careful not to talk about it. (Actually, the lesbian S/M community has a designation of Daddy, which is specifically sexual. However, most lesbians are reluctant to accept anything identified with the S/M community, especially when the world at large might think we are acting like men.)

The Mother/Father issue plays right into our worry that lesbian sex has something to do with female/male roles. We do inherently accept a lesbian version of sex-role stereotyping, even though we deny it. The laughter at Rikki's memorial gathering reflected this belief. And at the same time, the preoccupation with not appearing as any "type" or "role" undermines our exploration of our sexual inner selves.

This notion becomes an issue with lesbian sex because the stereotype of female as passive and male as active does not make sense in the lesbian world. I contend that lesbian sex has nothing to do with female/male sex. In lesbian relationships, one partner may be passive today and active tomorrow. The mood might change in the midst of sex, and the partners may change their activity. A lesbian may change her primary way of having sex with a new partner.

We worry that something will be found out that relates us to the girl/boy thing. How can the heterosexual paradigm fit when a lesbian is likely to be someone who straps on a dildo, makes love to her partner, and then takes it off and lets her partner do the same to her? We can be top in the streets, bottom in the sheets. We can be an ultimate femme who is a top. We can be androgynous and have lesbian lovers of all types and engage in all kinds of sexual activities.

We are struggling for self-definition in a culture that has kept our consciousness in a tight-fitting box. This box contains the only sexual models that the majority thinks are acceptable. We are stuck in a world that has a male-centered gender construct. It has its historical roots and is reinforced in the modern filters of psychology, sociology, and anthropology. And finally, it is endlessly reflected in the culture.

Our presence in the world as female sexual beings in relation to other females is a complete confrontation of this cultural stereotype. Simply by being with other women we defy heterosexual standards. Lesbian sexuality innately exposes the limitations of these traditional gender definitions. We have complex inner lives reflected in our taste in clothes, women, sex, and sex toys. We break all rules. Unfortunately, we also are inculcated with the same world view as straights, one based on the polarities/dichotomies of male-defined gender stereotypes.

It is my feeling that our lesbian sexuality, our gender expression, our actual sex lives exist outside that box. Yet our consciousness is still forced into it. This thinking undermines our sense of well-being. We make apologies for our way of being sexual, and we try to fit it into some pattern. We try to explain it in the dichotomies of the culture; or in reaction to them, we claim it is the opposite. It is neither. Lesbian sex is outside anything we have been taught. It is difficult to think in what terms lesbian sex actually exists.

Not unlike the people who first said the world was round when conventional wisdom held that it was flat, I am talking about a revolutionary change in consciousness. We must learn to conceptualize our lesbian sexuality in a circle—the moving around and around that seems never to stop on one point, but always to be moving to another position. We must think in terms of a circle: no beginning and no ending.

The laughter at our butch sister's wake reflected a narrow vision of how a lesbian can be. A mother? Yes, she was, one of the best we have known. One of the ones we treasured when she was here and mourn now that she is gone. She was a butch woman who flew in the face of convention. I do not presume to speculate on her sexual life; I am interested in exploring the imagery of "Butch Mother."

As the rest of the world is busy creating its slow changes in the sex roles of women and men, lesbians have been busy living a sexual revolution. No one has been paying attention, of course, because we are outlaws, outside the conversation. And we have not found language yet to describe what this revolution is really about.

Our unique situation is not addressed in the dominant culture. We are seen, paradoxically, as both prudes in the queer world (gay men, of course, are perceived as more sexually active) and as nymphomaniacs in the heterosexual world (which thinks we are having sex with each other all the time). Even within our own family, lesbians have few words that specifically refer to our sexual identities: *butch, femme, androgyny.* All these words carry baggage.

The homophobic responses butch lesbians sometimes experience within the lesbian community mirror the disdain they feel from the rest of the culture. The femme lesbian is often mistaken as a straight woman and accused of trying to "pass" in the dominant culture. In the 1970s many feminist lesbians created an androgynous image as a reaction to what we saw as male-identified sex-role stereotypes. This powerful and obviously useful new alternative for our sexual expression gave many lesbians a way of better expressing who we felt we were. (Even the word *androgyny* puts the male principle first in the mix, though. Why don't we use *gynandry?*)

I contend that there are many more sexualities than butch, femme, and androgynous. To begin with, our sexuality includes many aspects of our lives that make a rich tapestry. Sexuality means everything from our sense of ourselves, our stance, our attitude, our attraction to others, to how we have sex, what we think is a turn-on, our vulnerable areas, who we have sex with, how we attract others, what sex acts we participate in, how much we want to make love to someone else, and how much we want to be done by them.

We may be nervous about telling those truths of our sexuality because we have been unconsciously accepting the majority culture's opinion that our sex is wrong. But standing up to the majority by not dressing, acting, or having sex as women are taught to will only enhance our sexuality. At the same time we also have to reinvent categories to help us understand who we are.

Lesbians have a great advantage in that we are not locked into a system that makes one of us more or less powerful than the other simply because of our gender. However, how do we cope with the reality that within our lesbian culture we have different gender identities? How do partners articulate and demonstrate these differences without parodying the roles of straight women and men? Does a question exist in the back of our minds that we may be performing a parody if we use a dildo with our lover? Can a woman be a top and use a dildo, and wear short hair and jeans and not be seen as male?

How do lesbians let each other know who we are without the world's recrimination? The fact that some lesbians wear their hair short and dress in what are considered men's clothes throws some people into homophobic rage that leads them to harass, beat up, and sometimes kill these women. What do we think people are seeing in a simple matter of style? They are seeing male wannabes who intend to be sexually aggressive with women. That may not come out in conversation, but lesbians are seen as a challenge to the mother/father, passive/active, female/male cultural archetypes.

My concern is that we might not see suitable alternatives to androgynous gender expression. The pain that comes with not seeing ourselves reflected in our culture is immense. The agony of feeling out of place all the time, the pain of being rejected even by our lesbian sisters, makes some of us believe that our gender identity must be male. Many women believed as girls that they were male-identified because that was the only alternative to female.

I believe there are thousands of genders. We have a sense of who we are at a very early age. As the socialization process takes place, we must try to fit into the narrowly defined sex roles that our culture assigns us. I believe that in some cases, our essential natures are socially constructed out of us. Many women have to go through an elaborate journey of dismantling this construction to find their way back to their essential nature as women-loving women.

While heterosexual gender stereotypes tend to be rigid, lesbians have gender identities that are liberating. We have an opportunity to do everything differently. We are held to no standard. We may keep the gender vision we had as a young child. We may be fluid in our gender expression, changing with a lover or with age or with different political awareness. There is nothing chaining us to the rules of biology. We are the errant gene; we are their biggest nightmare.

We do pay a great price in our revolutionary lives for being sexual outlaws. We lose our families of origin, we are fired from jobs, our relationships are not taken seriously, our children are taken from us. People make up who we are and what we do with each other in bed. In the absence of our truth, they hate us in their ignorance.

At the beginning of an affair or new relationship, we are acting on impulse. After the initial fever dies down, we begin to have self-conscious sex. We commonly stop having sex as the months and years go by because we do not have a core sense of our sexuality that feels valid to us. Our essential sexual nature has been demeaned or denied. Our unique gender identification is missing. We don't have role models. We often cannot access the emotional strength to re-invent ourselves at night after a long day in a world that hates us.

It is difficult to begin talking to our lovers about our doubts and fears. This silence between us comes from a long tradition of having our reality annihilated by the majority culture. In addition, the 1970s brought a feminist lesbian standard that monitors and judges sexual activity among women, as if it were possible to make us con-form simply from a political analysis. Both these phenomena make us fearful of telling our sexual truths.

In a sense, we are scared to be lesbians. We police our behavior and even our thoughts, so we won't find ourselves out there by acci-dent in what we think is girl/boy territory. We obliterate traces of what we think may be heterosexual behavior while measuring our behavior completely by that standard.

I find it fascinating that if someone asks lesbians to describe our-selves with adjectives, we tend to answer in stereotypical ways that have little to do with how we really are. In *The Lesbian Erotic Dance,* I presented the results of a survey that showed that, if given a list of human characteristics, lesbians most likely described butches as dominant, masculine, athletic, forceful, assertive, or aggressive. Femmes were described as feminine, gentle, affectionate, warm, ten-der, or helpful. Androgynous women were described as individualis-tic, adaptable, independent, yielding, self-sufficient, or self-reliant.

In the November 1994 issue of *Dykespeak,* a Bay Area lesbian newspaper, a letter to the editor made reference to "lesbian sex experts who, by their own admission, have sex with men." My name was included in this list. This rumor has been floating through the lesbian community for some time. I have heard it on both coasts, and have been asked about it on national television. Individual lesbians approach me about it. My lover once overheard someone in an audience say, as I came out on stage to speak, "Oh, I didn't know she was straight." The comment was a result of my appearance alone. Now I begin all my speeches with "I'm JoAnn Loulan and I'm a lesbian. Are there any other lesbians here?"

I have not had sex with men since I came out twenty years ago. However, on my own scale I am a No. 1 femme and proud of it. I identify as a femme bull dyke—that is, a strong, political, powerful, loud, proud dyke in a dress. Yet my gender identity as a revolutionary lesbian makes me suspect in my own community. Our stereotypes about what a real lesbian is will likely override any information we may receive to the contrary. Visual images are powerfully wrapped up in the heterosexual paradigm.

How do we get past the stereotypical belief that there cannot be a Femme Bull Dyke or a Butch Mother? The question becomes how to get back to our essential lesbian sexual nature to create the sex lives we want. How can we get out a dildo without the thought that this is a penis substitute? How can we want our lover to lie on her back and let us come at her without thinking of the heterosexual stereotype? How can we claim our own territory?

We need to create a language to express what most of us know and live, but cannot seem to explain to anyone else or even to ourselves. The old language simply constricts and limits us. There are categories of lesbians. There is no reason to eschew categorization. In fact, I think it is powerful. Ever since a critical mass of us has established a category of "lesbian" by standing up, coming out, and simply saying, "We are lesbians," we have been coming up with common ways to define that group. We need more ways to define ourselves.

It is my contention that on the 1–10 butch/femme scale, we do indeed know the difference between a 2 and a 3 or a 4 and a 9. The question is how to explain these differences when they aren't based on appearance or sexual activity. What are the differences, exactly? They include attitudes, various gender identifications, ways of holding ourselves, ways of seeing ourselves as the object or the objectifier. The point is supporting each other to be and become all that we want. Acting in ways that turn us on. Coming on to our lovers in ways that turn them on. How can we love each other and continue to feel good?

As a spiritual teacher has said: If you want to keep your cow, give it a bigger pasture. If we want to keep the creativity and excitement that have always been lesbian, then we must be open to larger truths. We must create words that express our reality. We need to accept that the World of Lesbiana is round, and it includes Butch Mother and Femme Bull Dyke living vibrantly among us.

FURTHER READING

Burana, Lily, Roxxie, and Linnea Due, eds. *Dagger.* San Francisco: Cleis Press, 1994.

Butler, Judy. *Gender Trouble.* New York: Routledge, 1990.

Faludi, Susan. *Backlash.* New York: Anchor, 1991.

Feinberg, Leslie. *Stone Butch Blues.* Ithaca, N.Y.: Firebrand Books, 1992.

Foucault, Michel. *The History of Sexuality.* Vol. 1. New York: Vintage, 1980.

Grahn, Judy. *Another Mother Tongue.* Boston: Beacon, 1984.

Loulan, JoAnn. *The Lesbian Erotic Dance.* Minneapolis: Spinsters Book Company, 1990.

Nestle, Joan. *A Restricted Country.* Ithaca, N.Y.: Firebrand Books, 1987.

Nestle, Joan, ed. *The Persistent Desire: A Femme-Butch Reader.* Boston: Alyson, 1992.

Ortner, Sherry, and Harriet Whitehead, eds. *Sexual Meanings: The Cultural Construction of Sexuality.* New York: Cambridge University Press, 1981.

EIGHTEEN

DOUBLE TROUBLE

Lesléa Newman

"Trash, Flash," I say, reminding my beloved that it is time to put the cans by the curb. "In a second," she grunts as the Starship *Enterprise* zooms across our TV. Ten minutes later I plant myself in front of Counselor Troi's cleavage to remind her again. "Next commercial," she promises.

Why don't I just take out the garbage myself? Because rubbish is a butch job.

Yes, Flash and I are a bona fide butch/femme couple. Contrary to popular belief, butch/femme did not disappear with the beehive hairdos of the fifties. No, we have not changed our lifestyles, only our hairstyles (thank God). Only in our case, it's femme/butch. Just because Flash wears the pants in this family doesn't mean she's always on top.

So what makes me the femme and Flash the butch? Is it that, unlike Flash, I have never been called "Sir" once in my entire life? Is it that, unlike me, Flash hasn't worn a skirt since 1967, the year she shed her nun's habit? No.

It's just something you're born with. According to family legend,

257

my first words were, "Got any mascara?" Baby Flash, on the other hand, went through her childhood with holes in her jeans and frogs in her pockets. I am thrilled to have found Flash, who truly appreciates the femme that I am, unlike my last girlfriend, who forbade me to wear high heels (except in bed). Flash is the butch of my dreams. As soon as I met her, I knew I would marry her. As soon as we started dating, Flash cut her hair as short as she had always wanted to, and I started wearing my skirts tighter and my heels higher. At our wedding, there was never any question about who would wear a dress and who would wear trousers. As they say in *Glamour Dyke* magazine, "The femme is the picture, the butch is the frame."

Some lesbians think the whole butch/femme thing is passé. I pity those girls who take out personals looking for a woman, but "no butches, please." At first I thought they meant "no bitches, please." But when I caught on, I couldn't believe it. Don't you girls know that any butch worth her weight in Brylcreem will do anything to please her femme? The first time I read a "no butches" personal, I was relieved. At least I could stop worrying that some young lipstick lesbian would pull Flash right out from under me—after all, a good butch is hard to find. But then I got mad. How dare anybody underestimate our darling butches after everything they've done for us? Even though we femmes have to put up with straight men coming on to us all the time, it's my butch who puts herself in danger just by walking out our front door in her freshly pressed trousers and black muscle shirt. And when Flash and I go out together, it's double trouble. It's obvious that there's something going on between us, though some people aren't quite sure what. Whenever we eat out, our servers always stumble. Sometimes they'll say, "What'll it be, ladies?" even though Flash is no lady. Other times they'll say, "What can I get you guys?" even though I am certainly not a guy. If I was asked for advice, I'm not sure what I'd tell them to say. "Two for lunch, Lesbians?" just doesn't sound right.

And so to solve the problem, we often eat at home, which means there is a lot of garbage to be taken out. And here it is, 8:30 P.M. on

Sunday and Counselor Troi is lying in sick bay with the lovely Dr. Crusher about to examine her. It would be cruel to disturb Flash at a time like this. And so just this once, I take out the garbage myself. No sooner am I back in the house than the phone rings. "Lesléa," my neighbor Mitzi says, horrified, "was that *you* taking out the trash?"

"Yes," I admit, reluctantly. "Flash is knee-deep in *Star Trek* and I let her get away with it. But just this once."

"That's a relief," Mitzi says. "I saw you out my window, and my whole take on butch/femme was instantly destroyed."

Not to worry, world. Butch and femme are here to stay.

NINETEEN

BLACK LACE HAIRBOW

Greta Gaard

It was a black lace hairbow, worn at a time when such hairbows were in fashion for femmes of all sexualities, and I was wearing it all right. I wore that hairbow all during one particular summer, while dating a talented hockey dyke. Whether we were out dancing, skating, or hiking, my hairbow signaled femme power. In defiance of heteronormativity, I scooped up my hair with black lace to please women only: my lover and myself.

At summer's end, I received an offer not to be missed: an extended climbing trip with two of the best male climbers around. In the weeks before the trip, the three of us climbed together as much as possible, practicing various setups for the anchors, rappelling, multi-pitch climbs, and different routes. On these practice climbs, my hair-bow served many purposes. It marked my femme strength and style; it kept the hair out of my face during some precarious moves; and—based on my method of climbing chimneys, which requires using not only hands and feet but occasionally the back of my head—the hair-bow was dubbed my special "fifth hold."

At the end of August, we set out for the Needles of South Dakota, where we climbed pinnacles of quartz and signed summit registers with pencils sharpened by our teeth. I became enamored with this setting of physical strength, the late summer sun, and perilous adventure, whose embodiment seemed to be Dave himself, always grinning or whistling. Somewhere between a three-pitch climb in the Needles, Mt. Rushmore, and Devil's Tower, we became lovers. When the trip ended, we drove home across South Dakota, laughing lustily and singing along with a song by Two Nice Girls—something about how one woman's queer life had been complicated by the love of a strong man.

Little did I realize just how complicated mine would get.

Back in the small town where I worked, the climate chilled for more reasons than autumn. A few weeks after my return, one co-worker approached me to whisper, "I've heard you're dating a MAN! But of course that's just a filthy rumor," she concluded, inviting explanation from me. I confirmed She backpedaled, wished me happiness, and left hastily. Then my ex-from-hell broke her vow of silence and telephoned me to see if it was true. Sweetly, I reminded her that even she had dated a man before dating me, a segment of her life conveniently deleted from the databanks of collective memory, since she had dutifully denounced the relationship and all men thereafter. The conversation ended as pleasantly as it had begun, and I continued to date Dave.

In public with Dave on Saturday afternoons shopping, or Thursday nights at the theater, I felt suddenly watched, judged. While queers worried about hiding their sexualities in this homophobic little town, my concerns went the other way: I didn't want the lesbian community I still cared about to monitor me holding hands with Dave, laughing with him, having breakfast. Determined to maintain lesbian connections, I went to the coffeehouse alone, leaving Dave to fend for himself by playing pull-tabs and watching football in the local pub. Women still spoke to me there, but they never asked about my personal life—a strange omission in a town of that size. Of course, they knew.

Meanwhile, another community was also taking notice. Co-workers who had been intimidated by my politics or my partners suddenly became friendly. At the symphony or in restaurants, employees who knew me by name now addressed their questions to Dave alone, while I stood by, strangely silenced. I still wore my lace hairbow, but it had taken on a different meaning. My femme strength had been mistranslated by all these viewers to mean heterofeminine submission, and the flood of their misreadings seemed to drown out my own erotic.

Luckily, just when I was about to throw in the hairbow, I met Beth. For her, Dave and I were clearly visible as queers. It was Beth who joked that we should find him an extra-large T-shirt that read, "I'm not a lesbian, but my girlfriend is!" It was Beth who brought me back to dancing at the gay bars. Finally, it was Beth who gave me a way of describing my sexual orientation as a composite of biological sex, gender identity, gender role, sexual identity, and sexual practices. With these components, I could finally name my sexuality to myself and to others: woman, female, femme, lesbian, and bisexual.

It's been four years since my last bisexual dating experience, and I've been merrily monogamous with a woman for the last three. Of course, thanks to Beth, I've still got the hairbow.

THE PUBLIC WORLD

TWENTY

LESBIANS IN CORPORATE AMERICA

Maria De La O

Before large numbers of middle-class women heeded the feminist call of the 1970s to get out of the home and enter professions, the image of the woman who climbed the ladder of corporate success was already well-worn. The antithesis of the ideal, nurturing mother, she was often unmarried, childless, and stereotyped as mannish, domineering, and power-hungry— in other words, she was seen as a dyke. The image was damaging enough for heterosexual women, so it certainly gave lesbians in the business world every reason to play it straight.

Since the 1970s, society has told women that it's okay, even expected, to work outside the home. We now have new stereotypes, like that of the superwoman, a creature of seemingly boundless energy who can take care of both her work and her family with ease. As visibility of women in our professional workforce steadily increases, issues like sexual harassment and advancing beyond the glass ceiling are now serious topics for discussion.

During the past few years, gay rights groups have been pushing gay, lesbian, and bisexual workers to come out and have successfully lobbied companies to do something about workplace discrimination based on sexual orientation. Some companies have responded by officially sanctioning gay-employee organizations and newsletters. Others have added "sexual orientation" as a category to in-house diversity training sessions that have traditionally dealt with race, gender, and religion. Still others have revised their equal-opportunity policies to ban discrimination based on sexual orientation. And the most progressive companies, spurred by policy enacted by the Lotus software development corporation in 1991, have given domestic-partner benefits to employees who are in same-sex relationships. These packages, sometimes also offered to unmarried heterosexual couples, attempt to equalize the benefits that married employees and their spouses receive through the company, such as bereavement leave and health insurance.

These efforts have had a snowball effect. As more and more companies welcome gays, lesbians, and bisexuals, more and more CEOs are deciding that, to compete for the best and brightest employees, they must match or beat gay-friendly policies offered by similar companies. At the same time, according to a 1992 survey of 1,400 gay men and lesbians in Philadelphia, 76 percent of gay men and 81 percent of lesbians hide their orientation to some degree at work.

In the midst of all this change, why are lesbians still playing it straight? What strategies are lesbians using to get ahead, or just to survive, in the business world? Are the issues that are important to lesbians in corporate America more allied with those that are important to gay men or to women in general? To find some answers, I went to the source: I interviewed fifteen lesbians in their twenties and thirties who work as professionals.

WHY THEY DO WHAT THEY DO

The women I interviewed all work in a strictly corporate environment—that is, they are not in academia, the government, or the military, or self-employed as lawyers, doctors, writers, or therapists.

While these white-collar professionals might have similar educational backgrounds, skills, and incomes as people who work in corporations, they do not work in the same business milieu.

The women I interviewed also grew up in a generation where, for the first time in the United States, it was commonly presumed that little girls could grow up and have careers. This expectation was true both for women who grew up in middle- and upper-middle-class families as well as for those who could only aspire to middle-class status. I interviewed women whose backgrounds ranged from lower to upper middle class. For the most part, they do not link their sexual orientation to their professions or to their specific areas of interest in business. In other words, I did not find any jobs that are perceived by lesbians as preferable because they are "lesbian fields." Like most people, these women decided on a career based on their interest in the work and their financial needs.

Emily is typical. Now a thirty-three-year-old project manager for a large computer company, she grew up in a lower-middle-class Pentecostal white family. By the time she attended college, it was no longer a rarity for women to want to enter the engineering professions.

At her longtime job in a somewhat stuffy corporation, she has worked both in a small, conservative Colorado town and in the liberal San Francisco Bay Area. Explaining her career choice, she states matter-of-factly: "I knew even before I came out that I was going to have to take care of myself financially. The thought of marrying someone to take care of me financially never entered my head. So I went for a bachelor's degree in electrical engineering, which, in 1979, was not only the degree to have but something I enjoyed."

Sara, who at thirty-one is the CEO of her own health instrumentation company, has another fairly typical response: "I do what I love. I knew at an early age I was going to be a scientist. Nothing could stop that." One gets the feeling that nothing much could stop Sara. Although she is now a successful professional, she grew up in a "relatively poor" white family, the last child born to parents in the mountains of Arkansas before they moved to Texas.

Another thirty-one-year-old woman, Margot, a transportation engineer, wryly explains: "I always wanted to be an engineer, and my parents, good Chinese parents that they are, they very transparently thought, 'Thank goodness, she can find a good job and support herself.'"

Margot went to school in Oregon, but moved to California when she got her first job and never left. She now lives in Santa Cruz, a small coastal town known for its large population of lesbians. Although she has gotten several out-of-town job offers since moving to Santa Cruz, she says, "I've dismissed the thought of potential jobs based on what town or state it would be in."

Although what originally attracted these women to their careers was not related to their lesbianism, almost all of them say that it influences where they choose to live. Not surprisingly, it is important for most to live and work in or near urban centers with large lesbian communities. Most manage to do this fairly easily because the majority of big businesses are located in or around major metropolitan areas.

Some also say that their sexual orientation directly influences not only the area of the country in which they work but also the *company* for which they work. For example, Yun is a twenty-three-year-old Taiwanese American who grew up in an upper-middle-class Jewish and Italian suburb in Massachusetts. Although she sports a military-style haircut and wears Doc Marten boots to her Silicon Valley job, she hasn't directly told any of her nongay co-workers about her sexual orientation. She says she would eventually like to reveal her lesbianism to her colleagues. She feels positive about being a lesbian in the computer field, an industry that has recently gained notoriety as a leader in progressive policies aimed at lesbian and gay workers: "I feel like I do have more opportunities in the computer field, because there are a lot of companies that support same-sex partnerships, which is great. This is partly also why I chose to work at [my company], because it is so supportive of sexual diversity."

Although many computer companies have instituted gay-friendly policies to tap lesbian and gay talent, they don't all welcome gays and lesbians. Emily describes herself as out to her boss and her co-workers, but she is still somewhat wary of letting the entire company know about her sexual orientation. She says that at her job, at one of the oldest and most traditional companies in the computer field, she doesn't expect to rise to the top levels of the corporate ranks because "to advance you have to be male, Mormon, and married."

Although Emily is thinking about switching careers in a few years, she will stay with her current company for the time being. Her corporation's traditionalism has not made her seek a more progressive employer, but it has influenced where she works within the company.

The stringent dress code within certain departments in her company encourages her to stay in her present position, in research and development, where she can arrive at work wearing jeans, a black leather jacket, and hiking boots: "I landed in R&D sort of by accident, but I stayed in R&D because I can be myself—butch—and have fun. Although I am somewhat interested in marketing, I would never want to work in marketing because I'd have to dress up all the time."

CORPORATE HOMOGENEITY

Yun and Emily allude to one of the most important aspects of working within a company: fitting in. Although leaders of U.S. companies like to invoke ideas about "American individuality" and "ingenuity" while pointing to other countries, chiefly Japan, as places where corporations quash difference and encourage a cookie-cutter mentality, few U.S. CEOs encourage much diversity within their workforce. Employment decisions, including promotions, are made not just on the basis of who can do a job but on the basis of who can do the job while getting along smoothly with his or her co-workers. Company parties or events are more than just opportunities to let off steam: They are also forums for bosses and workers to evaluate one another in a different context, and, depending on what takes place, social events become tools to bond a corporate community.

Employees are often expected to bring their spouses or dates to company events. As James Woods explains in his book, *The Corporate Closet,* this expectation creates a double standard. When heterosexuals bring a spouse or a date to a party, they are perceived as fulfilling a societal expectation. When a gay man or lesbian brings a partner to a party, he or she is perceived as calling attention to his or her sexuality.

This double standard can result in a high level of stress for lesbian or gay employees who are expected to attend company events. Vickie, thirty, is an athletic fourth-generation Californian. Although she is out to most of her department co-workers at her job as an electrical engineer, she dreads company social events: "The biggest stress comes around company party time. Even if I go to these, which I try not to, my partner and I have to constantly watch our behavior. We limit touching and other displays of affection."

For jobs that require contact with other organizations or the general public, like sales or advertising, the stakes are even higher. Corporate leaders are likely to hire someone they feel reflects the company's values—norms that are typically not female and certainly not lesbian. As Vickie puts it, "Being out can hurt your advancement possibilities if your boss doesn't like gays and lesbians or if being gay or lesbian is seen as embarrassing to the company or not compatible with leadership."

Since being a woman may already be a mark against them, many lesbians in corporate careers feel stress about letting the people they work with know about their sexual orientation. Whether out or not, virtually all of them say that they feel they have to be better employees than their counterparts, strictly by virtue of their gender. "I don't have the luxury of doing an okay job. It will be perceived as less than okay no matter what I do," Vickie says.

Sara, the scientist, is not out at work and says she learned her lesson about being a woman early on: "I learned in college that I had to be a better student because I was female in a male-dominated field. I think you are always proving your worth when you don't fit the 'norm' of society. This makes you more acceptable to others. 'She's a good employee, even though she's. . . .'"

The women I interviewed say that many day-to-day issues they face are more in line with issues important to women than to gay people in general. Many feel they have been discriminated against or harassed because of their gender. When asked what the major issues for lesbians in the workplace are, they often mention sexual harassment and discrimination, credibility (both getting and maintaining it), wage parity, and promotions.

THE IMPORTANCE OF A CONFIDANT

The expression *out* is one of the more muddling terms ever invented to describe ourselves. A person can never come out once and for all because she or he will always meet new people. Depending on their overall awareness of gays, lesbians, and bisexuals, these people are likely to assume that their new acquaintance is heterosexual until they are corrected. Therefore, most of us are always somewhere between out and in—although some people are kicking loudly at the closet door while others are silently collecting dust.

The reasons for the disparity in strategies are fairly clear. While gays and lesbians have made some progress in terms of social acceptance during the past twenty years, mainstream society is still not a safe place for most gay people. In fact, according to a recent *Time* magazine poll, 53 percent of the American public considers homosexual relationships between consenting adults to be "morally wrong"; 32 percent say they are against passage of equal-rights laws to protect homosexuals against job discrimination; and 21 percent say that they would not buy from a salesperson whom they knew was lesbian or gay.

But few lesbians can manage to stay in the closet to everyone, or even to everyone at work. I discovered that even lesbians who consider themselves the most in the closet had some sort of co-worker confidant—either a fellow gay person or a sympathetic straight. (Of course, lesbians who have not revealed their sexual orientation to any co-workers do exist.) For these women, confidants provide valuable relief from the stress of inhabiting the corporate closet. Sometimes, successfully confiding in one co-worker makes them want to come out to more people at work.

Erin, twenty-eight, is a software developer in Seattle. A self-described "funky nerd" who wears glasses and likes dressing in shorts and Doc Martens, she shares an office with someone she describes as a "Christian family man." They talk throughout the workday, but before she came out to him she felt that there were many parts of her life that she could not discuss. When she finally got enough courage to tell him that she is a lesbian, to her surprise he simply reacted with an "I thought so." She says that he has been very supportive and that they discuss gay issues practically daily. Their conversations are often joined by other gay employees. She has come out to additional people at work, but only to those she thinks will react positively.

Other times, even a very supportive relationship with a confidant does not encourage the coming-out process. The friend simply functions as someone to share secrets with and, if he or she is a longtime employee, someone to rely on to give accurate information about attitudes within the company about gays.

Sara confides in one of her three business partners. Though she is not yet out to the other two partners, whom she describes as "relatively closed-minded," she says that she plans to come out once their small business is more stable. Her confidant is a gay man, and they usually talk about their relationships and gay and lesbian issues daily. "I do enjoy having someone to talk with and feel I can identify with. This is important," she says.

Margot says that everyone knew that she was a lesbian at her previous job. At her current job, she is out only to a couple of individuals, however, because she was warned about the department's conservatism and homophobia by her workplace confidant, a sympathetic straight.

Amanda Kovattana

For a year, in Palo Alto, birthplace of Hewlett Packard and Silicon Valley, I had the rare opportunity to write for a straight audience as a lesbian. My vehicle was the *Palo Alto Weekly*, a free newspaper delivered to homeowners in five surrounding towns. When the paper actively solicited people of color to write a column, I proposed that they spice up their attempt to diversify and offered myself as a woman of "some color" who was willing to write from a lesbian perspective. It was a measure of the paper's liberal stance that they took me on.

My first column was entitled "Tales of a Media Slut," an account of my search for role models in the media as a young, biracial, lesbian immigrant. I was thrilled to have a voice in the community I had lived in since I was ten years old. The local lesbian and gay population wrote me letters of praise, just for being visible, especially since the column included a photograph. Strangers stopped me on the street with friendly hellos. My co-workers were amused to be able to tell their friends they worked with the notorious town queer. My boss, who had participated in the civil rights movement of the 1960s, drew parallels in support of my activism. Homophobes wrote anonymous letters quoting the usual biblical passages and phoned the newspaper demanding that it stop publishing the opinions of a pervert. My parents had mixed feelings. Though I had been out to them for some years, they didn't know whether to be proud of me or apologetic when their friends mentioned having seen my column.

My second column, "Ten Good Reasons to Be a Lesbian," generated a handful of protest letters, mostly from men who were outraged that I had pointed out that lesbians didn't have to take care of men. The paper was delighted at the response. But when I addressed more serious issues of identity versus assimilation, I exceeded the paper's tolerance level. The editor asked me to cut out the personal details of "motorcycles vibrating between our legs" and stick to issues the public would understand, like Clinton's waffling on gays in the military. When I continued to write about lesbian life rather than political issues, the paper terminated my column. Somehow it was permissible to have strong political opinions, but the line was drawn at descriptions of queer folk living their "radical" lives.

PROFESSIONALISM AND THE CORPORATE ATMOSPHERE

For people who are expected to conduct themselves professionally in their jobs, the coming-out issue is more complicated because private matters, especially those involving sex, are not seen as an appropriate topic for everyday office discussion. As Margot puts it, "[talking about sex] doesn't happen much among the engineers, at least when I'm around. I do hear the secretaries and other clerical staff talk about it, but I make it a point to not get involved, because I'm a manager and it wouldn't be appropriate."

Margot adds that she works almost entirely with men, which may be part of the reason why her colleagues do not often discuss sex or their personal lives with her. For the same reason, she avoids talking about her personal life with them: "One of my rules is to keep personal and professional lives separate, and I would do this whether I was gay or straight. I believe that, as a woman, bringing the personal into the professional will affect your credibility. The good old double standard."

In workplaces where the talk is mostly about business, lesbians do not usually find obvious opportunities to out themselves, even if they so desire. Conversely, if they do not want to come out, they may be able to avoid the subject of their sexuality with little effort. Even if they are not currently out, all the women I interviewed say that they would tell the truth if a co-worker or boss asked whether they were lesbian. Some admit that they wish someone would ask, just so they could get their secret out into the open. But people don't ask. Even if employees suspect that a co-worker or manager is a lesbian, few directly question her. The effort toward professionalism probably plays a significant role in continuing this "don't ask, don't tell" environment.

THE STRESS OF THE CLOSET

The reasons for corporate lesbians to stay in the closet are fairly obvious. Women who have managed to rise to levels of authority within their companies may rationally fear that their opportunities for advancement, or even their very jobs, could be threatened by coming out. That a large percentage of public opinion is still against lesbians and gay men is not the only intimidating factor. Although many companies have drafted nondiscrimination statements, they are the exception rather than the norm. Furthermore, gays can rarely look to government for protection—forty-two states still allow employers to fire people simply for being homosexual.

Even lesbians who work in states like California that outlaw discrimination based on sexual orientation say they believe that nondiscrimination is often little more than "words on paper." They fear that coming out could endanger their job security.

Margot summed up common coming-out fears. She is wary of "being sabotaged at work, reducing my effectiveness, having my decisions questioned, resistance to any changes I propose, having to defend my personal life instead of my professional decisions, not getting support from upper management, and affecting chances at promotions."

For some, the nature of their work explicitly precludes them from coming out. Sara, who started her own company because of the restrictions that went with many science jobs, explains: "My previous job was with a government laboratory. I held a top-secret security clearance. I would have been denied clearance if it were known I was a lesbian." That, combined with the fact that she worked with many fundamentalist Christians, was why she left the job.

Lesbians who describe themselves as out, as well as those who do not, say that the primary advantage of coming out is that it alleviates stress. Since the women I interviewed were, on average, out in most other aspects of their lives, they found that staying in the closet while on the job was an effort. Those who are not out say they hope to come out at some point. They all would be out in their current jobs if they felt that they could be without jeopardizing their careers.

There are a few basic strategies for lesbians who try to keep their sexuality a secret at work. While few gay women blatantly lie about their lesbianism, many use subtle techniques to mislead people. These techniques include using the noncommittal pronoun *they* or other vague words to refer to a significant other or failing to correct people when they assume heterosexuality.

Sara describes her technique: "I avoid conversation regarding my sex life and use generalities to confuse the situation or 'play along.' If a worker mentions a date I've had, they generally will say *he*. I don't correct them. I don't personally say *he*, but I let them assume they are right."

Erin, who describes herself as about "fifty percent" out at work, explains her changing strategy this way: "In the past, I had referred to my partner as *he* simply because when I mentioned her first name, Jo, many people assumed that I meant *Joe*. I have since corrected this with the people that made the incorrect assumption. I no longer refer to my partner as *he*, but I do sometimes refer to her as 'my roomie.' So people are aware that I am living with a woman, but I let them draw their own conclusions about what type of relationship we have."

Other lesbians just avoid discussing their personal lives at all. Margot says she can usually deflect the infrequent questions about herself: "Questions about personal life are rare. I never let the conversation get too deep, and usually if the conversation comes my direction, I redirect it. Most people prefer to talk about themselves, so it's an easy thing to do."

Whether it's by using subtle and misleading heterosexual indicators or simply avoiding talk about personal life, these are extremely difficult strategies, considering the number of vagaries necessary to deflect an ordinary Monday's worth of questions about weekend activities. Besides the stress of lying, either directly or indirectly, it is difficult to go beyond just being co-workers and form meaningful friendships when a person can't discuss her life away from the office. Usually because of these reasons, some lesbians decide to come out.

COMING OUT

Coming out is a continuous process, and often quite without drama. It's usually not the kind of thing one does over the company P.A. system. Usually, it simply happens by becoming friends with a co-worker and trusting him or her. As Erin's friendship with her Christian officemate illustrates, sometimes the result is even better than imagined.

Some women say that it is easier to come out smoothly, without shocking announcements, when they are in a relationship and can just introduce the partner rather than proclaim a sexual orientation. As Emily says: "It is much easier to be out when I'm seeing someone. Otherwise it just sounds strange."

Openly gay women who work in the business world say that they tend to try to make their sexual orientation accepted and "normal" to heterosexuals by focusing on the common ground of relationships, whether with someone of the same or the opposite gender. It's a tactic that psychological research supports. Gregory Herek, a psychologist at the University of California at Davis, claims that antigay feeling is lower among people who know gays and can relate to them on a one-to-one basis.

Although Margot is not out now, she was out at her previous job. There, Margot says, she was friends with her co-workers and regularly brought her girlfriend to her employer's home for dinner parties: "They just knew about it after a while because of my bringing my girlfriend to social functions, for instance, or having her call me at work, or only having female friends stop by, obvious butch types, or call. It was a gradual process and I don't recall a specific incident. They just made the assumption I was after a while. I never had to explicitly say it."

Margot says that she is a little afraid to be out at her new job because of the "redneck" atmosphere there, and is thus vague about her personal life. However, she almost wishes they would get to know her enough to figure it out. She admits to hinting at her lesbianism: "I don't 'femme out' at work, I have rainbow stickers on my car, [and] I recycle *The Advocate* in the break room."

But stressing common experiences while maintaining a sense of individuality can be a tightrope walk. Vickie says that she tries to focus on the commonalities between herself and the heterosexual men who outnumber her at work without being a hypocrite: "I try not to compromise my beliefs and to stay true to who I am. It can be a difficult compromise, since, let's face it, I'm not exactly like everyone in my group. In fact, I'm not like anyone in my group. I try to draw similarities where I can, when I'm trying to connect with someone."

Once people are told about a co-worker's sexual orientation, or finally put the pieces of the puzzle together, it is often difficult to keep the secret. The women report that sometimes this situation arises because they start having trouble keeping track of whom they are out to and whom they are not, and at other times just because, as Emily says, people tend to "pass the information along."

Since relatively few corporations and states prohibit discrimination based on sexual orientation, some lesbians decide to bite the bullet and come out to their bosses before coming out to any co-workers. This is the strategy Emily used during the ten years she worked for her company before they added sexual orientation to their antidiscrimination policy. Every time she got a new supervisor, she went up to him or her and started the conversation with, "This shouldn't matter, but if it does, I need to know if you'll consider it my problem or the other person's problem."

Luckily for Emily, her managers always backed her up, but she does not attribute this solely to their gay-friendly attitudes. She thinks her case was helped by the fact that they needed her—because she was a woman at a site that was having trouble meeting affirmative action goals, and because she is a salaried employee rather than an hourly worker.

The newly emerging gay, lesbian, and bisexual groups in companies has undoubtedly encouraged lesbians to come out. At Erin's computer company, where she took a job partly because of its gay-friendly policies, she has become much more forthcoming about her sexual orientation. "It helps me to come out more knowing that people who are out are still accepted and treated with respect," she explains.

Emily was out for years before a gay group, still not officially recognized by her company, began at her workplace. Since the group succeeded in lobbying management to write up a new antidiscrimination policy, she thinks that more people have come out because they feel officially protected by management. In turn, as the numbers of out gays increase, the policy becomes less abstract and more effective.

LAVENDER VISIONS FOR THE FUTURE

As the women I spoke to stressed repeatedly, policy means very little without people to back it up. Without gays and lesbians who are out and educating nongays about issues important to us, an antidiscrimination clause might just be words in an employee handbook, able to be easily and subtly circumvented.

Some lesbians, spurred on by recent successes and by the reality of working in relatively gay-friendly environments, are optimistic about the changing corporate atmosphere for lesbians, gays, and bisexuals.

Ann Mei, a twenty-seven-year-old who recently marched with the first-ever gay contingent in the San Francisco Chinese New Year Parade, is one of these positive thinkers. As a software engineering manager, she came out to her entire company when she helped organize the corporation's gay, lesbian, and bisexual group, Lavender-Vision. Since then, she and other employees in LavenderVision lobbied the company to institute a nondiscrimination policy that includes domestic partner benefits. In speaking about the new benefits package, Ann Mei stresses the idea that, while it does not necessarily mean much on its own, the process of educating people about the policy has helped open minds and improve the environment for gays and lesbians in the company.

Considered somewhat of a gay community spokesperson at her workplace, Ann Mei doesn't mind the educator role, welcoming the chance to influence her co-workers. She has been quickly promoted and says that she sees no disadvantages in being a lesbian at her company. In fact, she thinks that she has made quite a few connections with company higher-ups through her work on the nondiscrimination policy.

Although Ann Mei is more optimistic about being out on the job than most lesbians, her reasons for being out are the same as those echoed by many women who are out or who would like to be. "I'm out because I don't feel comfortable lying, and I think it is critical politically to start changing people's attitudes," she says.

But most people don't work at a company that is as welcoming of lesbians and gays. And not everyone, even if she does work at a gay-friendly company, wants to become a gay and lesbian community spokesperson.

As my interviews with these women show, there is no one right way for gay men or lesbians to conduct themselves in corporate work environments. Depending on the geographical region in which one lives, the atmosphere for women and gays in specific fields or companies, as well as individual job security, lesbians have to choose for themselves whether or not to come out at work. Likewise, the way in which one comes out depends on personal style and professional constraints.

Without a doubt, lesbians are deciding more and more to come out to co-workers and employers. As they take tiny steps or giant leaps, it becomes easier for others to leave the closet.

FURTHER READING

Henry, William A. "Gays and the Limits of Tolerance." *Time.* June 27, 1994, 54–59.

Mickens, Ed. *The 100 Best Companies for Gay Men and Lesbians.* New York: Pocket Books, 1994.

Sloan, Louise. "Do Ask, Do Tell: Lesbians Come Out at Work." *Glamour.* May 1994, 242–43, 291–95.

Woods, James, and Jay Lucas. *The Corporate Closet.* New York: Free Press, 1993.

TWENTY-ONE

SHE TICKLES WITH A HAMMER

Donna Allegra

W e've all done it—nearly broken our necks off our shoulders just to get a good long look at the strong, sexy woman with the work boots and toolbelt. Whether she's the truck driver we're hoping is a diesel dyke, the carpenter with a hammer hanging at her hips, the telephone repairwoman with a pouch filled with delicious-looking tools, the efficient and competent stagehand—all these women have led countless lesbians to dream about having a trade. We imagine the independence and freedom offered by having a manual skill with which to earn our living. Sometimes our fantasy goes further; we itch to do this work in partnership with another dyke, or several. Maybe in our dream we would hang up our shingle as Wonder Woman Carpentry, Electra Electric, Persephone Painters. Or perhaps our business card would read Artemis Engineers, Martha and Mary's Household Repairs, Medea's Home Improvements: If it's broken, she'll fix it.

Why do we grant such power and glory to lesbians who do blue-collar work? It certainly starts with being of strong body and a strong enough mind to pursue a socially unsanctioned line of work.

There is also drama inherent in facing the challenge of antagonistic men and triumphing—a chance to be a lesbian heroine. An equally important spinoff is the satisfaction of pioneering paths for future women, a goal that's certainly in line with traditional lesbian ideals.

Nontraditional is the term used to describe women who do jobs once solely the province of men. Lesbians have always been in the forefront, blazing trails heterosexual women now take for granted, while many of these same heterosexual women disdain the feminism that freed them to have abortions, to work as lawyers or doctors, and to be self-supporting. Lesbians have always been at the cutting edge of movements for civil rights, abortion rights, battered women's shelters, self-defense, and women's participation in sports, and in the realms of nontraditional work. We are more likely to go against behavior deemed right and proper for women. Marty Pottenger, a carpenter who has worked in New York City for the past twenty years, speculates that "almost all the women who first went into those trades were lesbians because just having to figure out that you're a lesbian makes it possible to figure out what you actually want to do."

Just what are the concerns of those inspiring butch-looking women who take to blue-collar work to earn their livelihood? What are the labor pains of a lesbian in a nontraditional job?

My focus here is on construction workers only partly because I am a construction worker, and most of the women I've seen in blue-collar work are also in that industry. The more important reason is that even when I did secretarial work, the women who delighted me with the sight of their tools and work boots were generally tradesworkers.

The construction trades include sheet metal workers, carpenters, plumbers, ironworkers, painters, operating engineers, plasterers, lathers, and my trade: electrician. The work involves using hand and power tools. At times we also use our bodies as machines in order to get a job done. Mechanical reasoning is involved, a skill not taught to young women. Boys, however, routinely learn "shop" skills.

There are good reasons to work in the skilled trades—especially money. In 1991, women constituted 68 percent of all adults living below the poverty level. At the journey level of a trade—that is, after you've completed apprenticeship training—laborers, carpenters, bricklayers, plumbers, and duct workers make upward of $25 to $30 an hour, plus benefits.

According to the U.S. Department of Commerce, Bureau of Census, in 1988, women's hourly earnings were 74 percent of men's, and their annual income was 68 percent of men's. Money alone is reason enough to rethink becoming a secretary, schoolteacher, administrator, or sales worker—the leading occupations that women end up in. The paychecks in construction are persuasive, but they're not the only lure to a nontraditional career choice.

Molly Martin, an electrical inspector and former construction electrician, says, "I didn't want to do what the options were in traditional woman's work."

Women in construction report feelings of enormous satisfaction in the course of practicing their trades. You build and fix things; your labors make a difference and help bring a structure concretely into being.

The total number of women in the traditionally male trades is small. And not as many women construction workers as I had expected are lesbians, given the butch appearance of many of them. Perhaps my expectations had been too high, or I had underestimated heterosexual women's ambitions. I find the biggest drawback for an unabashed manhater like myself is that I end up working with more heterosexual men than I would have if I had worked in a traditional woman's field.

To any lesbian considering entering the construction field I would post this sign: Caution—Men at work. This world is far from any idea of lesbian heaven, and this work environment is psychically toxic to a woman who loves women. Many women who go into blue-collar work share the fantasy I had when I considered my trade. I imagined being on a crew with other butch women working in concert on a project we cared about. I've found instead, to my dismay, that I spend the bulk of my time with men who spout reactionary and male-supremacist beliefs, beliefs that go unchallenged.

In any blue-collar job, working with men is the biggest stumbling block you have to grapple with. The physical labor itself is never the problem. As any woman who works in what used to be a man's world will tell you, "It's not the work but the guys that present the greatest difficulties on the job."

Karen Bateau is a young woman whom I took to be a boy when I met her as a fourth-year apprentice. Karen says: "The hardest part is dealing with the sexism. It's the everyday stuff that no one questions. Most people would think that you were being really picky if you complained about what the guys say. I end up having to spend most of my time figuring out how to get along with boys. They have such different values than I do, and I think they're really backward in many ways."

Nanci Ezzo, a former telephone installer, said that what bothered her most about working with men was "the social disease: the homophobia, the racism, and the ignorance about it. They were so unaware of how sick they were. Around the time of Desert Storm, they were just gung-ho about blowing everybody up. They were so violent and so pro-war—they had no idea that there was anything wrong with them."

When I started in construction work, I quickly came to see that men become more offensive when they're among themselves than when they are in mixed male and female company. Construction work is one of the last bastions where the heterosexual male ethic is glorified without criticism. Misogyny is the law of the land. For example, one day on my job two men had been bickering all morning long. Just before lunchtime the foreman joked about them, "You should never put two women together." All the men laughed.

Most women in fields traditionally considered male territory are familiar with the following scenario. The guys are standing around during coffee break or waiting for the elevator. One guy is talking about how much effort he put into a task. He'll say, "My shirt was soaked, my arms and my legs were dripping, my balls were pouring like—" He has seen me and knows I am paying attention to the story, so he'll say, "Oh, shit. I forgot there's a lady on the job."

Through their language, male co-workers will let women know we are not in what they deem the proper place for females. That's the subtle version of the sexism. And then there's the overt kind: "Hey, homo"; "If it was easy, a girl could do it"; "Man, what'd you do to get such a tit job?" But I've been known to do a humorous turnaround of a phrase: "You must have some set of nuts to do this kind of work"; "Well, my pair of ovaries works pretty good." But most of the time I don't challenge the routine sexism that passes for friendly conversation among my co-workers. My experience has shown me the futility of attempting an honest dialogue.

But carpenter Bells Sandborn doesn't keep silent: "I open my big mouth. If I hear things that are offensive, I say I don't want to hear this shit. They're real careful about saying things that could get them in trouble these days, but they do other things. Someone has been jerking off every day in the Portasan. It would get cleaned up, but it'd be there again a few hours later. I know he was doing it for me."

These men also assume they can be familiar and flirtatious with the women workers, calling us "honey," "baby," "sugar," "sweetheart." Women in white-collar positions have had greater success in protesting verbal sexual harassment, but when blue-collar women speak up, the men become nervous. They regard us as uppity dykes—a compliment in my book. Many of us simply learn to be less prickly over the years. Electrician Karen Bateau feels: "It helps to grit your teeth to survive on the job, but I still don't like being called 'sweetheart' just so some fool can feel he is superior."

One of the great paradoxes for lesbian tradesworkers is that we end up working with the most sexist men. They act out the ideas of maleness around aggression and intimidation, and they embody the worst of male behavior from bragging about how drunk—or drugged—they got to talking about women as if our only function were to entertain and serve them, taking potshots at and making put-downs of other men in order to present themselves as superior.

Furthermore, blue-collar men expect the lesbians on the job to be an interested and attentive audience. Tradeswomen like Theresa Schwartz have often complained: "I feel like I'm on the job to practice therapy rather than be a plumber." Lesbians especially dislike being called upon to do what they consider, in Theresa's description, "straight girl mental-latrine duty." Or, as telephone installer Nanci tells it, "The men glom all over you because they're so emotionally needy."

In the perpetual discussion of sexism and harassment in construction, Molly, who is also the editor of *Hard-Hatted Women* and an editor of *Tradeswomen Magazine,* makes the distinction that "we get more shit for being women on the job than for being lesbians." I agree. I also feel more hostility from the men on account of being female than being black.

Nanci points out that "sexism and racism are all part of the same bundle of yarn." The racism, sexism, and homophobia intermingle so that one strand pulls the others in what Nanci identifies as "the societal sickness."

But as a white woman, Bells can report, "What I've opened my mouth about more than sexual harassment is racism on the job. Because I'm white, they'll say things around me. Basically the guys I work with are white racist motherfuckers and they think I won't say anything about it to them."

Molly adds, "Men are not as threatened by and hateful of lesbians as they are about gay men, so in a way, the sexism/heterosexism 'protects' us." Some lesbians speculate that in their homophobia, the men don't truly believe that lesbians don't want sexual involvement with men; hence, we aren't the threat that they feel male homosexuals are for them.

Still, we must perform a balancing act in order to get along with the men. On one hand, the very skills that make you a good worker become points for attack by male co-workers who cast doubts on your womanhood when you show more initiative, confidence, strength, or daring than they can be comfortable with. On the other hand, if we stand back and let a male co-worker handle a physically challenging task, we are viewed as bad workers. We are likely later to overhear male colleagues say, "She shouldn't be here if she can't handle the job."

Sylvia Robbins, a mechanical engineer, says, "What bugs me is that you still have to walk a line between being one of the guys and being ladylike, and I could never do this, even when I was straight. I always thought that there is a lot of humor in sexuality, but if you go too far [as a woman jesting, the men] freak out."

Nanci adds, "A lot of times the guys have no skill, but they act like they're God's gift to the universe, and like they know so much when they really don't know a thing. At least two out of every ten boys that I worked with were always like this. They thought they were just so great."

A man will often condescendingly offer a woman worker help if she shows any uncertainty about a task. His offer usually amounts to his showing off, coupled with his making the woman look incompetent. This so-called help usually costs her dignity. Many of the men want women to be unable to do the work so that they can step in and show how much better they are at it. As mechanical engineer Sylvia puts it, "I don't like working with men because they're piggish bastards and if they can do something better than you, they'll take tools out of your hands, and if you protest this, they say you're bitchy. You can't win with them."

Despite lawsuits that have inspired company policies to curb men's behavior, women still relate stories of outrageously unfair treatment and outright hostility. Bells Sandborn tells of her first job apprenticing as a carpenter: "I was sent to a job in an unheated building in midwinter. It was wet and freezing and dusty, and every other day we were sent home for asbestos contamination. There was one Portasan for four hundred men and me. The elevator was broken, and they put me hauling double Sheetrock all day, up and down three flights

Shelley Anderson

By the 1970s, the U.S. military no longer rationalized its witch-hunts against lesbians on the grounds of our mental illness. We were now kicked out because we were "morally unfit."

You can burn millions of people and leave the world a radioactive waste, you can bomb innocent women and children and remain moral enough for the military, but touch another woman's breast with love and you are morally unfit. Something was perverse here, and it wasn't me.

I had been an enlisted woman for two years. Then I went through ROTC in college while earning a degree in Women's Studies, compliments of the GI Bill. Going to the National Guard one weekend and volunteering at the battered women's shelter the next was schizophrenic. But I thought I had it all under control, safely compartmentalized.

I was wrong. My conscience bothered me. The arguments paced back and forth, treading a well-worn path up to the edge of a cliff: What was I doing, staying involved in this system designed to kill? If I didn't pull the trigger myself, I was helping others to kill. I was teetering on the edge of a cliff.

The thought of refusing to put on the uniform made me sick to my stomach. What would happen if I broke my contract for military service? Could the government put me in jail?

I argued with myself: I'm the unit's equal opportunities officer. Enlisted women come to me about sexual harassment, about racist insults. I can do some good if I keep my job.

Ironically, it was precisely because I held that position that I finally left. The National Guard wanted to send me to a training course on race relations. I needed it, but the hypocrisy stuck in my throat. Picture it: patting each other on the back, congratulating ourselves on the military's tolerance. As long as I kept my mouth shut, I could be part of the bonhomie. One whisper about my lesbianism, though, and I would be out so fast my head would spin.

Perversely believing that nothing in my lesbianism made me morally unfit for the military, I filed a claim as a conscientious objector. It was terrifying, but there's great freedom to be found in holding hands with fear. I had the experience of coming out as a lesbian to fall back on, which had taught me one very important lesson. When you are on the edge of a cliff, there's only one thing to do: jump.

of stairs." Ironically, women have had to show more courage protesting inhumane conditions for all workers because we are often placed in a trade's worst conditions to deliberately discourage us.

On account of the rampant sexism, many women—lesbians and heterosexuals alike—leave the trades. Bells had to keep the time of our discussion short in order to get back to studying for exams for a nursing degree. After eight years, Nanci has left telephone installation to become a massage therapist.

Still, there are some positive aspects to tell about a work life in the midst of rabidly heterosexist males. For example, there is strength in knowing that we can do this kind of work. Inherent in the skills of manual labor is the satisfaction of seeing a job done. We are also less subject to being domineered and bullied by men who have a knowledge of mechanical things. Their traditional territories and work prerogatives have been demystified because we have these skills, too. Learning any of the trades and taking on the challenges of the work is enormously absorbing. I love that I have learned to do what boys are expected to do. Here, as in so many other matters, the world is set up so that boys can have more fun.

Karen, the electrician, is enthusiastic on this point: "I can fix things, and that makes me feel really good because I never had any grounding in tools when I was a kid. I enjoy working with my body physically. Knowing how to operate in this world gives me something that I couldn't have gotten any other way. I've gained a lot in being forced to deal with people in a way that keeps me alive and my integrity intact. And the money is really good. You're just not going to make this kind of cash in regular women's jobs. They only let men make the big bucks."

Some women find the work romantic at first, but that notion generally wears off with time and experience. Still, tradeswomen love their work. Many value the advantages, such as not having to work unpaid overtime. When union workers work overtime, they are paid the rate of time and a half. We generally get health benefits and a pension plan that many people would envy. The job comes to an end after the workday. We are not like the lawyer or doctor who has to put in sixty-plus hours a week to attain wealth, or the editor putting in long hours for little pay.

Marty says: "Working with men, I learn confidence. You've got to hold your own. You don't get caught up in a lot of the nicey-nice and fake stuff with working-class guys."

Sylvia adds: "The plus side is when they see what I can do—the young guys—they have a lot of respect for me. I've learned that there are things I can't do, and I say it without apology. I've learned that what I can do, I'd better do it well, and what I can't do isn't that important. I've found that if I feel confident about it, they don't get pissed off."

Nanci reveals another aspect of the greater respect automatically granted to men when she says, "I also enjoyed being seen as one of the guys—that power, the loudness, that taking-over, the not-caring, the obnoxiousness. It's a lot of power, and I enjoyed that to a point."

While I have to do the bulk of the work to create positive relationships with my male co-workers, I enjoy a superficial companionship with some of them. Many lesbians realize we can have a feeling of camaraderie with the guys on the job without getting intimate.

Bells gives mixed reviews about working with men: "The men I've had the best working experiences with are older men. They seem to be less threatened and are willing to teach me what they know. The younger men are so threatened and so hostile."

Sylvia reports, "Once I have the human connection and nobody's stroking their dick, [being at work is] like being a little boy. You get to rig things, climb things, carry and test equipment. You look like you're doing an honest day's work."

Molly says, "I sometimes get along better with het men than I do het women or gay men. I've seen het women and gay men get along really well. Likewise, lesbians and heterosexual men. Men don't live as intensely emotional lives as women do, so if you want distance at work, you can bet they won't ask you about your life outside work. You can hide your emotional self from straight men for years."

Marty, who doesn't work in the confines of union work, is the only lesbian I know who socializes with men off the job. "I've had friendships where I can call them up for information and help. I've found humor is my keenest survival weapon—just to make jokes for my own self. I also don't try to get the men to like me, which some women do, but I don't cut the men off. Construction work is very dangerous, and it's in my own interest and everyone else's to stay in some contact because we can keep each other from getting hurt."

Heterosexual males can be, in some ways, less frustrating and disappointing to me as a lesbian than heterosexual women, whose main conversational focus is often heterosexual mating. Perhaps my expectations for heterosexual men are low. My guard is up around men, so I'm less often surprised, pained, anguished by them. Because I know my enemy, I can often enjoy him. Karen agrees: "I sometimes find myself in the bizarre position of defending the guys on the job as 'not so bad' when people assume that it's awful to work with such sexist jerks. At times, it is indeed awful, but because I know this context, I can see the good in them."

Despite these positive aspects, few lesbian blue-collar workers come out on the job. The men assume and worry that all tradeswomen are lesbian and want it to be proved otherwise. Molly says, "Het men don't know anything real about us as lesbians. They can't believe an attractive woman can be a lesbian. I told the guy I am good friends with that I am a dyke. His reaction was, 'You're not a lesbian. Lesbians are fat and ugly.'"

Even with other lesbians, it is hard to be open about our sexuality. Construction work is an industry where gossip can be a safety hazard. Some women fear betrayal from those women who want to gain favor with the men. Karen says, "All a woman has to do is mention to one guy that she thinks I'm queer, and it's all over. The whole town will be talking. It's actually a threat to your life because if the men know you're a dyke, they will take on this attitude that they have a right to be hostile and assaultive on you. It's like, 'So what? she's a dyke'—not a person anymore, and therefore not entitled to any human rights." Bells, who is not out on the job, says "the homophobia is getting more violent."

In San Francisco, the situation is less homophobic. Molly states, "Coming out on the job is empowering and freeing. You know they think you're a dyke and are talking about it behind your back. If you say it to them, they have no power over you for what you keep hidden or try to hide."

I myself have put up a mask that hints toward heterosexuality to protect myself from men acting out their homophobia. They might suspect that a woman who does tradeswork may be lesbian, but so long as they're not sure, I feel safer. I sense that the men want to know my sexual orientation as much as I want to know that of other women, but it's a matter of knowing who my people are. As Theresa says, "The men want to know if the woman is fuckable, and even if she is a dyke, they are challenged into believing that they are the ones who'll convert her."

A final paradox for a lesbian who has chosen tradeswork is that she will frequently encounter the butch heterosexual woman. When you hear accusations of lesbians trying to be like men, the speaker may well be describing a butch heterosexual woman who emulates the worst male behavior. A telltale sign is when I discover a woman playing the game of "Don't-upset-the-boys."

Karen describes her this way: "She walks like a dyke, talks like a dyke, but damned if I can be sure. She does a lot of emotional dick-sucking and breast-feeding to guys, which is basic hetero girl survival strategy. Okay, no woman wants to rile up the boys—males are even more dangerous when they're in packs. But dykes are more likely to be impervious to male flirtations. We don't get drawn in by the ways men fish for ego bolstering. You know how they set you up to stroke them while they sniff you out for pussy potential."

Molly agreed that such heterosexual tradeswomen are "just like men and want to be. They're not feminists. They're male-identified and are not pro-woman." Bells has a term for these butch heterosexual women: motorcycle mamas.

But because there are so few women construction workers, we become hungry just for the sight of some other women. It's therefore all the more disappointing if the woman I meet on the job is a male-identified woman or if she puts men first. Such a woman invariably denies that there is sexist aggression besieging us and excuses offensive male behavior.

As few of us as there are, there is a greater concentration of lesbians among blue-collar workers than in the pink-collar sector. And sometimes we identify each other by a certain look—some call it "gaydar." On whatever channel we pick up the lesbian blue-collar worker, she has an allure that excites us, sparks our hopes for greater strength, independence, and freedom. Perhaps it is the potential for greater power that is aroused by the sight of a woman who works a blue-collar job, but when she tickles you with that hammer, you know.

TWENTY-TWO

OUTING AND THE POLITICS
OF THE CLOSET

Victoria A. Brownworth

The term *outing* was coined by the mainstream press in 1989 to describe a tactic devised and adopted by some radical queers and promulgated by writers for the New York magazine *Outweek.* Writers at *Outweek,* including myself and editor/columnist Michaelangelo Signorile, refused to maintain the code of silence about famous, but closeted, gay men and lesbians. Among the famous people exposed by *Outweek* were the financier Malcolm Forbes, the Hollywood mogul Barry Diller, then Assistant Secretary of Defense Pete Williams, the columnist Liz Smith, and the actress/director Jodie Foster. No libel suits were ever filed against *Outweek;* people alleging libel must prove they are not what they have been accused of being.

Outing made *Outweek* notorious and created a political schism within the lesbian and gay community. Many younger and more radical Queer Nation–style gays and lesbians became proponents of the tactic, arguing that powerful but closeted queers actively supported the status quo of homophobia by staying safely in the closet while also enjoying their queer lives; that denial of their homosexuality allowed them all the benefits of heterosexual privilege denied to out queers. A clear case in point is Pete Williams, a closeted gay man who was the Assistant Secretary of Defense and spokesperson for the Pentagon during the Bush administration. He enjoyed his relationships with other men while the Pentagon ousted thousands of lesbians and gay men from the military for even the presumption that they might be queer. The Pentagon had no comment when Signorile outed Williams.

The political theory underlying outing posits that since the true number of lesbians and gays remains unknown because so many women and men are in the closet, heterosexuals are able to reinforce the myth that queers are a tiny and perverse minority undeserving of civil rights. This theory of the closet as a codifying element of homophobia and a way of denying civil rights to lesbians and gay men has made outing appear to be a bona fide and essential political method. In essence, outing was perceived by its proponents as fighting fire with fire; if, for example, the Pentagon was going to continue the ban on lesbians and gays in the military, then any closeted member of the hierarchy promoting that antiqueer policy, such as Williams, deserved to be targeted. Initially, outing was utilized only against gay men and lesbians who were actively participating in homophobic practices.

Proponents also defend the practice by citing the high incidence of teen suicides among young lesbians and gays. Isolation and homophobia are considered to be key factors in this trend. Activists argue that the dearth of positive role models for lesbian and gay youth contributes to their isolation. Knowing that there are a host of famous gay men and lesbians living productive and fulfilling lives would be of tremendous benefit to the younger generation of lesbians and gays, they assert.

But those who oppose outing find no justification for its use. Coming out is a private and personal decision, they argue, one that must be made by the individual and that can be quite traumatic. Some, like *The Village Voice* senior editor Richard Goldstein, *Outweek* arts editor Sarah Pettit (now executive editor of *OUT*), and former *Advocate* executive editor Richard Rouillard, have strongly denounced outing on the pages of their respective publications, calling it unconscionable or likening it to McCarthyism. Even the *Outweek* editorial board was split on the issue of outing—as was the community itself.

It is still the most radical queers who remain proponents of outing and utilize it as a political method. Mainstream gay men and lesbians have consistently disavowed the practice, even if they have privately enjoyed the results.

In the years since it has been adapted as a political tool, outing has primarily been used by gay men against gay men. I was the only lesbian to support it in the pages of *Outweek;* other lesbians found the practice questionable from an ethical standpoint and some even called it abhorrent. The lesbian philosopher Claudia Card questions whether the practice is ethical for lesbians to use and suggests that lesbians might be damaged by it, but she also notes that there is generally little discussion about outing among lesbians.

Lesbians have rarely been either the source or the target of outing. There have been widely circulated rumors about two highly placed women in the Clinton administration, neither of whom is married. But while I and other journalists have been asked to out these women, no one has done so, in part because neither of these women has promulgated antiqueer or otherwise homophobic agendas. On the contrary, both have actively engaged in helping the lesbian and gay community.

During the congressional hearings on Clarence Thomas's nomination for the U.S. Supreme Court, rumors also spread about the sexuality of Anita Hill. Many publications printed (as did a later book, *The Real Anita Hill,* which exonerates Thomas and states unequivocally that Hill "lied" about everything) suggestions that she was alternatively heterosexually promiscuous, heterosexually frustrated, or lesbian. As a 1994 book on the Thomas-Hill debate, *Strange Justice,* elucidates, Hill's sexuality was made a target to deflect heat from Thomas. Each of the accusations against Hill was meant to invalidate her claims against him, with the following theories: If Hill were heterosexually promiscuous, then it would be unlikely that she would be bothered by the behavior Thomas was alleged to have perpetrated; if she were sexually frustrated, then she might have welcomed his advances and been angered if he rebuffed her; and since lesbians are known manhaters, as a lesbian she would have misinterpreted benign heterosexual behavior as predatory. The accusation of her alleged lesbianism was even made at the hearings in a veiled way by Senator Alan Simpson, who warned of her "dangerous proclivities," *proclivities* being an encoded word from Simpson's generation for homosexuality.

The morning after Simpson made his comments, I was asked by two mainstream magazines to write a story outing Hill. It was clear from the direction the editors wanted me to take that if Hill were outed as a lesbian, whether or not she was one, her allegations would suddenly become far less credible and distinctly more controversial. I declined both requests. Outing in service to the state or to facilitate some other antiqueer agenda is not accepted by most proponents of outing. It alters the purpose for which outing was devised by doing damage to the powerless in service to the powerful.

But, as mentioned earlier, women are rarely the targets of these actions. The reasons for this are varied, but devolve most clearly from the differences between lesbian culture and gay male culture, as well as between male and female power within society as a whole. As women, lesbians have far less power—economic and political—than gay men. And so we are less likely to be in positions that would benefit others should they come out of the closet. There are, for example, no lesbian equivalents of billionaires like Malcolm Forbes and Barry Diller. The kind of power a man like Diller has over television and the movie industry is phenomenal; the kind of change he could effect within those industries is substantial.

Gay men are far more likely than lesbians to rise to the top of their professions in spite of their sexual orientation. The new trend toward neoconservatism among gay men (as exemplified by Bruce Bawer's *A Place at the Table* and Andrew Sullivan as editor of *The*

Hon. Paula J. Hepner

You don't know I'm a lesbian until I tell you; that's coming out. You don't remember I'm a lesbian unless I remind you; that's staying out. In thirty years, our society has learned not to expect those in authority to be white males, but we are light-years away from overcoming the presumption that they will be heterosexual. Remaining visible, even at the risk of being branded a "professional lesbian" or a "poster dyke," is essential to changing this perception.

I have been out since 1974, when I entered law school. In 1990, New York City Mayor David Dinkins appointed me, along with two other out lesbians, to the courts. Our presence has made the judiciary more representational of our society, and has given us an opportunity to educate our heterosexual colleagues. But because we have no distinguishing characteristics to identify ourselves, like gender or race, the attorneys and litigants who appear before us do not know we are lesbians. With the passage of time, those who once knew have forgotten.

Staying out is difficult for me as a judge because I am required by the Code of Judicial Conduct to behave in a manner that preserves the impartiality and independence of the judiciary. Therefore, I cannot wear a pink triangle on my robe or display a rainbow flag in my courtroom, since this would convey a bias or predisposition with regard to my cases.

My dilemma is how to stay out without violating the code of ethics. When interacting with other judges, attorneys, and court personnel outside the courtroom, I can refer to my domestic partner and drop phrases like "we lesbians" or "you heterosexuals." I can decorate the walls of my chambers with photographs of same-sex pairs figure-skating at the Gay Games. But when a man testifies that he beat up his ex-wife because "she was out with that 'bull dagger' again," and looks to me expecting approval, I must hide the outrage I feel. When a gay father withdraws his petition for visitation, saying, "I can't help who I am; she won't stop telling my children I'm diseased, and they're frightened to be with me," I must hide the frustration I feel. My invisibility allows the ex-husband to speak without the circumspection he might otherwise exercise before voicing a racial, ethnic, or gender epithet, and allows the father to presume that I am as homophobic as the mother of his children.

My experiences on the bench remind me that attaining full membership in this society for lesbians and gay men depends on our visibility. When we are visible, ordinary citizens can recognize us among their family, friends, neighbors, and co-workers. And when they do, it becomes easier to discard the stereotypes by which we have been characterized. They can see that we, too, live by spiritual, ethical, and moral standards, and that we share similar aspirations, hopes, and disappointments.

New Republic) and the rise of the gay Republican group, the Log Cabin Club, are good illustrations of this. Gay male neoconservatives state unequivocally that there is no difference between them and other white men (there are few men of color involved in this movement)—that no one would know they were gay unless they came out (which they don't necessarily advocate). From politicians to movie moguls, gay men have been able to attain success while maintaining their closeted lifestyles. Outing was devised with powerful men in mind.

Sexism has prevented women from achieving economic and social power equivalent to that of men. And since World War II, women who are career-oriented but unmarried have often been suspected of being lesbians; homophobia and sexism have become inextricably connected. In fact, the presumption of lesbianism has been entangled with feminism and women's struggles for job, economic, and political equity. While a man without a woman is not considered suspect in the work world, the reverse does not hold true.

Traditionally, lesbians have been invisible in society—in part because we are women and in part because patriarchal society has been unable to imagine two women together without a man. Lesbian invisibility has defined the perimeters of the lesbian closet. For generations, lesbians were able to live together in what historians have termed "romantic friendships." These relationships were really very similar to heterosexual marriages; because two women together posed no overt threat to society, there was no social proscription against these pairings. And because sex between women was, for the most part, unimagined and unimaginable, there weren't specific laws in the United Kingdom or the United States prohibiting lesbianism.

Conversely, gay men living similarly were perceived to have broken with patriarchal society and male tradition, and so were often targeted by the legal system. Because men were accepted as sexual creatures, prosecution for sodomy and other "crimes" of gay male sexuality was common, particularly when the man involved was not discreet about his sexual habits.

As female sexuality began to be acknowledged in the twentieth century, however, lesbianism became recognized as a social evil. Overt lesbian sexuality came to be denounced by religious and political leaders. Discretion—the closet—became a necessity; "romantic friendships" and so-called Boston marriages were accepted alternatives to heterosexual marriage for women only so long as they did not hint at actual sexuality. Because women were often seen as sexual innocents, many lesbian couples were able to live together in veritable marriages without societal disapproval. They could even express physical affection for each other in public so long as it appeared under the guise of friendship. Touching of almost any sort between men, however, has always been viewed with suspicion.

So in many respects, it was the distinctions between socially acceptable sexual behavior for men and women that defined the differences between lesbians and gay men and the evolution of the closet. Those distinctions remain today, despite over three decades of modern feminism and a quarter century of the lesbian and gay rights movement. Lesbians are still much more able to "pass" in society than gay men; they remain largely invisible to the society around them, their lesbianism undetected. The inability of a male-defined society to comprehend women-identified women has in some respects been an advantage for many lesbians; unless they declare themselves, society presumes them to be heterosexual. Consequently, the closet has become a comfortable place for many lesbians. Society still accepts two women living together without immediately assuming they are lesbians, largely because society still cannot accept the premise that women can live independently of men.

The confluence of being able to "pass," on the one hand, and being suspect as a single woman in the workplace, on the other, has created serious conflicts for lesbians who are in positions of relative power, such as politicians, corporate executives, and Hollywood studio producers. One well-known independent filmmaker was openly lesbian prior to moving to Hollywood. After her transition to the studio system, she retreated to the closet, denying her lesbianism in

Lee Lynch

The week before the November 1992 election in Oregon, I went to a fund-raiser. By then I was suspicious of every nongay who didn't wear a button opposing the ballot measure that would take away my rights, that would label me abnormal and perverse. And that night, something snapped. Would snipers pick us off as we left the fund-raiser? Was our house under attack? I fled into that dark night and sped home, switching on the radio to drown out my crazed thoughts. The oldies station played the Shirelles' "Will You Still Love Me Tomorrow?"

I felt the exaltation of that long-ago moment: the song that had been playing the first time I kissed a woman.

Can any nongay ever understand the rapture of coming out, of taking that small and infinite step beyond a world where we'd never fit in and that didn't make sense to us? Can anyone but a queer person comprehend the transformation that comes when the universe, which had been topsy-turvy, rights itself?

Now here I was, decades later, rushing home for reassurance that my world had not been destroyed. It was stupid. Alone I was more vulnerable, yet I had to walk through my fear, had to cross my unlighted driveway to the house that shelters my lover and me.

Just before the election, gays, going out at night, even in our relatively safe town, walked to our cars only in groups. Lovers woke in the middle of the night to whisper, "What was that sound?"

During the campaign, a man offered a lesbian grandmother a slander sheet about gays. "Are you voting yes on Measure 9?" he asked. *"Absolutely not."* "Why?" *"Because I'm a lesbian!"* she answered. Then he told her, in perfect seriousness, "That doesn't matter." She shakes her head as she repeats the tale to me. "And then something snapped. I started yelling and screaming at him right there on the sidewalk."

We all snap in our own ways. Lesbians and gays have borne the unbearable since the beginning of time. Yet no movement based on hate and fear can erase the sweetness of loving and living true to ourselves. Kissing in the shadows or in the full light of day, loving and being ourselves. There is no question that, once again, we will prevail.

interviews. The closet was, for her, the only place from which she could make films in homophobic Hollywood.

Such women fear the politics of outing, though they are unlikely to be caught in its snare. Outing is perceived by many lesbians to be a violation of the basics of feminism, a male tool in a male culture. Opponents assert that women are constantly denied freedom of choice over their own lives. They believe that a woman's lesbianism is nobody's business but her own. Yet it was feminists who defined the personal as political. And in a society where heterosexuality not only predominates but is the predication for nearly every aspect of social interaction, demanding equal attention to queerness would appear to make good political sense. And then there is the question of history: What about famous queers from our past?

I have personally outed only two living people. One case was inadvertent—I didn't realize when I wrote about this woman that she was not openly lesbian. The other woman I outed was working for the FBI and turning in women and men who were queer, to be fired for violating FBI rules. To me this outing was justified because the person was actively working to reinforce homophobia.

All the other people I have outed were already dead. And I would say that there are many historians who have done the same, even though they might not be advocates of the practice. The political queasiness many feel about outing the living doesn't extend as readily to the dead, even if it is in violation of the deceased's wishes. Yet outing is today an established research tool of queer history. Anyone who has written about Willa Cather as a lesbian, for example, has outed her, because she went to drastic lengths to disguise her lesbianism, making certain her private letters and papers were destroyed at her death. Others—Emily Dickinson, Elizabeth Blackwell, Eleanor Roosevelt—were secretive about their lesbianism, but history has revealed it. And there are certainly others, such as Gertrude Stein, who didn't identify as lesbians during their lives, even though they were notorious lesbians.

Do we, as a community, consider historical research that unearths the information that a former president was gay or bisexual to be out-ing that person, or do we consider that information essential to building historical documentation of lesbianism and homosexuality over time? Does outing have a different connotation when its subject is living than when she or he is dead? Does privacy die with the body?

Historians would argue that, yes, privacy does die with the body unless the deceased has made extravagant efforts to protect it. Yet Cather did just that and she has been outed for all the world. The very same arguments that proponents of outing have used to explain their methods are used by queer historians outing the dead: *Who* is lesbian or gay is a vital need-to-know aspect of our collective queer history. The end result of having this information justifies the some-what questionable political means. The very same arguments used by opponents of outing, that personal privacy is paramount and each person must be allowed to make her or his own choices about coming out, dissolve in the face of history. Those opponents have not demonized queer historians as they did the *Outweek* colum-nists—yet Michaelangelo Signorile and I and those we outed will all be history one day, too. How do we make distinctions between good outing and bad outing, and, regardless of how we make those dis-tinctions, aren't they ultimately extremely subjective?

In her book *Surpassing the Love of Men*, the lesbian historian Lillian Faderman refers to lesbian relationships in the centuries before our own as "romantic friendships." She is careful—too care-ful, some allege—not to "out" her subjects or place a revisionist con-struct on her interpretation of their relationships. But is it not equally revisionist to presume that the twentieth century invented lesbianism (where did Sappho come from?), and isn't it actually skirting the obvious issue to delete the word *lesbian* from the histori-cal record of these women's lives? Interestingly, Faderman is less care-ful (or less revisionist) in a more recent book, *Chloe Plus Olivia*, a huge compendium of lesbian literature by women from the seven-teenth century to the present. Does this qualify as outing?

Outing is actually not as new as current history, and its neolo-

Anna Livia

When I left London for California after a nasty breakup, my mother's advice rang in my ears: "If you want to meet new lesbians, Anna, it's no use sitting around on the doorstep. You have to join a club, take up a sport, learn a new language." But she wasn't figuring on the Bay Area, where they have a gay interest section at the local video store, and you can choose to attend gay traffic school instead of paying a fine if you get caught speeding on the way home with your movie. My problem was not lack of opportunity, but rather too much. Every street corner, every guidebook, seemed to hail the joys of lesbian sex. There was Good Vibrations, the sex store; Osento, the women's hot tub center; Ecstasy Lounge, the public-but-safe-sex club.

I turned on my computer and was greeted with a welcome to Berkeley's Lavender Graduate Group and a free list of the university's gay interest courses. If I preferred the more intellectual approach to dating, I could enroll in "Alternative Sexual Identities in Contemporary America"; if my subsequent activities led me into trouble, I could presumably seek free legal advice in "Sexual Orientation and the Law." Of all the course offerings, however, "Gender and Melancholy" would best have suited my mood as I sat doggedly on my doorstep puzzling over the personal ads. What exactly was an "NS SF SF brn/brn," and why did she want to alphabetize my spice rack? Clearly, it wasn't a lesbian guidebook I needed, but a lesbian dictionary. Maybe my mother was right about the need to learn a new language.

gisms, would suggest. At the beginning of this chapter I noted that the term was coined in 1989, but literature and life have provided examples of lesbians being outed long before most of us at *Outweek* were even born. What differentiates these examples from those of queer historians or queer activists is their perpetrators. Those perpetrators show the flip side of outing—how it is used as a destructive tactic intended to harm an individual, with no political, social, or historical benefit attached to the act.

In Lillian Hellman's play *The Children's Hour,* two young women, Karen and Martha, run a school for girls. A precocious student named Mary tells a lie in anger over being punished. She says that the women are lovers, that she has *seen* them making love. Inadvertently, however, she chooses "the lie with a grain of truth," as Martha notes late in the play; Mary has in fact outed Martha, who has been in love with the heterosexual Karen for years. Martha commits suicide after revealing her secret to Karen in the play's final act.

Hellman uses many metaphors in her play, which also attacks small-town mortality and deconstructs class differences. But a queer reading of *The Children's Hour* points to the terrors of the closet and the nature of what would eventually be called outing. Martha is closeted even to herself, unable to acknowledge her deep and passionate love for Karen because she knows it is "wrong." More important, because Karen has a fiancé, Martha also knows that her passion, even if acknowledged, will not be reciprocated. Rather than risk rejection, she lives with her secret. But as Hellman repeats throughout the play in various incidents with different characters, it is in the nature of secrets that they be revealed. A queer reading simplifies Hellman's script: No closet door can remain closed to everyone, and if the wrong person opens that door (a vicious and vengeful person, for example), outing is inevitable.

Outing was also a regular feature of the movie magazines that saw their heyday from the 1930s through the 1950s. In those scandal sheets, read by millions, actresses were regularly outed for their heterosexual behavior. But Greta Garbo and Marlene Dietrich were outed as lesbians, and false inferences were made about Katharine Hepburn after her androgynous roles in *Christopher Strong* and *Sylvia Scarlett*. While both Dietrich and Garbo were notorious for their affairs with women, Hepburn was then romancing a married man: Spencer Tracy. These tabloids did minor damage to these women's careers. In fact, Hepburn would no doubt have been more damaged by being outed as the other woman in Tracy's marriage than by insinuations of lesbianism.

Comparable tabloids in today's market have also taken to outing celebrities. A recent target was country megastar Dolly Parton. Like Dietrich sixty years earlier, Parton responded to the accusation with a shrug and a "so what?" While denying that she was involved with the woman the tabloid mentioned, Parton noted that she indeed spent a lot of time with the woman because she enjoyed her company and stated unequivocally that if she *were* a lesbian she wouldn't care who knew. She repeats both the accusation and the rebuttal in her autobiography.

Parton's response, while certainly in keeping with her down-to-earth honesty, is the exception rather than the rule. Few women accused of lesbianism so coolly answer the charge. In 1989, Whitney Houston's publicity people issued nearly forty statements denying that the singer's relationship with then longtime companion Robin Crawford was lesbian.

Outing can also come from an unexpected source: a former lover. That was the situation the married tennis star Billie Jean King found herself in when a former paramour sued her for palimony. King admitted to the relationship but never admitted to the charge of lesbianism. The scandal significantly damaged her career: She lost the advertising endorsements that comprise about a third of most athletes' incomes, as well as any chance at being a sportscaster.

And outing has even more sinister aspects. Revisionist historical views indicate that a presumption of lesbianism fueled some of the hysteria during the Salem witch trials. Many of the "witches" were outed by the adolescent girls who initiated the craze. All accused the women involved of causing them physical or sexual torment. The McCarthy hearings of the 1950s made communism and homosexuality synonymous. Senator Joseph McCarthy equated the two and in his quest to rout Communists, outed many a true queer and accused many who weren't. While McCarthyism was at its peak, countless women and men were destroyed by those accusations.

In 1993, conservative Topeka renegade Reverend Fred Phelps, a virulent homophobe and defrocked Baptist minister, began a campaign of outing women in the local government and businesses. Sending newsletters, picketing outside offices and restaurants, and organizing protests on the streets of Topeka, he led a campaign to rid the town of lesbians. (Phelps also picketed outside the funerals of gay men who had died of AIDS.) An organized effort by both straight and queer targets of his campaigns leveled lawsuits at Phelps, but he is a skilled attorney, as are several of his thirteen children. He was able to quash each of the suits filed. Because his targets included straights within Topeka society, however, the majority of the town rallied behind the lesbians and gay men he had outed. Phelps so angered Topekans with his outing tactics that a bridge between the queer and straight communities was formed, and many queer Kansans outed themselves in solidarity with those Phelps had attacked.

Similar outing tactics have been used by other members of the religious right in states where antiqueer initiatives have been placed on the ballots, such as Washington, Oregon, and Colorado. These uses of the tactic have alarmed mainstream lesbian and gay activists and further polarized the community about outing. But radical activists—some using the Topeka incident as an example—make the claim that if queers come out themselves, they can't be threatened by a would-be Fred Phelps or a former lover.

Lesbian celebrities who have come out publicly say the move has been the most freeing of their lives. And while they don't pretend that coming out eliminates homophobia, they do assert that being openly lesbian doesn't have to damage one's career irreparably.

Martina Navratilova, Melissa Etheridge, k. d. lang, Roberta Achtenberg, Linda Villarosa, Alice Walker—these are all famous lesbians who have been able to maintain their celebrity, or in the case of Achtenberg, their political cachet, while declaring their sexual preference.

Indisputably, outing is a problematic political weapon, one that can be used as easily by homophobes as by the queer community itself. Many lesbians assert it is antifeminist, while others claim it devolves from feminist political theory. In the early days of the National Organization for Women in the 1970s, lesbian members were outed and purged from the organization. NOW's then-president Betty Friedan argued that these women would damage the fragility of feminism and the mainstream image of the organization with their "obvious" lesbianism. In 1991, NOW president Patricia Ireland, who is married but also in a long-term relationship with a woman, was outed by the *New York Times*, which argued the media's right to know.

Did either of these outing experiences damage feminism or the individuals involved? Feminism is always threatened in the mainstream by associations with lesbianism, but it has managed to perpetuate itself nonetheless. Ireland has weathered the storm well, and most of the lesbians purged from NOW actually gained lesbian political cachet from the experience. But some lesbians who were purged from the fledgling NOW remain furious to this day about the experience of having their sexual choices divulged and then used as a reason for expulsion from the organization, citing homophobia and heterosexism. As for Ireland, she said her private life should remain private.

One of the reasons outing remains such a potent political tool stems from changing attitudes about what is private. Does a public figure like Ireland have the right to keep secrets about her personal sexual life—particularly given her role as titular leader of the nation's feminists? Isn't it important, perhaps even vital, that women know whether she is a lesbian or bisexual, whether she has children, or even whether she has ever had an abortion? Aren't these relevant bits of information to have about a woman who is speaking publicly for the women of the United States?

In mainstream politics the gloves have come off on personal privacy issues; there *is* no privacy for public figures, queer or straight. But mainstream political activists, particularly the assimilationists, assert that sexual choice and sexual privacy are, or should be, synonymous. In a country where it is illegal to be a lesbian or gay man in over half the states, however, there can be no true sexual privacy. In fact, the U.S. Supreme Court basically stated this in the 1986 ruling on *Bowers v. Hardwick,* which upheld Georgia's sodomy statute in a case where police had raided the home of a gay man at dawn and found him in the midst of consensual sex with another adult male. (The case could also be perceived as one of state-orchestrated outing.)

The outing controversy will only be settled by time and history. As long as people remain in the closet, there will be people with a variety of motives eager to pull them out. Conversely, as more people choose to come out of their own volition, the power of the closet and secrecy over lesbianism or homosexuality will be eroded.

Back in the mid-1970s, the lesbian theorist Charlotte Bunch wrote an article on lesbianism for *Ms.* magazine. In her piece she noted that until the charge of lesbianism carried no political weight—that is, until no woman cringed at being called a lesbian, until it was no longer a threat—lesbians would not truly be equal in this society. Bunch's commentary still applies.

Lesbians have a long and complicated history with outing, one that spans centuries. In this century the power has shifted. We are no longer doomed to be the victims of a child's accusation—whether in Salem or in the workplace. We are no longer doomed to the choice of Martha in *The Children's Hour*—outed to death. As more women come out publicly, there are more examples of happy, fulfilled lesbians. Ultimately *they* will bring about the annihilation of the closet—and with it the need for outing as a political device.

PART FIVE

THE LESBIAN BODY

TWENTY-THREE

HEALTH CARE ISSUES

Karen F. Kerner

Although lesbians and straight women share many of the same health care concerns, some issues are unique to lesbians. In addition, lesbians often perceive or experience interactions with health care providers differently. Lesbians are specifically concerned about breast, ovarian, and cervical cancer; sexually transmitted diseases (STDs) and AIDS; chronic fatigue immune dysfunction syndrome (CFIDS); pregnancy and alternative insemination; obesity; and substance abuse. Aside from specific medical conditions, lesbians must also consider crucial issues such as our inclusion in medical research, barriers to access to care, the influence of traditional Western medicine, the pioneering role of gay and lesbian clinics, outreach to and education of underserved lesbian populations, and the reeducation of providers. The inevitability of health care reform means we must work to ensure our inclusion in a system that will bring both benefits and restrictions to our lives.

ACCESS TO CARE

Imagine you're going for your annual checkup, an appointment fraught with fear and dread above and beyond concerns about your health and your ability to pay. The pelvic exam might leave you hurt and embarrassed, you hate to get on the scale, you're afraid you'll forget all the questions you want to ask. Your doctor may want to know if it's possible that you're pregnant. If you tell him you're a lesbian, you'll run the risk of incurring his wrath, loathing, or just plain ignorance.

I am a lesbian physician who has been practicing in busy urban emergency departments since 1979. I consider myself a knowledgeable and sophisticated consumer of health care. Yet, until four years ago, I thought there was nothing incongruous about my seeing a male gynecologist. At that time, I began to experience very irregular and scant periods, hot flashes, mood swings, and dry skin and hair. I was forty-seven. It didn't take a medical degree to figure out what was going on. After a few months of classic symptoms, I went to my doctor and told him I thought I was beginning menopause. His first reaction was, "Are you sure you're not pregnant?" I told him I was very sure and why. His next statement was, "You're too young for menopause!" By the time I finally convinced him, I felt as if I were the doctor and he the patient. At the end, he threw a package of hormone pills at me and told me to make a follow-up appointment when I had finished the pills.

I never went back. Luckily, I had resources that allowed me to find a woman health care provider who would treat me like an adult, take my questions seriously, and accept my sexual orientation. But what about "the stone butch who can't deal with having her breasts touched, and who can't deal with having a vaginal exam"? demanded Carmen Vasquez, policy director of New York's Lesbian and Gay Community Center. What about lesbians who are less fortunate, live marginal lives, and are automatically excluded from mainstream health care delivery? What about poor women, lesbians of color, intravenous drug users, HIV-positive women, or "outlaws" like sex workers, leather dykes, and cross-dressers?

How many women and how many lesbians experience ignorance, indifference, disapproval, overt discrimination, and even abuse by so-called health care givers? We don't know exactly, but many studies show that lesbians are more likely to cancel appointments, fail to follow up on referrals for specific problems, and avoid routine checkups because of past discrimination or because they fear coming out to a health care provider. "We have horror stories to tell," reports Cuca Hepburn. "We acknowledge how difficult it is for most of us to confront the medical establishment."

Our negative expectations are realistic, as demonstrated by clinicians' reactions to frank revelations of lesbian lifestyles: inappropriate prurience, embarrassment, disgust, rejection, and/or immediate referral for psychotherapy. Confirming what most of us know firsthand, Patricia Stevens, an R.N. and Ph.D., reviewed the clinical literature on health care providers' attitudes toward lesbians from 1970 to 1990. She found that many lesbians reported "intimidation and humiliation" upon disclosure of their sexual identity. Heterosexual doctors often attempt to trivialize our sexual identity by declaring that who we sleep with doesn't matter, and then denying visitation to hospitalized women by their partners or lovers because they are not "family."

There is also an issue of confidentiality about one's sexual choices. If the patient wants her sexual identity kept out of the medical record, this is her privilege. Some physicians use discreet coding to identify a lesbian, with her permission, in the medical chart. Records are not as sacred or confidential as they should be, so although my personal feeling is that pertinent information concerning a lesbian's health care should be on the chart, I would leave the final decision to the patient.

Apart from discomfort and fear, many women are barred from regular care by economics. Women earn considerably less than men, and as lesbians, we may have chosen nontraditional, less-well-paying careers. Also, lesbian partners usually cannot share health benefits or have each other's children covered, as do married heterosexuals.

Fear of health care encounters and avoidance of routine care may be a life-threatening risk to the lesbian with a breast lump or an abnormal Pap smear. The average time between Pap smears for heterosexual women is less than a year; for lesbians it's almost two years. Unfortunately, obstetricians/gynecologists, those clinicians most likely to deliver both basic primary care and essential cancer-screening services to all women, have been found to be among the most homophobic of all doctors. Lesbians are also less likely to seek regular gynecological care because most of us don't get pregnant. According to Dr. Katherine O'Hanlan of the Gay and Lesbian Medical Association (GLMA), more than 80 percent of lesbians never conceive. Women who are pregnant are usually forced to seek medical care, if only at the moment of giving birth. Afterward, it is likely that they will have follow-up visits for themselves and their children, and will continue their care with routine pelvic and breast exams. In sharp contrast, "crisis medicine," the practice of seeking care on the spur of the moment for emergency conditions, is the dangerous solution that many lesbians have accepted.

CANCER

The fact that few lesbians become pregnant may present health care problems for them. For example, the risk of developing breast cancer is increased for women who have never been pregnant, who defer pregnancy until later in life, who have never breast-fed, and who had early periods or late menopause. Also, it seems that the more children you have, the lower your risk, and having both ovaries removed before menopause also lowers your risk. In other words, the more you menstruate or ovulate, the higher your risk. Susan Love, in *Dr. Susan Love's Breast Book,* cautions that breast cancer is a "multifactorial disease," with so many interacting causes that no solitary factor can be isolated. But many lesbians fall into a higher risk category because we do not have children or we put off pregnancy until later in life.

Risk is also dependent on other factors which may have nothing to do with being a lesbian. It increases with age, a positive family history of breast cancer, and with high-fat diets. Genetic risk factors involve about 30 percent of breast cancer victims. Lethal radiation and estrogen treatment have been implicated as well.

In 1992, Suzanne Haynes, chief of the health education section at the National Cancer Institute, postulated an increased risk of breast cancer for lesbians based on the higher prevalence of obesity, alcohol consumption, and smoking in the lesbian population, practices that have been linked to breast cancer. Other researchers, notably Judith Bradford and Caitlin Ryan in their *National Lesbian Health Care Survey* (1988), confirmed that lesbians seem to drink and smoke more than heterosexual women and, even more significantly, that rates of alcohol and tobacco use do not decline with age in the lesbian population, as they do with straight women. Sharon Deevey, a researcher who studied older lesbians and reviewed studies from the 1970s and 1980s, stated that older lesbians were "invisible because of the triple minority status of their age, gender and sexual orientation." Her surveys revealed that alcohol consumption, extra weight, and skepticism about traditional medicine emerged as specific issues for older women.

No scientific studies tell us whether lesbians are actually heavier than straight women, but lesbians may be less concerned with weight than was previously thought. Generally, those most anxious about their weight and body image are those seeking the approval of men—that is, gay men and straight women. Susie Orbach, author of *Fat Is a Feminist Issue,* believes that to many women, "fat represents substance and strength," allowing us to feel "big and authoritative." It would make sense, then, that in a homophobic and patriarchal society, lesbians would seek reinforcement and validation of their choices via weight gain.

Some risks for breast cancer overlap with those for ovarian cancer, so lesbians are often declared to be at higher risk for this disease as well. Ovarian cancer can be "silent" until it is too late for definitive treatment. There is often no pain or detectable lump, as with breast cancer. A lack of obvious symptoms emphasizes the importance of regular pelvic exams and general checkups for all women. Positive family history is a major factor and increases the risk greatly. However, unlike breast cancer, birth control pills, rarely used by lesbians, seem to lower the risk for this disease. Both ovarian and breast cancer occur more frequently in white, affluent, European or North American women, perhaps because their diets are higher in fat and they tend to put off pregnancy and to have fewer children than do poorer women. Despite these statistics, when women of color develop breast cancer they tend to be diagnosed much later and have a much higher mortality rate than do white women. Delayed treatment, often resulting in rapid deterioration and death, appears to be directly related to lack of access to cancer screening and routine primary care. In this eleventh-hour approach to treatment, women of color, whether straight or gay, often find themselves in the same situation as many lesbians.

We have often been told that lesbians won't get cervical cancer because we are not in any of the important risk groups. It is mistakenly assumed that we never have sex with men, are likely to be monogamous, and don't have genital warts or human papilloma virus (HPV) infections. There are even gynecologists who believe Pap smears to be unnecessary for lesbians, because only women who sleep with men could become pregnant, get STDs, or develop cervical cancer. This is like signing a death warrant for lesbians, especially when a 1993 report from the Centers for Disease Control (CDC) confirms that some strains of HPV have been "strongly associated" with cervical cancer. These conditions are often diagnosed by gross visual examination, colposcopy (using a kind of microscope to look at the cervix), or Pap smear. Informal communications from many American practitioners reveal that HPV might be the most common STD seen in lesbians. It is the third most common STD among all

Margaret Robison

I wanted to smash my fist
against the dashboard of the car,
to do such violence to my hand.
I'd wanted so to hold
my new grandson in my arms,
but my spastic left arm
only drew my clenched fist
hard against my chest.
What confusion of rage and tears I felt.
Now my hand rests on my thigh,
palm up. Fingers curled.
Vulnerable like my grandson
who curls and uncurls his fingers,
yawns a milky yawn, relaxes
into sleep again.
My left hand, part of all
the seasons of my life, it helped me
tie my shoelaces the first time. It
  grasped

the rough rope of my swing, brought
my schoolbooks home, and closed
my suitcase when I left for college.
Did the Australian crawl.
It gathered wildflowers from the woods.
Pulled weeds. Baked bread.
Held my children. Drove my car.
Cut my husband's hair.
After my divorce, it held
the banister as I climbed down
the courthouse steps. It caressed
the face of the woman who became
my lover then. Now
it dangles from my arm, assuming
the importance of a bookmark
marking the end of one chapter,
beginning of the next.

groups in Britain, noted in a 1990 paper that also emphasized the high prevalence of HPV and herpes simplex virus (HSV) in lesbians. In addition, HPV is rivaling chlamydia as the most rapidly increasing STD in the general population in the United States.

Cervical cancer is usually asymptomatic and almost 100 percent curable in its early stages. As with other cancers, successful treatment depends on early detection, in this case, primarily via a yearly Pap smear. Obtaining this simple test is as easy as getting an annual checkup—which may be difficult, unheard of, or impossible for many lesbians. In addition, no one knows the effects on the cervix of constant battering by penetrating sex toys and fists. It may be that (although when used with latex barriers, this practice does not transmit STDs) repeated minor trauma to the cervix predisposes lesbians to inflammation, infections, and cancer.

STDs AND AIDS

Sexually transmitted diseases are so much less common in lesbians than in straight women that some practitioners feel it is a waste of time to test us for them. But it is crucial to prevent, diagnose, and treat STDs in lesbians. We are less likely than heterosexuals to worry about chlamydia or AIDS, less likely to practice safe sex, and less likely to be routinely tested for HIV. Although uncommon, genital diseases can be transmitted from woman to woman, especially in the presence of open sores or inflamed tissues.

Lesbians are often reluctant to talk about what we do in bed. As Amber Hollibaugh, director of the Lesbian AIDS Project of the Gay Men's Health Crisis, put it, "it's very controversial for a lesbian to talk about whether or not she uses sex toys, she fucks men, or whether or not she rims or is rimmed by her girlfriend." But it is precisely our sexual activity that defines our risk. Plain and dirty talk about sex, as featured in 'zines like *Bad Attitude* and *Taste of Latex,* is read by only a minority of women. Even the more mainstream magazines, like *Deneuve* and *On Our Backs,* which feature fiction and factual pieces about lesbian sex, do not have wide circulation. There has been little general information about safe sex between women, except for Pat Califia's *Sapphistry* and *The Lesbian S/M Safety Manual.* Only very recently have such works as *The Lesbian Sex Book* by Wendy Caster and *The Good Vibrations Guide to Sex* by Cathy Winks and Anne Semans provided basic information for women having sex with women. Now that we know that lesbians can get AIDS, safe sex videos and workshops proliferate, and organizations like the Lesbian AIDS Project and the Women's Caucus of ACT UP provide essential information to sexually active lesbians. Unfortunately, these services are not usually offered by the health care establishment.

Although these sources are available to those who seek them out, a false sense of security still keeps women from accessing the information. Despite a growing awareness that there are lesbians with AIDS, many of us believe we are safe from the transmission of STDs or HIV. Women who use penetrating sex toys or engage in S/M practices involving urine or feces, fisting, whipping, cutting, or piercing are at risk because of breaks in the mucosal and skin barriers that usually protect us against infection. In the same way, untreated STDs provide a potential route for HIV transmission because disrupted genital tissue is more likely to bleed during sexual activity.

Women who identify as lesbian but also have sex with men are often hesitant to admit it; thus they deny their contact with a potential reservoir of AIDS and other STDs. Because of fear of being labeled politically incorrect, embarrassment about having been raped, or shame at having traded sex for money or drugs, these women may keep quiet about their heterosexual activity. Several recent studies from the United States and Europe reported a significant percentage of women partnering with women who had unprotected consensual sex with men in the preceding three years. Not surprisingly, many of these men were close friends and were gay. A significant number of the men were also intravenous drug users; it is unclear how many of the women were also drug users. According to Joyce Hunter, president of the National Lesbian and Gay Health

Victoria A. Brownworth

It was midwinter and bitterly cold the morning I had the first tumor removed from my breast. It was one month before my twenty-eighth birthday, and still dark when I arrived at the hospital. My teeth were chattering from cold and fear, and I was shivering all over. My surgeon, a tall, attractive blonde woman with a slight Austrian accent, greeted me cheerily, dressed in green surgical scrubs and a string of opera-length pearls. She told me she would make as small an incision as she could, that she would remove only what she had to. The pearls gave me hope that she would do as little damage to my breast as possible.

For months I had had a pain in my right breast and a heightened awareness of it, a sensation I didn't have in the other one. What I had was a tumor the size of a child's fist, a tumor that showed up as an ominous white splotch on the mammography X ray.

On the day I casually mentioned the pain, the sensation, to my doctor, he examined my breasts thoroughly. Then he took from the pocket of his lab coat a plastic card with graduated-sized holes cut in it and placed it over my breast. He held it up to me, pointed to the largest hole, and said, "You have a mass this size. You need to see a surgeon."

Surgery followed: one and then another, eighteen months later, after the tumor grew back. Most of my breast tissue had been removed. After the second operation, my formerly pale-pink breast was hard and black as macadam, and a long, plastic drain hung from the scar, blood and fluid leeching out of the wound for days.

The odd thing is, I never actually felt frightened, despite the chattering teeth and the quaking of my body on the morning of the surgery. I accepted that these operations would happen and that I might die, as my great-grandmother had, of breast cancer. Instead, like too many women, my concerns lay with the image of my body, rather than the possibility of my death. I had beautiful breasts and I was proud of them, as I might be of a flashy new car—I didn't want them damaged. Rather than worrying about how I might look in a shroud, I worried about how I might look to present and future lovers with the deformity of a scarred or missing breast. I wanted my beautiful body to stay beautiful.

Ten years later, three of which have been spent acutely ill, I feel differently. Now I would trade body parts for health, trade almost anything for what I now recognize as the superb good health I had when I first met the surgeon.

Now I know more than I would like to about illness, dying, death. My surgeon, the blonde with the pearls, got breast cancer three years ago. She has left her brilliant career as one of the top surgeons in my city. Now she goes to art school, now she reconstructs her life on canvas.

She does fine work. Ten years later, my breasts are still beautiful. The scar is nothing more than a fine white line, a pale pink slice of memory. And survival.

Foundation, lesbian adolescents were especially likely to have anal intercourse with their gay male teenage friends. (See her chapter in this volume.) Substance abuse leading to an altered state of consciousness invariably produced a denial of the dangers of HIV and STD transmission and a disregard for safe sexual practices in the young adults who were studied.

In addition to chlamydia and HPV, women can pass a variety of infections to one another, including HIV, genital HSV, gonorrhea, syphilis, bacterial vaginosis, trichomoniasis, candidiasis, viral hepatitis, and some intestinal parasites. Most sexually transmitted infections are present in semen, vaginal fluid, and/or blood (including menstrual blood). Some are also found in feces and urine. Of course, crabs (pubic lice) and scabies (mites) are also transmitted from person to person, often during sexual activity, but these are more properly considered superficial infestations, not infections. Some researchers have postulated that CFIDS, the chronic debilitating condition that has sometimes been referred to as "our AIDS" because it affects many lesbians, may be a viral illness sexually transmitted between women.

Those of us involved in front-line patient care have begun using gloves and gowns to prevent transmission of blood- and bodily fluid–borne disease between patient and clinician, assuming everyone we touch could be infectious. So, too, should we assume everyone we sleep with, male or female, is capable of transmitting a serious or deadly disease and practice safe sex accordingly.

One risk for HIV transmission that is becoming increasingly important to lesbians who want children is alternative insemination. Fifteen or twenty years ago we could fill a container with the fresh semen of a gay male friend and use a turkey baster (hence the term "baster babies") to introduce the ejaculate. Today it is clear that without prior testing for HIV and STDs, this casual practice is no different from having unprotected sex with the sperm donor. As April Martin cautions in *The Lesbian and Gay Parenting Handbook,* using frozen semen from a sperm bank ensures that the donor was tested at the time of collection and again six months later. (See Heather Conrad and Kate Colwell's "Creating Lesbian Families" in this volume.)

Until recently, the notion of HIV transmission between women was treated as a joke by the medical establishment. A scattering of clinical notes in mainstream medical journals in the 1980s reported the possibility of infection between lesbians when one partner was an intravenous drug user. The implication was that if one partner was shooting up, her lover must be sharing her needles. No one believed that one woman could pass the infection to another through lesbian sex. Although there is not yet enough evidence to determine the true incidence of HIV transmission between women, we are beginning to see papers on lesbians and HIV presented at the yearly International Conference on AIDS. In New York City, a Bellevue Hospital/Community Health Project study in 1989 con-cluded that false assumptions about lesbians' lack of risk for HIV transmission "can lead to tragic misdiagnosis by providers and lack or risk awareness by the women themselves."

Once a woman, straight or lesbian, is diagnosed as HIV-positive, where is she to go for treatment? Most AIDS clinics and treatment centers were created and developed for gay men. Understandably, a woman might not be able to get proper counseling or gynecological care, and might feel uncomfortable, in this setting. The situation contributes to the negative reinforcement that pushes sick women away from the providers of care.

WHAT WE NEED TO KNOW

It is important to remember that the health issues specific to lesbians overlap with those of straight women, and are implied rather than based on hard scientific data. To the casual eye, breast cancer is epidemic in the lesbian population. It could be that this condition is simply epidemic among women in general. At present we don't know the true incidence of breast cancer among lesbians. We can only extrapolate from our knowledge that most lesbians will never become pregnant and that women who do not bear children are at higher risk.

Much of our information comes from surveys, often self-administered, whose results cannot be viewed as more than a trend. Studies are written based on questionnaires, or retrospective samples, whose conclusions tend to be self-fulfilling prophecies. Samples are frequently too small, and often include mostly well-educated white urban dwellers. Indeed, this population is the most accessible and the most likely to perceive a benefit from answering questions. In addition, there are no age, ethnic, or socioeconomically adjusted control groups of heterosexual women.

The National Gay and Lesbian Task Force (NGLTF) Policy Institute published an Action Plan for Lesbian Health in 1993 that included the following recommendations to the Health and Human Services (HHS) Department:

Lesbians must be included as subjects, reviewers, and researchers in all studies on women's health.

Lesbians must be included as a specific subgroup of women in all treatment and prevention initiatives for women's health care.

Sexual identity and activity questions must be included in all surveys.

HHS must create a fully funded office on Lesbian Health Care.

The NGLTF also made specific recommendations to the CDC regarding inclusion of lesbians in breast cancer and cervical cancer prevention plans, HIV risk-reduction programs, and STD studies. The CDC was encouraged to expand its definition of *lesbian* to include more women than simply those who have had "only female sex partners since 1977." The National Institutes of Health was strongly urged by NGLTF and GLMA to include lesbians in all women's health research, especially long-term studies of the causes of death and disability in women, like the Boston Nurses Health Study and the Women's Health Initiative.

There is a desperate need for rigorous prospective studies and clinical data on lesbians with respect to specific health issues. Research on AIDS must focus on multiple-risk categories for women and more comprehensive case reporting. More information is needed on lesbian sex practices. The Lesbian AIDS Project's Women's Sex Survey is a good model, providing more specific data than previous studies on practices like vaginal and anal fisting. We must determine how many lesbians have breast cancer or CFIDS, and whether the incidence is higher or the same as in the general population.

Substance abuse by lesbians is another area that deserves more thorough research. As many as 7 percent to 35 percent of lesbians have been reported to abuse alcohol in at least three separate studies in the late 1980s, although these figures have been challenged as much of the data was gathered in lesbian bars.

We also need to know why so many lesbians are in psychotherapy. There are no data that show that psychological problems are more common in lesbians than in heterosexual women. Are we all so miserably depressed and dysfunctional that we need to lie on the couch and bare our souls two or three times a week? Or is the desire for therapy a logical reaction to the stress of being in the closet, coming

Kitty Tsui

My best friend has been dead for eight years. How can that be? Seems like just yesterday we talked on the phone, walked on Baker Beach, took a sauna at Finilla's, ate Vietnamese-style crab with our hands. But she's been dead for eight years. And I still miss her.

Anita Oñang and I were friends for thirteen years. I met her in the early 1970s when she was part of the Women's Press Collective. She wore her hair short and rode a BMW. She loved to dance, shop, smoke dope, and fish on the Berkeley Marina. But mostly she loved women and she loved to eat.

We were sisters, buddies, best friends. We planned to grow old together. But that was not to be. Cancer took her when she was thirty-six.

The memorial service was March 8, 1986, at the wedding site in the Oakland Rose Garden. Linda Tillery was to sing, and I was asked to speak.

Where would I find the words? What could I possibly say that would convey the scope of my grief, the depth of my love?

As we didn't always live in the same city, or even the same country, and since one or the other of us was often broke, we communicated by mail. I decided to use her words, culled from letters written between 1977 and 1985, for the memorial ceremony.

"I send you my hope and strength and love in your time of difficulty and sorrow. I send prayer and bright sun fire yellow, white, red flame of candlelight to embrace you. Incense rises to the highest, the highest where we all come from and where we all eventually will return.

"I love you from afar and miss your sweet self. Thank you for your love, so true. We have shared a wealth of love together, of growing, knowing, opening. We grew countless times . . . touching, giving, struggling, loving over and over. . . . Our circle is complete and eternally unbroken. So many thanks to the Divine Force that continues to unite us as family, as friends for all time. A year is a year is a year. . . . How I love you and hold you close. You will always be in my heart. Don't forget me. Till we meet again, I love you. Anita."

It was a gray day, shrouded in mist. Incense rose in great clouds to the sky. As I spoke her words, I looked out at the crowd of women. Femmes in dresses, hair coiffed. Butches in suits and starched shirts. Anita would have been pleased to see us, her family of friends, gathered together to celebrate her life.

Dear Anita: I love you. I miss you. Write to me in my dreams.

out to face discrimination and rejection, suffering gay bashing, or simply living as an outsider in a homophobic world? We just don't know. Lesbians often lack the usual social supports available to other women: family, co-workers, and religious and social organizations. Lesbian support, when present, usually comes from friends, partners, and lesbian/gay community organizations.

Finally, lesbian battering by female partners is a problem often denied by victims and ignored by the rest of us. Hate and bias crimes against us appear to be generally underreported; on college campuses, however, lesbians report being victims of assault twice as much as straight women do. Lesbians and gay men may be the most frequently assaulted group in the nation, but we need better statistics to determine whether this is true.

HEALTH CARE REFORM AND GOALS FOR LESBIAN HEALTH

Reform must ensure some basic rights. First, everyone must be covered; next, benefits must be comprehensive. There can be no restrictions for preexisting conditions; nondiscrimination clauses must include sexual orientation and must include health care practitioners as well as patients; and, most important, coverage cannot be taken away.

The NGLTF, in its Health Security Act Analysis published in March 1994, recommended that all lesbians be officially designated an underserved population because of "access problems . . . fewer screening exams . . . [which] may lead to poorer health status." In order to provide adequate health care for all, there must be community outreach by health care professionals to traditionally underserved groups within the lesbian population: poor women, women of color, the S/M community, older women, the physically disabled, those who are HIV-positive, and sex workers. These women are not going to make appointments for regular checkups, get their Pap smears and mammograms, or follow up on emergency visits without assistance from providers.

Providing education and information to empower lesbian patients to take charge of their lives and their health has been a function of many of the pioneering lesbian and gay clinics in this country. Organizations like the Whitman-Walker Clinic in Washington, D.C., Lyon Martin Health Services in San Francisco, and the Lesbian Health Program of the Community Health Project in New York City have contributed greatly to the ongoing primary care of thousands of women. Government funding for community health clinics for lesbians would allow for expansion of these vital services in urban centers and rural areas. Advocacy by peers can help those women who may be hesitant to speak out to their providers. Not every health care consumer is aggressive enough to present her clinician with a list of questions and symptoms. Some patients will benefit by having one or more women accompany them as facilitators, ensuring that they get answers to their questions.

The managed care/health maintenance organization (HMO) setting that is becoming the norm will permit less access to the primary provider of one's choice. There will be fewer providers to choose from, so it will become more difficult for the lesbian patient to get what she needs from her doctor. HMOs must make it possible for lesbians and gay men to select practitioners who are knowledgeable about and supportive of our health issues. There are several ways for this to come about. One is the education of health care professionals about our special needs. Government agencies, hospitals, and medical associations must be involved in dispelling health practitioners' ignorance about our lives. The school curricula in the medical, nursing, and health professions must include sections on lesbian and gay lifestyles and self-criticism and sensitivity-training sessions for students. National associations like GLMA and its local affiliates are already supporting openly gay and lesbian physicians.

We must also be allowed to pursue reasonable alternative treatments and therapies and to get reimbursed for them. The American Medical Association currently calls such unconventional methods "unproven, disproven, controversial, fraudulent and questionable approaches to solving health problems." It seems that practitioners offering massage, acupuncture, biofeedback, aroma therapy, psychic healing with crystals, and chiropractic services appear at every lesbian festival and in every urban neighborhood noted for its lesbian residents. This proliferation is clearly the result of distrust of the traditional doctor-patient relationship and, with it, of many Western health care practices. Women often report that their choice of alternative treatments is a direct result of their fear of disclosing their sexual orientation to a traditional provider.

As this country moves toward health care reform and Congress grapples with conflicting demands, the agenda for lesbians and gay men must be clear. Our goals are simple: Improve our access to health care; increase our use of the system, especially for preventive care; and improve the physical and mental well-being of the lesbian population.

Although we must be committed to improving and transforming the existing health care system, perhaps the truly healthy lesbian nation can be achieved only by our own work from within. To this end, the creation and expansion of more feminist and lesbian health care settings must be our ultimate goal.

FURTHER READING

Brady, Judy, ed. *1 in 3: Women with Cancer Confront an Epidemic.* Pittsburgh: Cleis Press, 1991.

Califia, Pat, ed. *The Lesbian S/M Safety Manual.* Boston: Lace Publications, 1988.

Caster, Wendy. *The Lesbian Sex Book.* Boston: Alyson Publications, 1993.

Gage, Suzann. *A New View of a Woman's Body.* West Hollywood, Calif.: Feminist Health Press, 1991.

Hepburn, Cuca, and Bonnie Gutierrez. *Alive & Well, A Lesbian Health Guide.* Freedom, Calif.: Crossing Press, 1988.

Lorde, Audre. *The Cancer Journals.* San Francisco: Aunt Lute Books, 1980.

Love, Susan M. *Dr. Susan Love's Breast Book.* Reading, Mass.: Addison-Wesley, 1991.

Orbach, Susie. *Fat Is a Feminist Issue.* New York: Berkley, 1990.

The ACT UP/New York Women and AIDS Book Group. *Women, AIDS and Activism.* Boston: South End Press, 1992.

White, Evelyn C., ed. *The Black Women's Health Book.* Seattle: Seal Press, 1994.

OTHER RESOURCES

Lesbian AIDS Project
Gay Men's Health Crisis
129 West 20th Street
New York, NY 10011
(212) 337–3532

National Gay and Lesbian Task Force
Publications Department
2320 17th Street, N.W.
Washington, DC 20009
(202) 332–6483

National Lesbian and Gay Health Foundation
1638 R Street, N.W., #2
Washington, DC 20009
(202) 797–3578

National Women's Health Network
1325 G Street, N.W.
Washington, DC 20005
(202) 347–1140

Sex Information Education Council of the United States
130 West 42nd Street
New York, NY 10036
(212) 819–9770

Outlaws and Addicts: Lesbians and the Recovery Movement

Jane Futcher

Recovery, according to *Webster's,* means getting back something you've lost—maybe your physical health, maybe your sanity. Seems innocent enough, something most lesbians can agree is good. And if you haven't attended a recovery meeting yourself, chances are you know a dozen women who have. If they're not in Alcoholics Anonymous or CoDependents Anonymous, maybe they've tried a newer program, like Women for Sobriety or Save Our Selves. If it works, no harm in trying, right?

Some say there's a lot of harm in trying. If you read *Changing Our Minds: Lesbian Feminism and Psychology,* by British lesbians Celia Kitzinger and Rachel Perkins, they'll tell you that recovery programs are a tool of the patriarchy and that "acceptance within the lesbian communities increasingly appears to depend on the extent to which we are prepared to define ourself as victims—scarred by the currently fashionable wounds." These fashionable wounds, aided by the various recovery groups they've engendered, say the authors, have obscured the true source of lesbian pain: oppression by the patriarchy. Instead of "raising one's self-esteem, loving one's inner child, surviving one's toxic family," lesbians, they argue, will find true healing only by engaging in lesbian feminist political action to topple the patriarchy.

Kitzinger and Perkins are not in recovery themselves and show little interest in talking with lesbians who are. If they did, they would find themselves in conflict with many thousands of recovering lesbians across the country (and around the world) who would consider it demeaning and downright dangerous to describe life-threatening addictions as "fashionable wounds." Consciousness-raising groups and political action committees, these recovering lesbians would argue, won't do much for the alcoholic or addict who'll die if she can't find support for her sobriety.

While the debate continues on how best to help lesbian addicts and alcoholics, the problem grows to epidemic proportions and affects lesbians of all ages, races, and ethnicities. In her article in *Out/Look* magazine, "Getting to Serenity" (summer 1988), Ellen Herman writes that the rate of alcoholism and drug addiction among gay men and lesbians is about three times as high as the rate in the general population—"about one in three compared to one in ten."

Why so many lesbians become problem drinkers and drug users is still unclear. I interviewed twelve lesbians for this chapter. They were all friends, or friends of friends, and ranged between the ages of twenty-eight and sixty-eight. None believe that their sexual orientation was the sole cause of their substance abuse, but many feel the two are closely related. The link is internalized homophobia. After a lifetime of hearing, reading, and experiencing negative messages about homosexuality, many lesbians use addictive substances and/or behaviors to escape the guilt and abysmally low self-esteem these messages engender.

"I drank because I was embarrassed and never felt like I was normal as a kid and a teenager," says Judy, a management consultant who's been sober for six years now. "I was very busy hiding from myself, from my lesbianism, from my drinking, and from my mother and *her* lesbianism. In college and through my twenties, I learned how to *act* normal and led a double life—dating the boys and loving and bedding the women."

Sally, a thirty-six-year-old secretary, drank alcoholically at fifteen: "I used to drown my emotions or keep them under control. I guess there was a time when I tried very, very hard to make my thoughts of falling in love with women vanish by ingesting drugs of all kinds." With sobriety and her membership in AA, which she joined over fifteen years later, Sally "could *begin* to accept [her]self as a lesbian."

In my own case, alcohol provided temporary relief from the self-hatred I felt for loving women and girls. At eighteen, when I agreed, under pressure from my parents, to make my "debut" into society, I drank at every debutante party I attended. Although I had never liked drinking, the Scotch and champagne helped me relax around men and stop worrying about my crushes on women. Long after I came out as a lesbian, at twenty-six, I continued to drink to numb my guilt and inhibitions. More often than not, my dates with women began by getting high at a lesbian bar.

For many years, bars were the only places where lesbians could meet and socialize, which certainly played a role in the drinking of most of the middle-aged women I interviewed. "I came out when *dyke* was synonymous with hard drinking," says Ray, a writer who has been sober for over twenty years. "Pretty much everyone did."

Pam, a fifty-something doctor who has been clean and sober for six years, also socialized in bars: "For a long time, lesbian bars were virtually the only social scene for lesbians, and this gave many of us lesbian alcoholics a greater opportunity to *indulge* our addiction. But I don't think bars *created* our addiction."

For the late Rikki Streicher, former owner of Maud's, a popular Haight-Ashbury lesbian bar that thrived in the 1970s, the recovery movement had a sobering effect on business. By the time Maud's closed in the late 1980s, much of Streicher's clientele "had gotten more middle class, moved to the suburbs, and bought houses."

Many had stopped drinking, and "there were no young people coming up behind them." Where were the younger lesbians? According to Streicher, "instead of going to bars to meet people, a lot of lesbians went to twelve-step meetings. They picked meetings where they'd find people that were like themselves."

A place to meet, says *Out/Look* writer Ellen Herman, is particularly important for lesbians and gay men: "Twelve-step programs provide at least one thing that all people—but especially stigmatized people—are desperate to find: a predictable, safe place in which to feel safe and accepted."

In March 1983, about the time Maud's was beginning to lose some of its allure as a place for lesbians to meet, I quit drinking. I'd been out late with a lesbian I was mad for, watching the performance of a (straight) cabaret singer I loved in secret, and both women rejected me. The next morning I woke up with a pounding head, a fluttering heart, and the resolve to try sobriety for a few months.

At an office party not long after, I confessed to a lesbian co-worker that I was dying for a drink. She persuaded me to go that night to a lesbian AA meeting in Berkeley, where she'd asked her (recovering) lover to meet me. "But I don't think I'm an alcoholic," I whispered, envisioning the proverbial roomful of hardened gutter drunks.

That night I was surprised and a little overwhelmed by what seemed like hundreds of lesbians in a church parish house, drinking coffee and herb tea and calmly discussing some guidelines for recovery. It felt about as safe as a drunk landing at a bar on a Saturday night without a drink in her hand. Of course, that's about what I was. I bridled at the sexist language and Christian bias of the official literature, but I returned to those meetings for several months, lured, in part, by the sheer excitement of being among so many lesbians.

Although I did not become a regular member of that Thursday night fellowship, I found a lot of support for recovery in the San Francisco Bay Area lesbian community. In addition to lesbian AA and Narcotics Anonymous meetings, there were lesbian drop-in groups for codependents, overeaters, incest survivors, children of alcoholics, sex and love addicts, and almost anyone else with a problem. Women's music festivals offered "chemical-free" seating; nationally recognized authors discussed recovery issues at lesbian bookstores. In every gay newspaper in town were hot personal ads written by sober lesbians of every shape, age, color, dildo length, and boot size—looking for same.

Support for sobriety in lesbian communities continues today. Muses one lesbian activist, "I can't imagine that the Woodstock revival [had] sobriety support and a chem-free section!" Says Pam, "It's becoming more socially acceptable to *not* drink." Tonya, a lesbian psychotherapist in AlAnon, agrees: "I find lesbians are conscious of drinking, drugs, and smoking cigarettes and are careful not to impose on anyone."

All this support has helped Sally stay sober: "There are many lesbian dances that are alcohol-free. This is good. If no one is drinking at an event, I feel much more comfortable, and to me it means that every woman can have fun and relate to each other on an equal level without the need for a drug to make it easier."

Clearly, we've come a long way since the 1960s, when Ray first realized she had a drinking problem. "Strangely, AA never once occurred to me, and I suspect this was because I was a lesbian. I felt agencies or help available to straight people were not available to me."

Today, as Ruth, a lawyer and member of AlAnon, points out, even the "celebrities" of the lesbian community have taken the wisdom of the program into their cultural work. One of those celebrities is JoAnn Loulan, whose annual talks draw standing-room-only crowds at San Francisco's annual Living Sober conference for lesbians and gay men in recovery. In an interview in *Out from Under: Sober Dykes and Our Friends,* Loulan explains why community support for lesbians in recovery is so important: "Alcoholism has such a bad rap, and a 'lesbian alcoholic,' who wants to be that?" says Loulan. "It's two of the worst things you can be, according to the majority culture. To admit that is really scary. We need to give support to one another to admit it."

Admitting that *I* was a lesbian and an alcoholic was difficult, particularly when I ventured beyond the lesbian community into some nonlesbian AA meetings in the bedroom community north of San Francisco where I live. I felt like a minority of one. People shared about their husbands and wives and divorces and seemed to assume that everyone else in the room was heterosexual. I rarely spoke, and usually went home feeling lonely and isolated.

At the only lesbian/gay AA meeting in my county, I felt uncomfortable again. The gay men joked mostly with each other, and the lesbians seemed to cruise newcomers instead of welcoming them. When at last I found a lesbian-only meeting just a few minutes from my home, I again returned home depressed. There were only eight of us there, and each one seemed gloomier than the next.

Perhaps things would have been different if I'd spotted someone I was attracted to. After all, cruising goes on at straight meetings. Why shouldn't it happen among lesbians? But Ruth disapproves: "I have seen a lot of lesbians use the meeting to find a lover, and I think that is a mistake. The primary purpose of the meeting is spiritual, not to pick people up. You get distracted. And it can ruin a meeting if you break up, because you may have to stop going to that meeting to avoid seeing your lover."

Such tales of heartbreak and infighting at lesbian recovery meetings inspired a friend of mine to ask me recently whether lesbian recovery meetings might be too ingrown and narrow, a minority within a minority that has limited itself by socializing only with one another. Pam, who goes to both straight and lesbian meetings, doesn't think so: "In lesbian meetings you have a solid community of interests. There are many things that you feel free to talk about that you wouldn't talk about, even with gay men there. And if you work the steps, relationships that develop in that atmosphere—which is social *and* spiritual—have a better opportunity to last and to grow. So the long-term result of lesbian meetings is the opposite of ingrown."

For others, all-lesbian meetings are simply too intense. Karen's self-consciousness around lesbians makes going to lesbian-only meetings awkward: "I feel less comfortable in that setting. It's easier for me to get along with gay men."

Although I never did find the "perfect" AA meeting, I was able to stay sober without AA. But five years after I quit drinking, when a lesbian relationship that was supposed to last a lifetime exploded in my face, I began to attend a straight AA meeting at 7:00 A.M. nearly every morning for three years. I shared openly as a lesbian, and although I continued to feel like something of an outlaw, I began to be more comfortable. I knew my lesbianism was not accepted by everyone at the meeting, but the principles of AA, which require that members tolerate, if not love, each other, shielded me from the in-your-face homophobes.

I've since learned in AA that part of my problem in finding a meeting I liked stemmed from a malaise that is characteristic of alcoholics and addicts and seems particularly rampant among lesbians. Recovery programs call it "terminal uniqueness," which means we feel so different and so isolated from other people that we never feel comfortable anywhere, and our very survival is threatened. Internalized homophobia, masked by years of drinking and suddenly exposed in sobriety, can escalate this feeling of uniqueness to such painful porportions that no meeting, no matter who is present, feels safe or comfortable to lesbians. Today, when I share in nonlesbian/nongay twelve-step meetings, I still find that my palms sweat and my heart races when I'm about to reveal my sexual orientation. This is a pressure that heterosexual women in recovery never have to face.

Although many heterosexuals have become more sensitive to recovery issues than they used to be, not all heterosexuals in recovery are sensitive to issues of sexual orientation. Several of the women I interviewed have felt stigmatized and rebuffed in twelve-step meetings. "I always believed in the twelve-step phrase 'principles before personalities,'" says Sally. "But there have been times when recovery program people I didn't even know have made negative remarks to me about my sexuality as a lesbian. This was hurtful because of my *trust* in fellow program people. I thought rigorous honesty was to be encouraged, but not as an excuse to verbally attack someone."

Despite the homophobia she's encountered, Sally feels she can count on AA when she really needs to. But Diane is angry. As a newcomer to AA three years ago, she was devastated by her breakup with her lesbian lover of twelve years. When she tried to talk about it in straight meetings, "people told me not to talk about my ex-lover. They didn't seem to understand that my relationship was a marriage, as important to me as their marriages were to them." Diane tried to educate straight AA members about lesbianism. For a while things improved, but not for long. "So many things felt so bad that I swallowed them," she explains. "A woman and a fat woman and a butch—I had people in my face all the time. I could never really tell the truth and survive a meeting."

Diane quit AA and now goes to a women's recovery meeting in San Francisco. It's called "A Feminist Alternative to AA," and is based on a program outlined in Charlotte Davis Kasl's book, *Many Roads, One Journey: Moving Beyond the 12 Steps*. Kasl, a psychotherapist who has been in recovery herself, believes that twelve-step programs reflect the biases of the white, heterosexual males who founded AA. "Bill Wilson [AA's principal founder] based the steps and the Big Book on the experiences of a hundred white men and one woman," writes Kasl. These upper-middle-class alcoholic males, she believes, needed a program to smash their "arrogant, resentful, controlling" egos. But she thinks this prescription is wrong for most women: "People who have been victimized and oppressed need to *build* a sense of ego and affirm their power in order to take charge of their lives. Reminding people of their faults and reinforcing humility hardly seems the remedy for a person who has little sense of self, feels ashamed for being alive, and self-blames for just about everything that goes on."

The ninth step—making amends to people you've harmed—is an important part of AA's recovery process, but one that Kasl feels is often inappropriate for minorities. Asale, a black Latina woman interviewed in Kasl's book, explains why it offended her: "It may be that I need to make amends to someone, but that was not what I needed to hear the first day I walked into a twelve-step group. I need to get to that place for myself. When I walk in and see a lot of white people, I think of all the ways white people need to make amends to people of color. So when those phrases are thrown at me, my defenses go up."

According to Gail Hromadko, a psychotherapist who has worked extensively with lesbians in recovery, many lesbians of color find that issues and feelings around ethnicity that have been numbed for years by substance abuse or addictive behaviors start to emerge in sobriety. A predominantly white twelve-step program may be a tough place to heal those feelings. "The more removed you are from the dominant culture," says Hromadko, "the harder AA and most recovery programs will be."

Poor women and lesbians of color also face overwhelming environmental pressures, she adds: "Relapse is incredibly common. In my day, you didn't relapse. Today, for lesbians of color who are dealing with multiple pressures, there's a lot more slipping and sliding. Being too rigid about relapse is unrealistic."

Younger lesbians are another population at risk, says Rhonda Ceccato, former clinical director of the Women's Alcoholism Center in San Francisco: "The majority of the younger lesbians I see are poly-drug-addicted. There's a lot of heroin and IV drugs. A lot of sharing needles. At the same time, there's this veil of unconsciousness around AIDS." Many of Ceccato's younger lesbian clients avoid twelve-step meetings: "They say it's too white, religious, and middle class for them. Ten to fifteen years ago, recovery was a real movement in the lesbian community. Younger lesbians today are more radical and out there and are doing it their way. These women don't feel like they fit in AA. They think only wimps are in AA."

The age at which lesbians *quit* drinking may not be as significant a factor in their recovery, says Hromadko, as their age when their drinking *peaked*. She believes recovery is harder for lesbians whose drinking peaks in adolescence, before their identity is fully formed. When these women get sober, as Hromadko did in her early twenties, they have no "self" to return to, no developmental foundation to fall back on. "I'd never accomplished anything," Hromadko explains, "I didn't have a job. I'd never dated. I didn't know who I was."

Part of knowing oneself is feeling comfortable with one's sexuality, an issue that lesbians of all ages must deal with in sobriety. The process can often be confusing and painful. "Many lesbians have never had sex sober," Hromadko asserts. "And they don't have any stage models for intimacy and for how relationships develop. If you're heterosexual, you date, go steady, and maybe get married. Relationships occur in a cultural context. But these rituals don't exist for lesbian relationships, and lesbians can get so intimate so rapidly, particularly when they're drinking, that the questions don't get asked—like 'Where are we in this relationship process? Are we in a committed relationship? What are our goals, as individuals and as a couple?'"

Sorting out sexuality and relationship issues without alcohol, drugs, or addictive behaviors can have a chilling effect on the sex life of lesbian couples. JoAnn Loulan comments: "When we have two people together who are homophobic, who are lesbians, who are sober, whose bodies are exhausted, who are physically and spiritually depleted, who are women who aren't supposed to know anything about sex or being sexual to begin with, I mean, it's an absolute wonder we have sex at all, in the best of conditions."

Sexual feelings do return, says Loulan, although most lesbians in recovery find they must make big changes in their lives: "You are going to have to rewrite your own history. You are teenagers again, and it's a pain in the ass, but you are."

For lesbian addicts and alcoholics, rewriting one's personal history means, at the very minimum, not drinking and drugging. But for lesbians recovering from "process" addictions, like codependence and other so-called relationship addictions, the revisioning process may be more elusive. "In AA, you just don't drink," says Ruth, of

AlAnon. "But it's not so clear-cut for a codependent. You can't just cut people out of your life. . . . I try not to be controlling and not to think obsessively about what others think of me. But as a lesbian, that's hard sometimes, because I'm often wondering how the straight world views me."

How the straight world views us as lesbians has, until very recently, been overwhelmingly negative. Add to that the label of alcoholic or addict, *et voilà*—as Loulan puts it: "Who wants to be that? It's two of the worst things you can be according to the majority culture." No wonder recovery looks so good to so many lesbians. Addicted, we have lost some of the most important things in our lives. We've lost tangibles, like jobs, housing, health, and families; and we've lost intangibles, like self-esteem, pride, and integrity.

Kitzinger and Perkins argue that recovery programs can't restore those lost qualities or address the fundamental political basis of homophobia and women's oppression. But in my case, being sober has fostered a desire and willingness to take responsibility, to become *more* politically active, to work for change and social justice. Since getting sober, I have written two books on teaching antihomophobia in schools and social service agencies, volunteered at a battered women's shelter, and co-founded a gay/lesbian/bisexual newspaper. I plan to do much more.

I hope that we who have survived the pain of dual stigmas—lesbian and alcoholic/addict—will lead the fight against injustice. For we know how it feels to lose, and we know how it feels to regain what we've lost. In the end, it is this dream—the dream of health, self-respect, and freedom—that has drawn so many lesbians into recovery. With hard work and a lot of luck, that dream will keep us sober.

FURTHER READING

Black, Claudia. *It Will Never Happen to Me.* New York: Ballantine Books, 1987.

————. *Double Duty: Dual Dynamics Within the Chemically Dependent Home*. New York: Ballantine Books, 1990.

Herman, Ellen. "Getting to Serenity: Do Addiction Programs Sap Our Political Vitality?" *Out/Look: National Lesbian & Gay Quarterly*, Summer 1988.

Kaminer, Wendy. *I'm Dysfunctional, You're Dysfunctional: The Recovery Movement and Other Self-Help Fashions*. Reading, Mass.: Addison-Wesley, 1992.

Kasl, Charlotte Davis. *Many Roads, One Journey: Moving Beyond the 12 Steps*. New York: HarperCollins, 1992.

Kitzinger, Celia, and Rachel Perkins. *Changing Our Minds: Lesbian Feminism and Psychology*. New York: New York University Press, 1993.

Kominars, Sheppard B. *Accepting Ourselves: The Twelve-Step Journey of Recovery from Addiction for Gay Men and Lesbians*. New York: Harper & Row, 1989.

Swallow, Jean, ed. *Out from Under: Sober Dykes and Our Friends*. San Francisco: Spinsters Ink, 1983.

————. *The Next Step: Out from Under, Volume Two*. Boston: Alyson, 1994.

TWENTY-FIVE

WHO CARES? LESBIANS AS CAREGIVERS

Jeannine DeLombard

The Graying of America. AIDS. Sharon Kowalski. The sandwich generation. These have become buzzwords for the current caregiving crisis in the United States, a crisis in which lesbians occupy a central, albeit contradictory, position.

On the one hand, lesbians, like other women, are assumed to be naturally qualified to care for others: children, the aged, the sick. Indeed, research suggests that, as lesbians, we stand a much greater chance of being called on to care for our aging or ill parents than our heterosexual sisters do. Likewise, although lesbians are considered to be at low risk for contracting the AIDS virus, we are disproportionately represented in the caregiving network that has emerged in response to its spread. On the other hand, the case of Sharon Kowalski serves as a grim reminder that, unless we take careful legal

This chapter is dedicated to the memory of my Aunt Jean Prochaska, who died of cancer in July 1994. She taught me a great deal about what it means to care for someone, as well as how to live and die with grace and dignity. Although we never discussed my sexual orientation, Auntie Jean treated my lover with affection and repeatedly demonstrated her respect for our relationship.

precautions, we can easily be stripped of our right to care for those to whom we may feel closest—our lovers. Lesbian caregiving in the United States is a catch-22. For if as women we are not only expected but often obliged to care for others, as lesbians we are denied the basic civil rights that would allow us to do so on our own terms.

Like most words, *caregiving* takes on different meanings in different contexts. Here I will focus on informal long-term caregiving, specifically, the care that (usually) untrained lesbians provide for their elderly or ill parents, their lovers, and their friends with AIDS. As America grays and the products of the lesbian baby boom come of age, lesbians will undoubtedly join the ranks of the sandwich generation (those who, "sandwiched" between an older and a younger generation, provide care for both simultaneously) on an unprecedented scale.

Although a great deal of research has been done on women as caregivers, there is virtually none on lesbian caregivers. In this chapter I rely heavily on the experiences of individual lesbian caregivers, and extrapolate, where possible, from existing heterosexist research. I hope this preliminary sketch will delineate the outlines of lesbian caregiving while illustrating the pressing need for more substantive, empirical research on this subject.

CARING FOR THE ELDERLY

The film *Eat, Drink, Man, Woman* depicts three daughters living with their widowed father. Each silently struggles with her sense of responsibility to him and to her sisters, while at the same time seeking autonomy for herself. All three assume that their frail father will soon need care and that the oldest daughter, a mousy high school teacher with little hope for romance, will be the one to provide it. By the time the final credits roll, however, everyone is living happily ever after: The daughters *and* their father have been paired off into happy hetero units. (We are left to assume that the father's new young wife will become his primary caregiver when and if the time comes.)

Art imitates life—to a point. Experts have found that most families in the United States adhere to a rigid caregiving hierarchy in which heterosexual spouses (usually wives, given both women's longevity and their tendency to marry older men) are the preferred primary caregivers. But a higher percentage of daughters than either husbands or wives ends up caring for the elderly, according to a 1987 report prepared by the House of Representatives Select Committee on Aging. The responsibility for caregiving tends to fall to those adult children *perceived* to have the fewest demands on their time. This explains why daughters are four times more likely than sons to become primary caregivers: Our patriarchal culture assumes not only that women are naturally more suited to fulfill nurturing roles but that men's careers and income are more valuable than those of their female counterparts. (The gerontologist Elaine Brody finds that adult children caregivers perform "gender-appropriate" roles: Sons help out with money management, home repairs, and decision making, while daughters provide the bulk of day-to-day hands-on care.) It also explains why unmarried daughters—whether widowed, separated, divorced, or never married—are more likely than their married sisters to take on primary caregiving responsibilities, and why never-married daughters are the most likely to become primary caregivers (as well as the least likely to receive assistance from other family members, according to Brody).

That so many lesbians remain closeted—and perhaps especially those in the forty-five-to-sixty-four-year-old range that composed 42 percent of all caregivers for the elderly in 1987—only exacerbates the situation. Because they do not feel comfortable sharing their sexual orientation with their extended families, many lesbians in committed long-term relationships may be incorrectly perceived by their families as having fewer competing responsibilities of their own and therefore as ideally suited to the role of primary caregiver. Even those lesbians who are out to their families may find that the importance of their relationships is underestimated or that the homophobia of individual family members makes cooperative caregiving difficult.

Take, for example, the situation of Rachel and Louise (not their real names), who have been lovers for four years. They would like to move in together, but each lives with and cares for her mother. Six years ago Rachel, who lives in Maryland, invited her then sixty-nine-year-old mother to live with her, despite the fact that her siblings, both of whom are heterosexual and married, lived near their mother up north. At the time, Rachel was not in a relationship. For years, she and her mother took care of each other, dividing up the cooking, cleaning, shopping, and gardening. Recently, however, Rachel's mother had a stroke that left her mute and partially paralyzed. Although she has regained the ability to move and speak, she tires very easily. As a result, she can no longer do her share of the house-work, and Rachel, who holds a demanding full-time job, must spend an increasing amount of time caring for her and for the house.

Rachel's lover, Louise, has an eighty-year-old mother who is recovering from a broken knee and several cracked ribs, and also suffers from recurrent bouts of pneumonia, frequent strokes, and regular fainting spells. Louise's three married brothers (with whom she is not open about her lesbianism) are not involved in caring for their mother. Louise has been forced to switch from full-time to part-time employment, because she can afford to hire a professional caregiver for only five hours a day. Louise's mother is in denial about her daughter's sexual orientation, which adds further stress to the time Rachel and Louise spend together at Louise's house.

Many caregivers, lesbian and otherwise, find their relationships with their partners an important source of support in this difficult and emotionally draining time. Rachel and Louise's relationship, however, only seems to exacerbate the stress they experience as care-givers. Rachel feels pulled by her work, her lover, and her mother: "I'm busy. . . . [My mother] lets me live my life. But it's still very dif-ficult. . . . I don't give her as much time as I should. I don't know, maybe it's just my old Jewish guilt coming out. But that's my biggest guilt, not spending enough time with her." Rachel also feels that Louise is being manipulated by her family and resents the limitations both women's caregiving responsibilities place on their relationship. She explains: "It's putting stress on me because I don't see any ending to this. I'm in a hard place. Not that I'm going to end the relationship, because I love [Louise] too much. But I feel like running. I just want to run away, period. I feel like a caged damn animal." Lack of insurance coverage means that Rachel, who describes herself as depressed, cannot see her therapist as often as she would like. As she puts it, "I'm living this every day, and every day I don't know how to cope with it."

Gretchen is a thirty-three-year-old only child. Although she lives in Philadelphia, about a five-hour drive from her parents' home in Virginia, she expects to become her parents' primary caregiver, even if they move into a retirement community, as planned. Although Gretchen 's mother is quite physically fit at sixty-seven, both parents are diabetics, and her father, who is seventy-six, is somewhat disoriented as a result of a series of strokes. For now, Gretchen sees her main caregiving responsibility as providing emotional support for her parents, especially her mother, who is depressed by her husband's condition. "I call them every week. I make sure that holidays and birthdays are observed, and that anniversaries get a card. I want to show them that I am a consistent and loving adult in their lives," she says.

But Gretchen has found that her mother's disapproval of her lesbianism has made it difficult to fulfill even such minimal caregiving responsibilities. Despite her commitment to observing holidays with her parents, Gretchen recently decided that she would not celebrate Christmas with her family, in part because Beth, her lover of two years, "is not welcome" in her parents' home. This preliminary conflict suggests that, unless Gretchen can work out a compromise, she soon may find herself forced to choose between her commitment to her lover and her commitment to care for her parents.

Debbie, who lives near Washington, D.C., is the legal guardian for her seventy-nine-year-old father, who recently moved from Arizona into a nursing home in Idaho. Her sister, who also lives in Idaho, visits their father occasionally, but Debbie considers herself his primary caregiver. Although she attributes her guardianship to complex family dynamics unrelated to her sexual orientation, she does find that her Mormon sister's disapproval of her lesbianism cheats her of what could have been a valuable source of emotional support: "I don't always sense that my sister is able to be [supportive]. She certainly doesn't want to know anything about my life, has never met my partner, and would be happier if that was the way it continued."

A related problem is that Debbie suspects her sister (who "handles her anxieties by telling everyone about her defective sister") of discussing Debbie's sexual orientation with nursing home personnel. Debbie, a nurse, already finds long-distance communication with nursing home staff difficult, and her sister's homophobia threatens to undermine Debbie's authority and ultimately to adversely affect the quality of the care their father receives.

Unlike Debbie, Pat has a sister who is supportive of her lesbianism. The two shared caregiving responsibilities for their mother and then their father, both of whom died of cancer. If her family relied more heavily upon her as a caregiver, Pat says, it is because of the three years she spent training to become a nurse, not because of her sexual orientation. Neither Pat nor her sister was involved in a committed, long-term relationship while caring for their parents. If they had been, Pat speculates, the caregiving dynamic would have been different: "Thank goodness I *was* single, that I could give the time that I gave and still maintain my life. If I had a family to take care of, they would have come first. There *is* a higher expectation [placed upon single women to care for their parents]." Pat, a thirty-nine-year-old African-American woman, is also aware of specific cultural expectations with respect to caregiving. She explains: "We are expected to take care of our own from day one, period. Somehow we as a community, as a family, are not *required* [to be caregivers], but it's kind of like a tradition passed down that if we don't take care of our own, nobody else will." For Pat and other lesbian caregivers of color, perhaps even more than others, "putting someone in a nursing home is the last resort," when such facilities are managed by and oriented toward members of the dominant culture.

CARING FOR PEOPLE WITH AIDS

Lesbians have been hard hit by the caregiving crisis that has followed in the wake of AIDS. In *Women and AIDS,* Diane Richardson observes that "the main impact of AIDS on the lesbian community relates to the way in which AIDS has been seen, wrongly, as 'a gay disease' *and* the way in which lesbians have been categorized together with gay men." Although lesbians are considered a low-risk group with respect to HIV, widespread public misconception about the virus means that lesbians are often subject to AIDS discrimination simply by virtue of our sexual orientation. This may explain, in part, why so many lesbians have become caregivers for people with AIDS, whether as professionals, volunteers, friends, or family members. Many lesbians see their AIDS caregiving as a form of gay activism. As Leah Chaplin, a volunteer at Philadelphia's ActionAIDS who has also cared for two friends with HIV, puts it, "I'm not an activist at heart; I get involved at a level which is comfortable, and for me that is in a caregiving, supportive way."

The other reason for lesbians' disproportionate involvement in the AIDS caregiving network is more personal than political. Rejection by their families of origin has led many lesbians and gay men to create new families among themselves. With AIDS' early targeting of the gay male population, many lesbians lost not only their close friends but those they considered, in a very real sense, family. Through their caregiving, they have responded to the AIDS crisis in a way that many gay men's families of origin could not or would not.

Gretchen believes that being a lesbian uniquely qualified her to provide emotional support for her two friends, Kevin and Thomas, who died of AIDS. "I'm family. I don't know if either of those men would have allowed a straight woman to be as close. . . . I feel that there's an intrinsic comfort level because I'm a lesbian." Kevin's family had a very difficult time coming to terms with his illness. "Kevin's sister was close to him," Gretchen explains, "but it was a different kind of thing: I was the gay sister."

AIDS caregiving appears to differ markedly from other kinds of caregiving. AIDS organizations provide their clients not only with therapy and information but also with more time-intensive services such as shopping, cooking, cleaning, and legal and financial counseling. And, rather than receiving care from a single overworked primary caregiver, a significant number of people with AIDS appear to receive support and assistance from a team of friends, family, volunteers, and professionals.

When her friend Peter became seriously ill with AIDS in 1989, Kelly cared for him alongside his mother, another friend, and volunteers from the local AIDS hospice. For almost a month, Kelly spent her "shift" sleeping on the floor outside the door to Peter's room all night, leaving in the morning for her nine-to-five job as the manager of a busy interior design office. Despite this grueling schedule, Kelly, who recently turned sixty, insists that because of the camaraderie she shared with Peter's other caregivers, she did not feel overly exhausted or stressed at the time.

Now, however, she still bears emotional scars from the experience. Although they received assistance from the AIDS hospice, Kelly and her fellow caregivers found themselves performing many of the most demanding tasks themselves: "We'd lift [Peter] up and put him on the commode, but after a while he couldn't do that anymore. Then we got to the diapers," she remembers. Such intimate exposure to her friend's disease-ravaged body left Kelly in a state of shock, the effects of which are still visible five years after his death. Her voice breaks as she recalls how Peter suffered from water retention: "His testicles—he couldn't even close his legs. . . . He just started to come out of his skin. His skin was literally separating. It was so horrendous what happened to him—I don't think I'll ever get over how [AIDS] disfigured him."

But despite the often voluntary nature of their involvement, many lesbians have mixed feelings about AIDS caregiving. Voicing an opinion commonly expressed by lesbian AIDS workers, Leah Chaplin says she believes that "if this epidemic had been the other way around, if the lesbian community had been affected, I don't think you would have seen the same outpouring [from gay men]. I think it's just the whole nature of women as caregivers versus men."

Gretchen agrees: "I think that lesbians have always been these little quiet nurturers. We just keep doing our thing and nobody even knows that we exist, and we are expected to keep doing it. Yet we are the last to get money for research to study our needs, our diseases, and our transmissions. And that pisses me off a lot. . . . I'm tired of us as a culture putting out so much and getting so little back. . . . How many lesbians will be at the AIDS walk versus how many gay men will be out defending Planned Parenthood or joining the next lesbian Take Back the Night march?" She sums her feelings up by observing: "Whether you're gay or straight, if you're a woman you're expected to be Mommy. I really get that from gay men as much as straight men. There's this expectation that I'm going to be there."

CARING FOR LOVERS

Perhaps the most famous lesbian caregiver is Karen Thompson, the Minnesota phys. ed. teacher who fought almost a decade for the legal right to care for her lover, Sharon Kowalski, who had been severely injured in a 1983 collision with a drunk driver. In *Why Can't Sharon Kowalski Come Home?* Thompson and her co-author, Julie Andrzejewski, describe how the combined sexism, homophobia, and ableism of medical institutions and personnel, the American judicial system, and Kowalski's own parents denied the two women access to each other and, in the process, denied Kowalski her right to

Emily Rosenberg

I loved my life as a dyke separatist. Then, in 1987, I heard about PAWS (Pets Are Wonderful Support), a group that helped gay men with AIDS take care of their pets. Well, if there are two things I love in this life, it's being queer and petting animals.

I hurried off to a meeting of eight queens and one fag hag, all talking about cat litter. I was in paradise. I spent the next four years with PAWS, which became an international model for offering pet care to people with terminal illnesses.

I had never met anyone with AIDS at this point, but a few years before I had been in bed for six weeks with hepatitis. I knew what it was like to be too sick to turn over or even to reach for a tissue. I was dependent on friends to nurse me and keep my house together. Most important, they fed my cat, Grey Wolf, who was often my only company through the long, lonely days in bed. Now there was a city full of young men who needed the security of their pets to go through a much more serious illness than mine.

Most people with AIDS assumed they would have to give away their pets when they got sick. And yet, being sick and facing death was when they needed their "best friends" the most. PAWS volunteers helped with daily care and eventual adoptions so that people with AIDS could keep their pets through their illness.

AIDS was transformational for all of us—whether we offered help or received it. Just as I moved out of separatism into a larger lesbian and gay world, I met people who had never known a gay person or had never met a person with AIDS. Walking the dog or grooming the cat for someone with AIDS opened up new worlds of friendship, compassion, and political activism. Animals were the common bond, and it was a safe way to become involved.

Today, as an activist in the women and cancer movement, when I start to get caught up in meetings, deadlines, and controversies, I try to remember that the heart of my work is to make sure that there is always a cat or a dog on the bed—an unfailing friend at every hour of the day and night for anyone with AIDS, cancer, or even a broken heart.

recovery. Kowalski and Thompson's disturbing experience has taught the lesbian and gay communities that we must utilize existing legal apparatus, such as guardianship and durable power of attorney, as strategies to force our families, the courts, and the health care system to recognize our relationships. (For more on this topic, see Ruthann Robson's chapter in this book, "Our Relationships and Their Laws.")

The experience of Thompson and Kowalski also serves as a reminder that, regardless of how young or able-bodied we may consider ourselves or our lovers, any of us could become patients or caregivers in the blink of an eye. Susan Hester and Mary-Helen Mautner discovered this sad reality eight months into their relationship, when Susan found a lump on Mary-Helen's breast. Over the next eight years, they negotiated the health care system as open lesbians and, for the most part, encountered no discrimination. "People really didn't challenge us or be funny about us," recalls Susan. "We were really fortunate. I feel like some of that had to do with the fact that we were white, middle-class, educated women. We had one or two instances where I feel like people were hostile to me, but they were the minority." Susan, who joined a straight bereavement group after Mary-Helen died from cancer, also believes that as lesbians, she and Mary-Helen were able to tap into a powerful support network that they would not have had access to otherwise. Indeed, this positive aspect of their experience inspired Mary-Helen to envision what was to become the Mary-Helen Mautner Project for Lesbians with Cancer.

Mary-Helen got the idea for the project shortly before her death, when she was at the hospital receiving a bone scan while Susan went to get their daughter at school. This rare moment of solitude (when Mary-Helen was diagnosed with cancer, Susan quit her job and began to freelance from home so that she could serve as Mary-Helen's primary caregiver) led Mary-Helen to imagine what it would be like to face cancer alone, without a lover or friends to depend upon. By the time Susan arrived to pick her up, Mary-Helen had written a page of notes outlining a project for lesbians with cancer, modeled after AIDS buddy programs. When Mary-Helen died, Susan requested that donations be sent to the proposed project. From the $4,000 that request generated, Susan, with the help of many Washington, D.C., area lesbians, has built a powerful organization with two hundred volunteers and $118,000 in funding. The organization provides direct services to lesbians with cancer, their partners, and their caregivers; education and information to the lesbian community about cancer; education to the health care community about the special concerns of lesbians with cancer and their families; and advocacy on lesbian health issues in national and local arenas.

Lisa Walker, who was diagnosed with breast cancer in 1991, and her partner and primary caregiver, Valerie Mullens, had a very different experience with the medical community, but they have also found the Mautner Project "invaluable." To say that Valerie and Lisa's encounter with the health care system has been difficult would be an understatement. "It's been a grand tour of hell," says Valerie. First, there was Lisa's lumpectomy, which left her in chronic pain and unable to do anything with her right arm. As a result, Valerie has been doing everything from making Lisa's phone calls when she's not feeling well to injecting her pet rabbit with antibiotics when he's sick. Soon after the lumpectomy, Lisa was diagnosed with cervical cancer, which required a hysterectomy. Next came a week of drug withdrawal, because Lisa had become addicted to the time-release morphine her doctor prescribed to lessen her pain. (She protested the treatment, fearing addiction, but her doctor ignored her, says Valerie.) Lisa then came close to having a heart attack when an anesthesiologist at her HMO's pain clinic administered local anesthesia (again ignoring Lisa's protestations), which produced a severe allergic reaction. For Lisa, this meant two weeks in the hospital's cardiac unit; for Valerie, it meant spending her vacation leave at Lisa's bedside. As a result of her allergies, Lisa had to have an angiogram without anesthesia. Valerie held Lisa's hand as the doctor inserted a catheter "the size of a pencil" into Lisa's inner thigh, and together the two women watched the video screen that showed the catheter entering Lisa's heart.

Throughout all these crises, Lisa has maintained a regimen of radiation and chemotherapy. (Lisa and Valerie's kitchen counter is lined with the nineteen medications Lisa uses regularly.) The drugs, Valerie says, have "screwed up Lisa's disposition." Remembering how a doctor once prescribed Lisa a drug that causes severe mood swings bordering on psychosis, Valerie says that, as Lisa's primary caregiver, she must not only minister to Lisa's practical needs but also "monitor reality" for the two of them.

Thanks to the Mautner Project, Lisa and Valerie knew to have a will and medical power-of-attorney and durable power-of-attorney documents drawn up at the very beginning of Lisa's illness. After repeatedly encountering sexism and homophobia from the medical establishment, Valerie now knows that "the issue of being a lesbian is one of the very first things you have to deal with when somebody gets sick." Like Susan and Mary-Helen, they have difficulty imagining how either of them could have negotiated the system alone. Valerie explains: "I go with Lisa for everything because of all the trouble [she's had]. First of all, she's a woman; she's also small. So people don't listen to her. . . . I've had to be so ugly and bordering on physically threatening to get things done for her. It's not an exaggeration. It isn't because I wanted to; it's because I had to." Valerie says she has learned to approach health care professionals on three different levels, depending on how gay-friendly they are: "First it's 'Hi, I'm Lisa's partner'; then it's 'Hi, I'm the power of attorney'; and then it's 'I'm the power of attorney, motherfucker, and you're going to do what I tell you to do.'"

Professional health care providers tend to "hold prejudiced views about lesbians and are generally condemnatory and ignorant about their lesbian clients," according to a 1992 study published by the journal *Health Care for Women International.* Valerie and Lisa's experiences certainly support this finding. Valerie remembers one time when she and two friends, one of whom is a doctor, tried to donate blood for Lisa. Knowing the women were lesbians, the hospital harassed them and refused to accept the blood, out of an erroneous (not to mention homophobic!) concern about AIDS transmission. Valerie claims that nurses at the same Seventh Day Adventist hospital avoided entering Lisa's room because she and Valerie "look queer." As a result, Valerie and their lesbian friends took over Lisa's care, including bathing her and changing her sheets. One time, when a nurse friend of theirs was visiting, Lisa's IV began directing fluid into her tissues rather than her vein, causing extremely painful swelling. Valerie recalls: "We rang the buzzer. We rang the buzzer. We rang the buzzer. They never came. My friend Nancy [the nurse] went ahead and took care of it. . . . When the nurse waltzes in half an hour later, Nancy, in jeans and a T-shirt, says, 'The IV was infiltrating. I took care of it.' This nurse says, 'Oh, okay.' Oh, okay? What the fuck! It was awful." Through its homophobia, the hospital staff added to, rather than relieved, Valerie's caregiving responsibilities. As she remembers it now, "unless I needed something that was a nursing function that I couldn't do, I'd do it."

Again like Susan and Mary-Helen, caregiving has been an important aspect of Valerie and Lisa's relationship almost from the beginning. The two women were involved only a brief time when Valerie convinced Lisa, then physically fit, to get health insurance. On her first covered visit to the doctor, Lisa was diagnosed with cancer. Valerie, who had lived alone for eight years and describes herself as "extremely independent," insisted that Lisa move into her tiny house immediately. She had seen her mother and her ex-lover's mother die of cancer, and she knew that Lisa's communal living situation would not be conducive to dealing with chemotherapy and radiation.

From the moment they moved in together, Lisa and Valerie have had to "prepare for the worst." Valerie describes how this has affected the development of their relationship: "We never had a chance to go through [day-to-day things] in a normal mode. You know, when you're living together and it's like, well, who does the dishes? Do you squeeze the sponge out when you're through? When you put the trashbag in, do you fold the edges down neatly? We never had a chance to do that." Valerie and Lisa each sees a therapist, and they attend Mautner Project support groups regularly; still, they found it necessary to seek couples counseling to help them deal with the stress Lisa's illness has placed on their relationship. Although Valerie prides herself on being a "realist," she admits, "I keep hoping things will settle down so that we can try to see what it's like to have a regular life."

Valerie is very positive about her decision to care for Lisa, but she is also honest about how caregiving has changed her life. Since she has used all her leave time caring for Lisa, she has not had a vacation in three years. Valerie says she feels much older than her forty-three years and that she is exhausted constantly. Lisa's illness has also restricted them financially: "I have to cut corners all the time. It's like, do I want this or does she need this? I have very few choices— and they're not my first or second choices most of the time." Still, like many other caregivers, Valerie values what she has learned from the experience and wishes she could have the best of both worlds: "I would like to be able to turn time back and undo all of this stuff, but I would like to be able to keep the knowledge that I have. I think I'm a better person, and I think Lisa's a better person."

Lisa's illness has also forced Valerie to be more open about her sexual orientation. Although she was always out at work, she seldom discussed her personal life. Now, since she may be called home to respond to a medical emergency at any time, Valerie finds that being out "is not a choice. Unless you want to compromise someone's health and life, you don't play those kinds of games." Comparing the treatment she receives at work with that of a male co-worker whose wife recently died of cancer, Valerie feels she is the victim of a double standard: "I don't think people gave him as hard a time. A lot of times he would just leave early in the day. Other people would cover for him, and nobody said anything." Valerie, however, not only must request permission to leave for a medical emergency but is routinely interrogated about the nature of the emergency. Just as it is the day-to-day inconveniences rather than the occasional crises that make caring for Lisa stressful, Valerie finds that the subtle, institutionalized homophobia she encounters both at work and in her dealings with the medical establishment is what makes being a lesbian caregiver most frustrating:

> I think they do harass everybody [about taking time off from work], but it's more difficult for me because it's stressful to have to worry about someone's reaction when they hear you talk about your personal life. Straight people don't go through that. The same thing with interacting with medical people. Every single time we've got to meet somebody new, we're both kind of like, "Oh, no." We go in and it's, "Well, who's this?" "This is my domestic partner." "Your what?" "My significant other." That's as stressful as having to deal with the disease: the constant worry and concern [about how you'll be treated as a lesbian]. And also the concern that it will affect [Lisa's] health. And it's not our imagination. Yes, indeed, it does happen, and it's not our fault. It's their prejudice and their bigotry—and it's real.

CONCLUSION

In its 1987 study of caregiving for the elderly in the United States, aptly titled "Exploding the Myths," the House of Representatives Select Committee on Aging found that the current era has created "greater pressures for caregivers than, perhaps, any time in the past," and that, contrary to popular belief, "far from abrogating their responsibility, family caregivers provide care for dependent family members, often at a great emotional and financial cost." The myth that the subcommittee was seeking to explode with this information is that we, as a culture, have lost sight of what Republican rhetoric would call our traditional family values. An examination of lesbian caregiving in the United States suggests that if, like other women today, many lesbians are engaging in nurturing and nursing, behavior traditionally defined as feminine, in the process we are also challenging the traditional meaning of the word *family* by expanding it to include our lovers and our gay and lesbian friends.

That all the women I interviewed for this chapter have served as caregivers more than once, and often on three or more occasions, suggests that caregiving is both a lesbian and a feminist issue—albeit a neglected one. Many of the women experienced depression, a loss of autonomy, and troubled romantic relationships as a result of their caregiving responsibilities. But most also reported that providing care for others inspired them to take better care of themselves, allowed them to come to terms with death, and strengthened their relationships with those for whom they cared. Perhaps Gretchen speaks for all lesbian caregivers when she says, "I feel like a sword that's been put in the fire: I'm being made stronger and sharper."

FURTHER READING

Brody, Elaine M. *Women in the Middle: Their Parent-Care Years.* New York: Springer Publishing Company, 1990. This study does a nice job of pulling together the demographic statistics and cultural values that place women at the center of informal caregiving networks.

Hooyman, Nancy R., and Wendy Lustbader. *Taking Care: Supporting Older People and Their Families.* New York: Macmillan/Free Press, 1986. Although this is one of the few books on caregiving with a special section on lesbian and gay couples, the authors do not seem particularly enlightened about queer realities. (They assume, for example, that gay couples will not have children of their own to care for them.)

Richardson, Diane. *Women and AIDS.* New York: Methuen, 1988. A good sourcebook on AIDS that deals specifically with lesbians and AIDS as well as AIDS' effect on women caregivers.

Sommers, Tish, and Laurie Shields. *Women Take Care: The Consequences of Caregiving in Today's Society.* Gainesville, Fla.: Triad, 1987. This product of a three-year study by the Older Women's League Task Force on Caregivers provides practical advice in a theoretical context, while advocating policy changes that would no longer take women caregivers for granted.

Thompson, Karen, and Julie Andrzejewski. *Why Can't Sharon Kowalski Come Home?* San Francisco: Spinsters/Aunt Lute, 1988. This memoir documents Thompson's battles against homophobia and ableism in her struggle to be granted guardianship of her lover, Sharon Kowalski, who was seriously injured by a drunk driver in 1983. Includes valuable legal advice for lesbian couples and reproducible legal forms for durable power of attorney.

OTHER RESOURCES

Mary-Helen Mautner Project for Lesbians with Cancer
   1707 L Street N.W., Suite 1060
   Washington, DC 20036
   202-332-5536   FAX: 202-265-6854

Contributors' Notes

JEANNE ADLEMAN, a more or less lifetime political activist, since 1972 has lived on the West Coast, where her community work has included the Women's Switchboard, the Women's Building, the 1987 and 1989 Old Lesbian Conferences, and, since 1986, the Advisory Board of Gay and Lesbian Outreach to Elders (GLOE). Her writing has been published in three anthologies and also appears in a book she co-edited, *Racism in the Lives of Women* (1995). She has been active in the Association for Women in Psychology and in the Feminist Therapy Institute, which she chaired from 1988 to 1990. In 1994, Jeanne was one of three lesbians over sixty to receive a Pat Bond Award as an outstanding member of the San Francisco Bay Area lesbian community.

DONNA ALLEGRA'S work has been anthologized in *SportsDykes, Woman in the Window, HomeGirls: A Black Feminist Anthology, Lesbian Love Stories, Volume 2, Contemporary Lesbian Love Poems, Out of the Class Closet—Lesbians Speak,* and *The Persistent Desire.* Her poetry and fiction have been published in several issues of *Sinister Wisdom; Common Lives, Lesbian Lives;* and *Conditions.* She has also contributed to *Colorlife!, Sappho's Isle, Gay Community News,* and *Sojourner.*

SHELLEY ANDERSON was born and raised in Florida, and now lives in the Netherlands. Her short stories have been published in anthologies in the United States and the United Kingdom, and her articles have appeared in over one hundred publications, including *Belles Lettres, The Advocate,* and *Out/Look.* While she enjoys Dutch national health insurance, she misses grits.

SYLVIA BLACKSTONE is a poet and a Buddhist who lives happily with her partner and their child in Northern California.

TERI M. BROOKS is a graduate student in clinical psychology at the University of Vermont, and is a member of the lesbian research group that authored this chapter. Her current research interests focus on examining factors impacting sexual activity in adolescence, with particular attention paid to assessing implications for the prevention of teen pregnancy and risky sexual behaviors. Clinically speaking, her interests center on working with adolescents in resolving identity issues, sexual and otherwise.

LAURA S. BROWN has been in private practice as a feminist psychologist since 1979, doing psychotherapy and forensic psychology. She has been a major contributor to the literature on lesbian psychologies, and has written extensively on feminist therapy theory, ethics, and practice, with special attention to the lesbian therapist working in lesbian communities. Her book on feminist therapy theory, *Subversive Dialogues,* was published in 1994 by Basic Books. She lives in Seattle with her partner of fifteen years.

VICTORIA A. BROWNWORTH is a Pulitzer Prize–nominated syndicated columnist for the *Philadelphia Daily News.* She is the author of eight books, including *Out for Blood.* She writes for *The Village Voice, The Advocate, OUT, The Nation,* and many other national queer and mainstream publications. She lives in Philadelphia with her partner of seven years, filmmaker Judith M. Redding, six cats, and a dog. She was outed at fifteen by the mother of her then-girlfriend and has been a radical lesbian activist ever since.

SANDRA BUTLER is the author of *Conspiracy of Silence: The Trauma of Incest* and the co-author of *Cancer in Two Voices,* which won the Lambda Lesbian Literary Award for Non-Fiction in 1991.

In addition to her work in the fields of child sexual assault and the politics of women's health, she is a co-founder of the Institute for Feminist Training.

KATE COLWELL is a forty-something lesbian and birthmother of a wonderful toddler. She works as a family practitioner in an urban public clinic in Northern California. She lives with her family in Berkeley.

HEATHER CONRAD is the author of the novel *NEWS*, as well as short stories and essays that have appeared in a variety of publications. She has an M.A. in creative writing from San Francisco State University and teaches English as a Second Language to adults in the Bay Area. She lives in Berkeley with her partner, Kate Colwell, and their son, David.

TEE A. CORINNE is the author of four books of fiction, including *Courting Pleasure* and *Dreams of the Woman Who Loved Sex*. Her artwork ranges from *The Cunt Coloring Book* to covers for recordings by Holly Near, Musica Femina, and Suede. She teaches memoir writing and is on the board of the Women's Caucus for Art.

D. BROOKES COWAN is a clinical sociologist who lectures in the Sociology Department at the University of Vermont and has a private psychotherapy practice. Dr. Cowan's academic and clinical work focuses on women's issues, especially reproduction and caregiving; gay and lesbian lifestyles and homophobia; and dying and death.

LAUREN CRUX, at any given moment, is a poet, photographer, psychotherapist, backpacker, cyclist, storyteller, or adventurer. Her poetry and prose have appeared in numerous journals and anthologies. She lives in Santa Cruz, California.

RINI DAS: "I was born in Calcutta, India, and lived the first twenty-two years of my life there. Since then I have stayed in Iowa, New York, Minnesota, and Belgium. Now I hover around *moi* partner in a quaint house in Columbus, Ohio. My writings have been published in a few anthologies and magazines like *Fireweed*. I have been labeled weirdo, game theorist, second-down batsman, seducer, mathematician, chatterbox, ex-wife, data analyst, poet, lesbian."

MARIA DE LA O recently graduated from Columbia School of Journalism and currently lives in San Francisco. Strictly speaking, she is a corporate lesbian. However, she works as an assistant editor at *10 Percent* magazine, a gay/lesbian/bi publication, where she flaunts her sexual identity openly. Her articles have also appeared in the *San Francisco Examiner, Deneuve,* and *The Advocate.*

TERRI DE LA PEÑA has written two novels, *Margins* (1992) and *Latin Satins* (1994). Her work has appeared in numerous anthologies, including *The Coming Out Stories, Chicana Lesbians: The Girls Our Mothers Warned Us About,* and *Another Wilderness: New OutDoor Writing by Women.* She is on the editorial board of *The Lesbian Review of Books. Territories,* her short-story collection, is forthcoming from Third Woman Press.

JEANNINE DELOMBARD is a doctoral candidate in the University of Pennsylvania's Department of English. She received an M.A. in Comparative Literature from Penn in 1994 and an M.A. in African Studies from Yale in 1991. She has contributed to the *New York Times Book Review, OUT, Girlfriends, Lambda Book Report,* and the *Washington Blade.* She lives in Philadelphia with her girlfriend, Laura, and their dog and cat, Bunky and Leroy.

BETTY ROSE DUDLEY is a fat dyke from Missouri with a working-class background. She now has a middle-class income and lives, works, and plays in San Francisco. She was on the editorial board of *Sinister Wisdom,* and has been published in *Sinister Wisdom, Common Lives/Lesbian Lives, FAT? SO!: A Zine for People Who Don't Apologize for Their Size, Fat Girl: A Zine for Fat Dykes and the Women Who Want Them,* and the *Utne Reader.* Her work has been performed by Fat Lip Readers' Theater and Mother Tongue Feminist Readers' Theater. She does not apologize for her size, or the space she takes up.

JANE FUTCHER lives with her lover, Erin Carney, in Novato, California. She is an editorial writer for the Marin *Independent Journal.* Her published novels are *Crush* and *Promise Not to Tell.* Her short fiction has appeared in *Afterglow, Bushfire,* and *Lesbian Adventure Stories.* "Not Wisely But Too Well," an essay on her own sobriety, appears in *The Next Step: Out from Under, Volume 2*, edited by Jean Swallow.

GRETA GAARD is an Associate Professor of Composition and Women's Studies at the University of Minnesota, Duluth. She served as co-chair for the Gay and Lesbian Caucus of the Modern Language Association from 1990 to 1992, and has published articles on antilesbian intellectual harassment, domestic partnership benefits at the University of Minnesota, and the importance of teaching lesbian and gay literatures. She is editor of *Ecofeminism: Women, Animals, Nature* (1993), and author of the forthcoming *Thinking Green: Ecofeminists and the Greens*.

E. J. GRAFF is a Boston-area writer whose essays and fiction have appeared in *The Iowa Review, The Kenyon Review, Ms.* magazine, the *New York Times, The Progressive, The Women's Review of Books, Out,* and several anthologies.

BEVERLY A. GREENE is a Professor of Psychology at St. John's University and a clinical psychologist in private practice in New York City. She is also an associate editor of a new journal, *Violence Against Women;* co-editor of *Women of Color: Integrating Ethnic and Gender Identities in Psychotherapy;* co-editor of *Psychological Perspectives on Lesbian and Gay Issues,* a new series of annual publications sponsored by the Division of Lesbian and Gay Issues of the American Psychological Association; and many other professional publications.

MARNY HALL has lived, worked, and played in the San Francisco Bay Area for twenty-five years. She has contributed to several anthologies and is the author of *The Lavender Couch: A Consumer's Guide to Psychotherapy for Lesbians and Gay Men.* Having just joined Internet, she is now busily researching lesbian sex in cyberspace.

CHERYL HALLER is a licensed clinical mental health counselor in private practice in Burlington, Vermont. She provides mental health services for lesbians.

SLICK HARRIS writes pornography in New York City. One of her short stories, "Shrink Rap," was published in *Trivia.*

SHEVY HEALEY, a seventy-three-year-old lesbian, is a retired psychologist, who now spends her time organizing, writing, speaking, and educating against ageism. She is a spokesperson and one of the founders of Old Lesbians Organizing for Change (OLOC). She and her seventy-six-year-old partner currently reside in an all-woman RV resort community in Arizona.

PAULA J. HEPNER has been a judge of the New York State Family Court since her appointment in August 1990. She is a founding member and president of the Association of Lesbian and Gay Judges, and a member of the Board of Directors of the International Association of Lesbian and Gay Judges. Judge Hepner has written a number of essays for legal journals, including "Minorities and the Law, Problems and Perceptions: Lesbian and Gay Judges, An Invisible Minority," "Out of the Closets and Into the Courtrooms," and "Offense Against Nature." She is a frequent lecturer to professional and student organizations.

JOYCE HUNTER is director of the Community Liaison Program, HIV Center for Clinical and Behavioral Studies, New York State Psychiatric Institute. At the HIV Center, she is Co-Principal Investigator for a research project with gay and lesbian adolescents, examining coming out and high-risk behaviors. She is currently the President of the National Lesbian and Gay Health Association. Ms. Hunter was also co-founder of the Harvey Milk High School, a school for lesbian, gay, and bisexual youth.

KARLA JAY has written, edited, and translated nine books, the most recent of which is *Lesbian Erotics*. She is editor of "The Cutting Edge: Lesbian Life and Literature," the only lesbian studies series in the world published by a university press. She has written for many publications, including *Ms.* magazine, the *New York Times Book Review, The Village Voice,* and *Lambda Book Report.* She is a professor of English and director of Women's Studies at Pace University in New York City.

YEMAYA KAURIALECTO is a forty-something lesbian mother of three currently living in Santa Cruz, California. She is a published poet as well as a freelance writer and is rigorously working on a degree in the school of life.

KAREN F. KERNER is an emergency medicine physician at Columbia Presbyterian Medical Center in New York City. She is a member of the Gay and Lesbian Medical Association.

AMANDA KOVATTANA was born in England and raised in Thailand. She is a freelance writer, currently finishing an autobiographical novel that explores the influences of her matriarchal Thai family and her bicultural/biracial heritage. She lives in the San Francisco Bay Area, where she became an American lesbian in 1977.

JACQUELINE LAPIDUS (b. 1941, New York City) spent most of her adult life in France, where she was active in international feminist groups. Since the mid-1980s, she has been shuttling between Provincetown and Boston, where she works as an editor. Her poems, essays, and reviews have appeared in numerous magazines and anthologies; her books include *Ready to Survive, Starting Over,* and *Ultimate Conspiracy,* as well as *Yantras of Womanlove* (with Tee A. Corinne).

JANET LINDER is a clinical social worker in private practice in San Francisco and a new member of the Board of Directors at her daughter's preschool. She lives with her family in Albany, California.

ANNA LIVIA was born in Dublin, grew up in Africa, spent eighteen years in London, obtained a Ph.D. in French Linguistics at Berkeley, and is now an assistant professor at the University of Illinois. She is the author of two collections of short stories and four novels, including *Minimax* and *Relatively Norma.* Her translation of *The Angel and the Perverts* by Lucie Delarue-Mardrus was published in 1995, and *Queerly Phrased,* a lesbian and gay linguistics anthology, will be published in 1996.

JOANN LOULAN is a psychotherapist, mother, lover, and public speaker in Portola Valley, California. She is the author of *Lesbian Sex, Lesbian Passion,* and *The Lesbian Erotic Dance* and the co-author of *Period.* She gratefully acknowledges the editing and advice of Margie Adam for this chapter.

LEE LYNCH is the author of several books of fiction. Her syndicated column, "The Amazon Trail," appears in over a dozen papers. She lives in rural Oregon.

PHYLLIS LYON, writer, sexologist, and activist, was a co-founder of the Daughters of Bilitis, the first national lesbian organization, which started in 1955. With her partner of more than forty years, Del Martin, she helped start numerous lesbian and gay groups, such as the Council on Religion and the Homosexual (1964) and the Alice B. Toklas Memorial Democratic Club (1972). With Del, she co-authored *Lesbian/Woman,* named by *Publishers Weekly* as one of the twenty most important women's books in the 1970s and 1980s. She is professor emerita of the Institute for Advanced Study of Human Sexuality, a San Francisco graduate school. Current interests focus on lesbian aging issues and politics.

JUDY MACLEAN is a freelance writer and editor in San Francisco. Her fiction has appeared in *Lesbian Love Stories, II* and *All the Ways Home.* Her humor has appeared in the *San Francisco Chronicle,* the *Washington Post,* and other publications. She also teaches writing at UC Berkeley Extension, San Francisco.

DEL MARTIN has been active in the lesbian, gay, feminist, and bisexual movements for almost four decades. With her partner of more than forty years, Phyllis Lyon, she was a co-founder in 1955 of the Daughters of Bilitis, the first national lesbian organization. With Phyllis, she co-authored the groundbreaking book *Lesbian/Woman,* now in a twentieth-anniversary edition chronicling the changes from the 1950s to the 1990s. Del also authored *Battered Wives,* which was published in 1976 and served as a catalyst for the battered women's shelter movement. Currently, she serves on the advisory board of Gay and Lesbian Outreach to Elders and is a member of Old Lesbians Organizing for Change.

PAULA MARTINAC is a writer, editor, and activist. She is the author of two published novels, *Home Movies* (1993) and *Out of Time* (1990), which won the 1990 Lambda Literary Award for Best Lesbian Fiction, and a young adult biography of singer k. d. lang

(1995). A former editor of *Conditions* magazine, she also edited the anthology *The One You Call Sister: New Women's Fiction* (1989). She lives in New York City.

MARY MEIGS was born in Philadelphia in 1917 and grew up in Washington, D.C. She is a painter and a writer. She moved to Quebec in 1975. She has written four books and is at work on a new book with the title *The Time Being.*

BETH MINTZ is Professor of Sociology at the University of Vermont. She has published in the areas of corporate power structures, intraclass relations, and the changing structure of the medical industry. She is currently working on a book with Esther Rothblum on lesbians in academia.

JESSICA F. MORRIS is a Ph.D. candidate in clinical psychology at the University of Vermont. Her dissertation research—about lesbian mental health and the coming-out process—is one of the largest surveys of lesbians ever conducted. Her dedication to lesbian activism includes being the founding vice president of the Lesbian and Gay Alumnae/i of Vassar College.

MARCIA MUNSON is a lesbian sex educator who has led workshops at the Michigan Women's Music Festival, the West Coast Music Festival, the Colorado Gathering, the Boulder Lesbian Connection, U.C. Women's Week, the Ft. Collins Monday Night Group, and San Francisco's Whiptail Lizard Lounge. She has a B.S. in Biology and an Instructor/Advisor of AIDS/STD Prevention Certificate from the Institute for Advanced Study of Human Sexuality.

LESLÉA NEWMAN is an author and editor with twenty books to her credit, including *A Letter to Harvey Milk, Every Woman's Dream, Writing from the Heart, Heather Has Two Mommies,* and *the Femme Mystique.*

AMY J. OJERHOLM is a graduate student in clinical psychology at the University of Vermont and a member of the lesbian research group. In addition to her interests in lesbian mental health, she is pursuing research in the areas of fat oppression and body-size acceptance.

DANA M. OSOWIECKI is a graduate student in clinical psychology at the University of Vermont. She is a member of the lesbian research group and the Stress and Coping Research Group. Current research interests include women's health psychology and women's sexuality.

DEBORAH PERKINS, proud Kentuckian, is a technical writer by day and aspiring essayist and novelist by night. She hopes to graduate from Northern Kentucky University sometime before she retires, in the year 2018. She and Ginger, her partner of nine years, eagerly await the day when every lesbian can safely proclaim aloud her love for womyn without fear of recrimination.

MARGARET ROBISON: "My books are *The Naked Bear* and *Red Creek.* A poet-in-residence in Massachusetts schools, I've taught women in prison and now lead writing workshops for women with disabilities. I have published in journals such as *The Virginia Quarterly Review, Sojourner, Disability Rag, Sinister Wisdom,* and *Negative Capability.*"

RUTHANN ROBSON is professor of law at City University of New York School of Law, teaching in the areas of constitutional law, law and family relations, criminal procedure, feminist legal theory, and sexuality and the law. Her work has been primarily focused on the possibilities of a specifically lesbian legal theory, as explained in the book *Lesbian (Out)Law: Survival Under the Rule of Law,* and she has written numerous articles in law reviews, periodicals, and anthologies. She is also the author of two collections of lesbian fiction, *Eye of a Hurricane* and *Cecile,* and a novel, *Another Mother,* about a lesbian attorney representing lesbian mothers.

BETH ROSEN is a psychotherapist living in New York City with her partner, Maryann King, and their daughter, Emily Rosen-King.

EMILY ROSENBERG: "I came out in 1974 at age thirty and never looked back. Being a dyke and being Jewish are the two best things in my life. Old dogs, a new love, and gardening keep me happy. I write when something needs to be said—fund-raising letters for nonprofits, friends' resumes, newsletters, occasional articles. Academic credentials are immaterial for this work, but I would love to study anthropology someday."

PAULA ROSS: "I was born in Detroit, Michigan, in 1947, the product of post–World War II and mass migrations of Black folks from the southern United States. I grew up among auto factory workers and plumbers, teachers and barbers, lawyers and doctors, a mix of working and middle class. The editor of three anthologies, I have also published fiction in *Conditions, Crossroads, IKON,* and *Word of Mouth, Short-Short Stories by 100 Women Writers.* A former television news reporter, I recently started my own business, Words by Design Editorial Consulting Services. My work and home life are split between San Francisco's Mission District and the more bucolic pleasures of Santa Cruz."

ESTHER D. ROTHBLUM is a professor in the Department of Psychology, University of Vermont. Her research and writing have focused on lesbian mental health, and she is former chair of the Committee on Lesbian and Gay Concerns of the American Psychological Association. Esther has edited the books *Loving Boldly: Issues Facing Lesbians* and *Boston Marriages: Romantic But Asexual Relationships Among Contemporary Lesbians.* She is currently working with Beth Mintz on a book about lesbians in academia.

SONDRA SEGAL-SKLAR is a writer who lives in New York City with her partner, Roberta, and their daughter, Rachel. Their godson Jesse, whom they raised together with others in a parenting collective, is now a young adult. As one of the artistic directors of the Women's Experimental Theatre, Segal-Sklar co-authored *The Daughters Cycle* trilogy ("Daughters," "Sister/Sister," and "Electra Speaks") and the play series *Woman's Body and Other Natural Resources* ("Food," "Foodtalk," and "Feast or Famine"). Her plays, poetry, articles, and commentary on social issues have been published in anthologies, professional journals, and popular magazines. She has produced several video documentaries on issues of relevance to women.

JUDITH P. STELBOUM teaches literature and women's studies at the College of Staten Island, City University of New York. She has had fiction, poetry, and essays published in *Common Lives/Lesbian Lives* and *Sinister Wisdom,* and is a reviewer for the *Lesbian Review of Books.* Recent work appears in the anthologies *Sister and Brother, Resist: Essays Against a Homophobic Culture, Not the Only One, Hot Licks,* and *Tangled Sheets.*

JEAN SWALLOW edited two anthologies on lesbians in recovery, *Out from Under* and *The Next Step.* She was the author of a novel, *Leave a Light on for Me,* and her shorter pieces, poems, narratives, and journalism have been widely published, both here and abroad. Before her death in 1995, she finished a book of photojournalism (with photographer Geoff Manasse) called *Making Love Visible: The Families of Gay Men and Lesbians.*

KITTY TSUI is the author of *The Words of a Woman Who Breathes Fire.* Her poems, essays, and short stories have been published in over twenty-five anthologies, including *Lesbian Erotics, Pearls of Passion, Chloe Plus Olivia, The Very Inside, Lesbian Cultures and Philosophies, Gay and Lesbian Poetry in Our Time,* and *Making Waves.* She has finished a historical novel, *Bak Sze, White Snake.* She is happily single again.

KATH WESTON is currently associate professor of anthropology at Arizona State University West and a member of the National Writers Union. Her books include *Families We Choose: Lesbians, Gays, Kinship* and *The Lesbian Issue: Essays from SIGNS* (co-edited). Her chapter in this volume is abridged from *Render Me, Gender Me* (forthcoming from Columbia University Press).

LOUISE G. WHITNEY: "I am an ex-member of the ruling class who was married to a man for twenty years. Many women lovers provided magic during that time. I am now a lesbian with three sons, a horsewoman, and a published poet."

KELLY JO WOODSIDE recently graduated from Pace University with a B.A. in English. She intends to pursue a career in publishing. A reformed intellectual, she is still lost between the moon and New York City.

Printed in the United States
60244LVS00003B/186